India and US on Terrorism

India and US on Terrorism

Jatin Desai

Commonwealth

India and US on Terrorism

First Published, 2000

ISBN 81-7169-616-3

Published by:
Ajay Verma
For Commonwealth Publishers
4831/24, Prahlad Street,
Ansari Road, Darya Ganj,
New Delhi - 110 002
Ph.: 3272541, 3257835
Fax : 91-011-3257835

Typesetting by:
Stylish Laser Typesetter
Delhi - 110053

Printed at:
Efficient Offset Printers
Shahzada Bagh, New Delhi-110035

Preface

War was once an extremely exclusionary activity. It was fought by the state, with its armed forces, often in a particular battle zone, against a like enemy—uninformed, with a clear command and control structure, and for clear political objectives. War was considered an honourable activity, and so the soldier was viewed with some respect, while the population was taxed so that the soldier might fight. But for all other purposes the three—the state, the army and the population remained separate, though sometimes the first two merged when various strong men ruled with an iron hand. While populations thus suffered the exigencies of errant kings or demanding dictators, war itself remained an activity that was outside the society at large.

Once the realisation dawns that terrorism today is a mutant of war, then the methodology of state reaction becomes that much simpler. All the panoply of options and policies that would normally come into play during a regular war needs to be considered here—keeping in mind always that terrorism has to be fought much more through the mind than by mere physical threat or persuasion. Thus a strong media policy is as important than equipping the armed forces with weapons and technology that is suitable for anti-terrorist operations.

It is therefore the responsibility of the states that form the "international community" to coax war again into its former boundaries. The realisation that even a super power or a regional power really has no defence against terrorism must finally push states into acting in their own interest. States supporting terrorism thrive on inter-state differences and competitive strategies, and have become adept at playing the one against the other to achieve their own covert objectives. While it is accepted that states will continue to adopt competitive modes of conduct in their relations with each other, the bottom line is that a cooperative strategy in tackling terrorism has to be made a "stand alone" objective by those democracies who still wish to retain a measure of stability in international relations. This alone can manage the phenomenon of terrorism. This book focus India-US contributions on terrorism more frequent and more systematic.

Editor

Contents

1

India and US on Terrorism

Following the recent intensive Indo-US consultations on terrorism, the two sides have already agreed in principle to form a Joint Working Group. Two senior MEA officials had visited the US in early September for consultations on Afghanistan and terrorism. The objective of the Joint Working Group is to make Indo-US consultations on terrorism, "more frequent and more systematic", diplomatic sources said. The group, which is expected to be set up early next year, will facilitate a two-way exchange of views and analyses between New Delhi and Washington about the current trends in terrorism in the region and the world. In a testimony before the US Senate in November, Mr. Sheehan had pointed to the shift in the centre of international terrorism from the Middle East to the subcontinent, in particular to Afghanistan and Pakistan.

The Clinton Administration has turned up the heat against the Taliban by getting the United Nations Security Council to approve sanctions against Afghanistan. Washington is also urging Pakistan to use its influence in Kabul to get hold of the terrorist, Osama bin Laden, now under the Taliban's protection in Afghanistan. Washington is also calling on Pakistan to moderate its own policy on Afghanistan and terrorism.

Mr. Sheehan told the Senate that Washington has

"repeatedly asked Islamabad to end support for terrorist training in Afghanistan, to interdict militants to and from camps in Afghanistan, to prevent militant groups acquiring weapons, and block financial and logistical support to camps in Afghanistan. We have also urged Islamabad to close certain madrassas, or Islamic schools, that actually serve as conduits for terrorism".

New Delhi would like to see the American approach on counter-terrorism expand its current limited focus on Afghanistan to include Pakistan's sponsorship of terrorism against India. Meanwhile, the United, States is bracing for a series of terrorist attacks against American targets world-wide.

The recent arrests of Algerian and Jordanian nationals with possible links to the terrorist networks in Afghanistan are the result of an intensified security alert worldwide against the feared terrorist violence at the turn of millennium, Responding to American pressures, the Government of Pakistan has begun to round up scores of Afghan nationals in Peshawar and Islamabad. An anti-terrorism convention with a new focus--targeting those who finance terrorism-was opened for signature on 10 January, 2000 at the United, Nations in New York. By the end of the day, the Convention had been signed by seven countries: Finland; France; Malta: Netherlands; Sri Lanka; United Kingdom and the United States.

The latest in a series of interlocking conventions intended to combat terrorism, the International Convention for the Suppression of the Financing of Terrorism was adopted by the United Nations General Assembly on 9 December, 1999 without a vote." It will enter into force when it has been ratified by 22 States., States who sign a treaty demonstrate their intention to ratify. Speaking at a press conference following its adoption, Philippe Kirsch, of Canada, who chaired the working group that drafted the legislation, called the Convention a model instrument. He pointed out that it recognizes the fundamental importance of the international problem posed by the financing of terrorism; it establishes the act of financing terrorism as an independent crime; it does not require that an act of terrorism actually be committed; and it contains important provisions on the liability of legal entities, such as organizations or groups-a new concept in the struggle against international terrorism.

The new Convention is intended to have "teeth". In today's electronic environment, huge quantities of money can circle the globe in seconds. If a significant number of countries become States parties, the Convention will provide powerful enforcement possibilities to governments who want to put an end to acts of terrorism. Every time terrorist monies pass through the territory of a State party, an international crime has been committed which can be prosecuted. The international community historically has been unable to agree on a definition of terrorism, as one man's terrorist is often another man's freedom fighter. Because of this difficulty, countries have taken the approach of creating the network of conventions which criminalize specific acts, such as setting bombs, kidnapping or hijacking airplanes. While this Convention does not specifically define an act of terrorism, it does come significantly closer. According to the text, it is a crime to provide or collect funds with the knowledge or intention that they are to be used in acts of violence targetting civilians with the intention of intimidating a government. This is a much broader category of crime than has previously been outlawed. A person is also guilty of an offence if he participates as an accomplice in such an act, if he organizes or directs others to commit such an act, or if he contributes in any other way to the crime.

In addition, the Convention makes it a crime to provide or collect funds with the knowledge or intention that they are to be used to carry out any of the acts described in nine previously adopted anti-terrorism conventions referred to by the Convention. States parties are required to adopt measures, such as domestic legislation, to ensure that the criminal acts described in the.

Convention will under no circumstances be considered justifiable because of political, philosophical, ideological, racial, ethnic or religious considerations. For the first time, the Convention specifically targets the financial sponsors of terrorist activity, rather than simply the actual perpetrators of the specific acts. Previously, the financial backers of such criminal acts could only be charged with aiding or abetting that crime. Under this law, it is not ever necessary that an act, of terrorism has taken place; according to article 2, the intention or knowledge of the use of the funds collected or provided is sufficient.

Proceeds from illicit activities, such as opium production or the small arm trade now often find their way to the hands of terrorists through a transnational "shadow banking" system. Front businesses, such as travel agencies's that can change currencies, are easily used to launder dirty money and to transfer funds. In the globalizing world, cooperation between transnational criminals and international terrorists is on the rise.

The Convention sets new limits on the banking secrecy traditionally provided by some countries, which has been such a useful tool for transnational criminals and terrorists. States parties will be required to take "all practicable measures," such as adapting their domestic legislation, to prevent the relevant offences, whether by persons or organizations. Banks and other financial institutions must identify account holders, and must pay special attention to unusual or suspicious transactions and report any they suspect may stern from criminal activity.

The Convention suggests a number of specific measures, such as requiring banks and financial institutions to verify the legal existence of a customer by obtaining proof of incorporation, or requiring banks to maintain transaction records for at least five years.

The Convention also calls for efforts to identify, detect, and freeze or seize any funds used or allocated for the purpose of committing a terrorist act, and asks that States consider establishing mechanisms to use such funds to compensate victims and/or their families.

States parties will be required to provide information to other States regarding the whereabouts and activities of suspects, or regarding the movement of funds, they must provide assistance when requested to obtain evidence in their possession. They should consider measures, such as introducing licensing for money-transmission agencies and monitoring the cross-border movement of cash and bearer negotiable instruments.

All the offences in the Convention are to be deemed "extraditable offences." But States may no longer refuse extradition on the grounds that the crime concerned is political in nature. Similarly, extradition may no longer be denied because the offence is of a fiscal nature, as the Convention specifies that none of the crimes it covers are to be considered fiscal offences. A plan by terrorists with possible links with Osama bin Laden to kill Americans and Western tourists in a hotel in Amman on the eve of the new millennium was foiled by the law enforcement agencies, American television network ABC reported on January 29. Quoting American and Jordian intelligence officials, it said the terrorists planned to place a radio controlled bomb at the Radisson Hotel in the Jordanian capital. The officials said they found radio controlled detonators and thousands of pounds of chemicals used to make explosives in a secret room on a farm outside Amman. Khalid Saeed Deek, 42, a possible participant in the plot, was indicted in Jordan on the charges of possession and manufacture of explosives. More details about him are emerging, the network said. He is also accused of "affiliation with" bin Laden suspected by the US of masterminding bombing its two embassies in Eastern Africa in which more than 200 people were killed.

Prosecutors were quoted as saying that Deek was also part of a thwarted attempt to massacre religious pilgrims in other locations in Jordan on the New Year eve. Deek, a citizen of the US and Jordan, has denied the charges and that he has ties with bin Laden, his lawyer Younis Arab said. ABC said in addition to the hotel bombing, the plan was to gun down pilgrims and tourists in Jordon, home of several Christian and Jewish holy sites on the New Year's eve. The sites targeted were Moses' reputed tomb at Mount Nebo, the Church of St. John where the Bible says Jesus was baptized and one of the border crossing between Israel and Jordan, ABC reported quoting unidentified sources. Last month, Jordanian officials arrested 13 people including 11 Jordanians, one Iraqi and one Algerian in connection with the alleged plot. Deek was arrested days later in Pakistan, charged with bomb making activities. He was later extradited to Jordan. FBI, ABC says, believes that the man behind all this is bin Laden. Deek admitted in a Jordanian court that he received military training in Afghanistan where Bin Laden maintains his camps and that he once shared a bank account with a man US investigators say is bin Laden's chief of military operations. The network quieted intelligence sources as saying that Deek's house in Peshawar in Pakistan was a "way station" for recruits going to and from bin Laden's camps.

Meanwhile, Canada will propose to the US that the two countries should coordinate preventative measures against international terrorism, the *Canadian National* Post newspaper has reported. Citing senior government officials, the newspaper said a plan will be presented to US authorities at a meeting next month. The plan proposes that the two countries should coordinate their policies on issuing visas, should share intelligence information, and establish common priorities on the investigation of suspects, the paper said. US legislators have been pressuring Canada to tighten controls along the border, between the two countries, following the arrest of alleged terrorists who entered the US from Canada.

2

Terrorism: Global Outlook

In spite of the spread of terrorist incidents throughout the world, the term has neither a precise definition, nor one which is widely acceptable. Like many political terms it is pejorative. Some governments are prone to label as terrorism all violent acts committed by their political opponents, while anti-government extremists claim to be the victims of government terror. It can have a moral judgement and the attaching of the label 'terrorist' to one's opponent can have a knock-on effect.

The media can exploit the term and they see the word as attention-getting to heighten drama. The imprecise nature of the term means that with some accuracy it can refer to a specific set of fear-producing actions which can serve a variety of purposes. More generally it can apply to similar acts of violence—kidnappings and hijackings—which are not intended by the perpetrators to be terror-producing.

The term is carelessly used—even by academic students of the subject—as a synonym for rebellion, street battles, civil strife, insurrection, rural guerrilla war and coup d'état. The indiscriminate use of the term not only inflates the statistics but makes understanding the specific character of terrorism and how to cope with it more difficult: Yet to some extent this is exaggerated because all the synonyms utilised by Laqueur denominate anti-governmental forms of violence. The concept of terror when discussed in the domain of international policy escapes definition. It is not that terror is intrinsically more difficult to define than any other political concept, but it does escape definition when it becomes embellished with value under political meaning. In historical terms, terrorism can't be a universal phenomenon and is a historical one emerging only at particular times and associated with particular developments in people's consciousness. Based partly on historical grounds and currently on political ones, the confusion over aims and definitions is very great.

Political sociologists argue that no definition can in principle be reached because the very process of definition is in itself part of the wider conflict between ideologies or political objectives. This cumulative research on an empiricist scientific model is not possible. The problem is not one of comprehensiveness or degree of detail of definition, but is one of the framework of the definition. Yet, lexicographically, to define is to explain something new by something old, adding the distinctive feature. In this way, the new object or phenomenon becomes embedded into a known framework of reference.

The definition problem has become far more than an exercise in semantics. The problem of ascertaining characteristics is vital if guidelines are to be established by which social scientists collect and evaluate data on strife incidents. The minimum consensus is now leading to some effective framework.

The question of the definition of terrorism is central to an understanding of the phenomenon and to the success of any rational measures directed against it. Confusion can arise over a seeming similarity of behaviour when a violent act is carried out by a politically motivated individual, a criminal or the mentally unbalanced. For example, is a member of Al Fatah to be equated with someone who explodes bombs in a commercial location or a deranged murderer? No one would deny that they all contain elements of terror, but does it contribute to an understanding or design of countermeasures to treat them all as instances of something called 'terrorism'?' Linking together all violent acts under the label terrorism could provoke repression which is unnecessary and fatal to the type of society it is intended to maintain. It is against this background that vague generalisations set in, born out of frustration at not being able to be more specific. Thus the phrase 'one man's terrorist is another man's freedom fighter' helps to delimit the boundaries of terrorism for purposes of academic research.

Terrorism is also a moral problem and definitional attempts are predicted on the assumption that some classes of political violence are justifiable whereas others are not. For instance, many academic students of terrorism find little difficulty in labelling an event as 'terrorist' without making a moral judgement about the act. Governments and lawyers and politicians find themselves unable to take such a detached view. It is hardly surprising that vacilations in policy characterise the responses of most individual states to terrorism, and there is complete failure of the international community to launch any effective multilateral initiatives to combat the problem. Even looking at the more general definition of violence (in relation to terror) it has been hard to encounter any pair of researchers in the field using the same definitions. There is not even any single tradition that has crystallised as the dominant one, with others competing for recognition. Hence violence has been defined in terms of force, coercive power, authority and legitimacy.

One of the problems of implementing criminal sanctions concerns acts of terrorism that produce a terror outcome by threats of violence, without actual physical injury to any human or non-human target. Legislative efforts to create a crime of terrorism at the international or state level have to include a definition that realistically mirrors the terror process. An effort to punish terroristic conduct by using an overly broad definitional or jurisdictional focus (as simply murder, attempted murder, threats or assault) is unwise and unworkable in the long run. At the national level, an attempt to prosecute as 'terrorism' many types of conduct that produce no actual terror outcome would seem politically and functionally unwise and constitutionally unsound. It goes without saying that a generally accepted definition of terrorism requires an element of 'terror' and a coercive purpose.

There is no consensus, nor even in many cases a recognition, that the discussion is carried out at cross purposes about subjects few have ever seen at the point of a gun. A paucity of data has never deterred the academic mind, rather, one suspects, the contrary. Thus attracted by the recent spurt of spectacular acts of violence, scholars have rushed into print almost as fast as the journalists, fashioning typologies, defining, explaining and usually prescribing. The definitional problem remains: who is a terrorist, and what is terrorism? The term is now pejorative, the label of the threatened. However, the world is full of situations where one group is pitted against another.

Terrorism is defined by the nature of the act, not by the identity of the perpetrators or the nature of their cause. All terrorist acts involve violence or the threat of violence, often coupled with specific demands. The violence is directed mainly against civilian targets. The motives are political. The actions are carried out in a way that will achieve maximum publicity. The perpetrators are usually members of an organised group, and unlike other criminals, they often claim credit for the act. And finally, the act is intended to produce effects beyond the immediate physical damage. "

The problem created is clear from the qualifying terms it uses—'often', 'mainly', 'generally' and 'usually'. These qualifiers allow for the injection of personal views in deciding whether a particular act is or is not 'terrorist'. On the other hand, defining terrorism by focusing on the nature of the act rather than on the identity of the perpetrators or the nature of their cause makes a substantial degree of objectivity possible. The Rand definition of terrorism implies that governments as well as individuals and groups may be terrorist. A survey of Rand chronologies indicates that very few examples of the use of terror by governments against their own nationals are included. Furthermore, incidents generally are not listed in which terrorists operate within their own nation against their own countrymen. For example, when Irishmen in Northern Ireland kill or otherwise terrorise each other the incidents are not included in the chronologies; when members of the Irish Republican Army kill Englishmen, the incidents are included.

The Central Intelligence Agency distinguishes between 'transnational terrorism' or 'terrorism' carried out by basically autonomous non-state actors, whether or not they enjoy some degree of support from 'sympathetic states', and 'international terrorism', which is terrorism carried out by individuals or groups controlled by a sovereign state. Whether or not a particular terrorist act was financed by a 'sympathetic' state or commissioned by a foreign government is usually so difficult to determine that the distinction would seem to be meaningless in the real world. Did Gaddafi 'control' or merely 'support' Carlos the Jackal? If the answer to that question is known it is so only through using the most sensitive and classified sources and methods and is probably not available to any ordinary scholar.

However, attempts by Congress to develop a viable definition of international terrorism have not, so far, yielded tangible results. Many definitions do not distinguish between common crimes and acts normally regarded as within the realm of international terrorism. For example, Section 202 of FIR 1179, 'A Bill to amend the Internal Security Act of 1950 to control and penalise terrorists and for other purposes', defines 'crimes of terrorism' as:

> espionage, sabotage, kidnapping, extortion, skyjacking, robbery, bombing, holding a person prisoner or hostage or any threat or attempt to kidnap, extort, skyjack, bomb, or hold prisoners or hostages, or any threat to do any injury to a human being, animal or personal or real property or any conspiracy to do any of the above in order to compel an act or omission by any person, or any governmental entity.

The United Nations has held discussions on terrorism for several years, and to this body the definition of a threat becomes feasible only when a particular activity, like skyjacking, becomes sufficiently onerous to a majority of the members of the three major blocs in the Organisation. In the case of terrorism, that stage has not yet been reached, judging by the failure of the UN General Assembly to agree on a definition of international terrorism. If the time ever comes when there is general agreement that international terrorism must be curbed, any definition adopted will have to be couched in universal, and not in pro-Western, terms. How to define the national security interests of the United States is a partially subjective question. However, it appears to focus attention where it is needed, on those terrorist acts which affect adversely American power, stability and security.

The UN argues that the imprecision of definition should not be allowed to render complete confusion desirable, and that a definition can be useful in leading decision makers to a comprehensive consideration of varying claims to authority in varying contexts of the terroristic process with greater insight into content, greater rationality in choice, greater overall policy realisation and greater efficacy during the process of authoritative response. Thus in the 1970s, the Secretary General's report on international terrorism reflected the need for a definitional approach by attempting to articulate certain basic definitional components. These included terror outcome, instrumental or 'immediate' victims, primary targets, violence and political purpose. Divisions, political differences and sectional interests have prevented agreement on this topic.

One of the central problems bedevilling international cooperation is the definition of terrorism. Because treaties are couched in legal terms they rely heavily on definitions acceptable to all parties. Debates on the subject have been acrimonious; in the 35-member UN General Assembly *Ad Hoc* Committee on Terrorism in its three prolonged sessions of 1973, 1977 and 1979, quarrels over the nature of innocence, acts of national liberation, modalities of state terrorism and motivation of actors have resulted in innocuoüs debates. Yet many member states of the UN believe terrorism to be an attack on the prevailing legal order, but are unsure how to respond.

International terrorism can be distinguished from purely domestic terror/violence by the presence of an international jurisdictional element. Transnational terrorism, a term that is often used erroneously—as a synonym for international terrorism—can be considered a subclassification with specific reference to non-state, non-political actors. It is the confusion and misuse of terminology that has complicated, at least from the legal perspective, an already badly misunderstood phenomenon. Although specially constituted UN committees have continually condemned acts of international terrorism in principle, they have exempted from the definition of such acts those activities that derive from 'the inalienable right to self-determination and independence of all peoples under colonial and racist regimes and other forms of alien domination and the legitimacy of their struggle, in particular the struggle of national liberation movements in accordance with the purposes and principles of the Charter and the relevant resolutions of the organs of the United Nations'. This exemption from the 1973 *Ad Hoe* Committee report on International Terrorism is corroborated by Article 7 of the UN General Assembly's 1974 Definition of Aggression. According to Article 7:

> Nothing in this definition and in particular Article 3 (inventory of acts that qualify as aggression) could in any way prejudice the right to self-determination, freedom and independence as derived from the Charter of peoples forcibly deprived of that right and... particularly peoples under colonial and racist regimes or other forms of alien domination.

Terrorism relates to any act performed by an individual or group of individuals that is designed to undermine the authority of a legitimate government or state. The Draft Proposal submitted by the Non-aligned Group of the *Ad Hoc* Committee on International Terrorism concerning the definition of international terrorism gives the equally clear impression that terrorism is related to the suppression of personal liberties of individuals by a ruling authority or military regime. Such opposing views of terrorism rely on the political context of the country providing the definition. In general, well-established, developed Western democracies are concerned with disruption of societal functioning by persons engaged in terrorist activity against the State, while relatively new 'underdeveloped' countries, often founded on the basis of revolution or protracted guerrilla activity, are concerned with oppression of indigenous populations and suppression or restriction of the freedom of dissent by repressive governments.

Perhaps, in the absence of an international definition, the West will go it alone as a community and act as a group against terrorism. The Gordian Knot can be cut only by an independent framing or norms by democracies—terror is the deliberate intentional killing and maiming of innocent civilians, so as to inspire fear to gain political ends. Under the Northern Ireland (Emergency Provisions) Act 1973, for the first time in UK Statute Law, terror was defined as the use of violence for political ends, including any use of violence for the purpose of putting the public in fear. This view was also held by Merlyn Rees, the then Ulster Secretary. Senator Henry Jackson and the Jerusalem Conference on International Terror defined terror as the deliberate, systematic murder, maiming and menacing of the innocent to inspire fear in order to gain political ends. Recently, consideration has again been given to whether democracies should convene a conference of all states which respect the principles of democracy and the rule of law. Especially useful would be the enforcement of an international convention against terrorism for which the European Convention on Terrorism would serve as a working model and which would cover the definition of terrorism as an international crime, the denial of political status for criminals so defined, common procedures for extradition, appropriate penalties and the exchange of evidence.

Governments often use the word 'terrorist' to describe their opponents, even when these opponents have not used violence. Guerrilla groups refuse to let themselves be seen by governments as terrorists and will prefer to call themselves guerrillas. The original use of the word as meaning someone who uses violence indiscriminately to achieve his ends can easily be forgotten. While it is easier for governments than for terrorists to legitimate their activities, terrorists often strive for legitimacy. Governments are portrayed as having substantial resources, and as rational beings whose actions serve a longer goal, while individuals have little social claim and are typified by mearge resources and frugal modes of violence, coupled with an irrational drive and a deranged mind.

The powerful in the Western world can label all sorts of violence against the State 'terroristic'. Despite the ambiguity and subjectivity that may surround an act of terrorism, there are certain characteristics that differentiate terrorism from other violent criminal acts. While the indiscriminate murders, maimings and mayhem associated with terrorism often appear to result from irrational behaviour by the terrorist, it is important to assume that violence, however barbaric, has its own rationality. This point may perhaps be difficult to accept but unless the responding forces and concerned officials do so, they will not be able to differentiate between terroristic violence and other forms of strife and will fail to understand the patterns that take place when the hostage-taker initiates an incident. Acts of terrorism are not to be treated as just another form of criminal violence.

Terrorism, by definition, is an act that seeks to influence a population significantly larger than the immediate target. Thus the quality of the public's understanding and its response to terrorism of all varieties is highly significant. One of the prime purposes of terrorist activity is to put a grievance on the public agenda. Ultimately, it is public opinion in a democracy that will help shape the political environment within which government officials must act. Thornton believes terrorism is the use of terror as 'a symbolic act' designed to influence political behaviour by extranormal means, entailing the use or threat of violence. In this view an insurgent group has to disrupt the internal relationship between incumbents and citizenry. Here, there is concentration on its extranormal quality, which can be placed above political violence such as riots. It is the extranormal nature of the use of terror that distinguishes it from other forms of political violence. The problem with this situation is in defining extranormal. Thornton then characterises its highly symbolic content which contributes to its high efficacy. Both Thornton and May divide terror types into two: the enforcement and regime of terror which is the service of established order to suppress challenges to their authority, and the siege of terror or agitational terror in the hands of revolutionary movements who wish to disrupt existing order and ascend to political power themselves. Both authors admit it is much easier to focus on a specific perpetrator than on an amorphous system. Groom is partly supportive in that he believes it is far easier to conceptualise the use of terror as a weapon to achieve a specific goal rather than as a form of regular and normal government.

The terrorist seeks instant gratification from his abominable act and takes pleasure in the attention occasioned by the consequences of violence. According to Fromm, political terrorists are more interested in destruction than they are in creation. Not only do they hate their enemies, 'but their destructiveness is protection against life itself'. What distinguishes terrorism from pure criminality in the statutes of afflicted countries is the focus upon particular consequences rather than upon mere criminal intent—whether it be in Israel, West Germany, Italy or Spain. A concomitant view—and as the Rand Corporation reiterate regularly—is that once a group carries out a terrorist act it acquires the label 'terrorist', a label that tends to stick.

Terrorism is a strategy whereby violence is used to produce certain effects upon a group of people. With special reference to substate terrorism this strategy is one of four 'ideal type' strategies, whereby a group out of power can effect violent social change, the other three being coup d'état, insurrection and guerrilla warfare.

To the terrorist the ends invariably justify the means. International conventions proscribing interference with air transport have had the effect of making aerial hijacking, for example, per se an act of terrorism. Likewise, by international and regional conventions, as well as domestic statutes, attacks upon heads of state, certain specified government officials and diplomats are categorised as forms of terrorism. The reasons for this derive from history, custom and tradition, but the end result has been to obscure the real nature of terrorist activity. The structural duality of terror/violence has also been a complicating factor. State or governmental terror has become far more pervasive and barbaric than individual or group terrorism. Only for the past two decades have social scientists been interested in terroristic violence. Some believed that it was a relatively rare phenomenon and others neglected it for different reasons. In studying and comparing violence in many countries, a broad generalisation can be concluded—that a little repression increases instability whereas a great deal has the opposite effect. Nevertheless, in saying this, although a good case can be made for a comparative study of terrorism, it has to be apparent that not everything can be compared with everything else.

In considering the link between terrorism and violence, it becomes clearer that many of the definitional problems plaguing analysts of terrorism can be found back in the scientific and ideological discourse on violence. It has been defined in terms of force, coercive power, authority, legitimacy, behaviour, motives, intentions, antecedents and consequences. It has been defined in terms of violation, violation of corporal integrity, violation of territorial or special integrity, of moral and legal decency, of rules and expectations and even violations of self-esteem, dignity and autonomy.

The distance between the defining social scientist and the political defining agency or the common language definitions can be a source of frictions and misunderstandings. While an author might use a narrow definition of violence to start with, the reader belonging to either the political defining elite or to the common language users group is likely to forget about the 'given' definition in the course of reading and introduce his own meaning, in consonance with his interests and experience. Looked at on a wider political scale, terrorism has been defined as violent Criminal behaviour designed primarily to generate fear in a large part of' the community for political purposes. When such behaviour hinges on the consciousness and concerns of the entire nation, then the nation becomes the community in the definition. The definition is deliberately 'innocentric', in that it labels as terrorists all those who use violent, criminal behaviour to attack the vital interests of Western countries.

In the international forum neither the Soviet bloc nor most Third World countries would be likely to vote in favour of a definition geared to Western interests. The

Soviet Union has an interest in trying to label all individuals and groups working against Western interests in a violent manner as 'freedom fighters' participating in 'wars of national liberation, not in terrorist acts. Many Third World countries achieved independence as the result of an armed struggle which typically began with terrorist acts, and as we have seen graphically in recent years, they are hardly likely to condemn many of the terrorists operating in the world today. Bearing in mind that not all violence is terrorism, but all terrorism is violence (psychologically as well as physically), there is a framework for defining terrorism as the use of force or the threat of force directed against innocent third parties for primarily ideological, financial or psychological purposes. Innocence is the quintessential condition of terrorist victimology, for the terrorist victim is not the ultimate target.

When political terrorists strike out at innocent third parties, their real intent is the destabilisation of governments and a demoralisation or even panic among the public-at-large. Anyone can be a potential victim, for to the idealist and the radical liberationist, no one is truly innocent. Thus one stands with the terrorists or against them; there is no middle ground. While the term 'terrorism' is often indiscriminately used and it is difficult to use accurately in a strictly legal context, it raises little doubt in the mind of the man in the street. Though definitional precision is difficult, terrorism is not hard to describe and for those who have experienced it, easy to comprehend.

Many lives are lost in natural calamities—epidemics and accidents, but those unfortunate people are not victims of evil designs. Evil lies in the human perception, how he behaves, acts and treats a person in captivity. It is when the value of human life is put at sake for some ulterior motive, that the nature and significance of victims becomes clear. Victim is thus a person harmed by person or as a result of an event or incident. This is what is meant by victims of terrorism. The-first requisite is that a person has suffered some painful injury or harm, physical or mental and that his or her name is linked with some reason or cause. Another element of the victim of terrorism is that an assault either tangible or intangible, is carried out by someone who is more powerful because of his position or because he is better armed or equipped than victim. Because interaction is aggressive, the victim is fearful and find himself/herself less powerful and helpless. In the face of stronger opposition in the victim normally responds with resignation or remorse or rage.

In order to fully understand and appreciate the problem of victims of terrorism it is imperative to realise that human life is not an item that can be wasted; it has value, some meaning and a purpose. Commitment to this value brings the terrorists, the victims, and the spectators together in a triangular relationship that crystalises modern terrorism and makes functions like hostage negotiations possible.

Countries which are alive to the value they attach to human life and individual rights, have figured prominently in dealing with victims of terrorism. In totalitarian states, placing less value on human life, terrorism is not a problem. Where the state does not value human life and where the aim is solely to kill we have assassination; where the victim does not value his own life, we have suicide; when he values it less than something else, we have martyrdom; where he sees himself as a soldier who accepts the risk of combat, we have a prisoner of war and finally, when no value is attached to individual human life, where the individual is ail insignificant, expendable creature where cruelty reigns, and where there is simply nothing to look forward to, we have in such a situation, a victim who like a pawn can be conveniently sacrificed to meet terrorist blackmail.

The victims of terrorism often stand as a symbol of he government under siege, and because media provide an extensive coverage to released hostages, once the traumatic incident is over, these victims exercise considerable influence over public opinion and public sympathy. Only a government or public that has deep under standing of these victims can act logically with what they say and do. If the public overreacts, it may result in harsh, counter-terrorist measures that may amount to playing into the hands of terrorists' design and may ultimately discredit the government.

On the other hand, if people, along With victims, identify themselves with the terrorists and their cause, it may undermine the morale and confidence of those in government, from policy makers to police, who must respond officially when an incident occurs. But a government that is aware of the outcome of human responses that may be manifested by a man and a woman under severe stress, including the stress of terrorist threat and captivity, will be able to make correct decisions about national policy on terrorism and appropriate and suitable means for managing terrorist incidents that occur.

There is another, even more pertinent, reason to appreciate the agony of the victims of terrorism. They are the persons who actually suffer. Public and government are mere spectators to the drama. Unfortunatcly the sufferings of the victims are not understood in its true perspective and are often forgotten when the climax of the monstrous episode is over. Since the terrorists' victims normally are the unwitting and unwilling proxies for an attack on the government it is natural that they merit direct government aid, attention and care. Care in the sphere where the victims suffer most: the ghastly imprints on the mind and spirit as well as physical damage to the body, and the emotional and psychological consequences in terms of human experience and behaviour. There is yet another pressing reason to consider the victim of terrorism.

The victim is a prize that is held in order to gain some tactical advantage elsewhere by way of bargaining for something that the terrorists want. Victim is a valuable possession which can bring terrorists good returns. The importance of the victim, if he is a single person, lies in his exchange value. It is thus the natural endeavour of the terrorists to snatch people having some connection with wealth fame or business. Otherwise the terrorists try to capture as many people as possible at a time, by way of hijacking aeroplanes, buses and trains. Victims are, however, always regarded as a commodity, a symbol of state authority without personality or individual value.

Once the terrorist incident has taken place, helping effort must concentrate on reducing the harm it causes. These efforts include the attempt to defuse the situation itself as early as possible with minimum loss of life. While concern for the victim's safety plays a major role in resolving the situation, many other political and situational factors influence decision makers. After the incident is over it is also essential to have a programme design, specific techniques and psychological primers that may be helpful in care and rehabilitation of hostages who have been put to great mental and physical strain and stresses while under forced detention.

As a law abiding citizen one should be as compassionate towards victims in general as the resources and the publicly-stated moral code of a nation should allow one to be. To re-establish the victims of terrorism we must extend our commitment to the value of human life by providing concern and advice to victims. Nation owes a lot to the survivors of the terrorist action, in that they had undergone a very strange and nerve-breaking ordeal, for no fault of theirs, and come back alive. These are the men and women who stood up against great odds, survived, and prevailed.

A hostage is like a handcuffed man, sitting on a heap of explosives, with the safety pin removed from the detonating device. There may be explosion any moment which may fragment the body of the hostage to pieces. Chances of survival are practically nil or very little unless a prudent person with guts and courage puts back the safety pin in the device before it ignites or wisdom prevails over the person who has the ignition mechanism in his hand. Between these two extremes of life and death lies a broad spectrum of stress and strain situations and reactions. Whether it is short or long term captivity all victims of terrorism share certain common features, both physical and psychological, including loss or limitation of freedom of action and loss of power over one's fate. While the different people involved may react differently, both physically and psychologically, certain patterned forces react against the victim's will to resist which produces anxiety leading to panic with little or no possibility for free movement or action. Victims correctly perceive that they are in danger of losing their lives, Nevertheless, in a captive state some kind of relationship, be it of hate or pity, to one's captor and some degree of affection or obligation towards one's family, arc induced.

The central point of any form of captivity is the loss of freedom to feel and move freely. Deprivation of freedom may be exacerbated by a high degree of physical restraint. The denial of free movements may take any form of torture. Some like the Nazis systematically tortured certain victims by mean,; of confinement in the so-called "Stenbunker", a cubicle so small that it was impossible to lie down or even sit down properly. Another version of Nazi torture was to force the victims to stand between two rows of electrically charged barbed wire for at least twenty-four hours. There are so many other forms of torture, which aim at depriving the person freedom of action.

A lesser, but intolerable, form of deprivation of freedom is to be watched constantly by the hostage takers. To be on display for twenty-four hours a day with no privacy at any time, is without doubt, a deep insult to human dignity and a serious blow to self-esteem. Such continuous watch inculcates feelings of revulsion, degradation, dehumanization and vague threat. Explicitly the victim feels impotent, confined, constricted and caged like an animal in a zoo. Despite difference of nationality, religion and race and may be for short durations, the victims are united in showing proud indifference, aloofness, and disdain to the inquisitive stares.

Another aspect of captivity is lack of power over one's fate. This makes any prediction for the future uncertain and any feeling of security impossible. In this respect normal criminal prisoners are well off. Whereas the criminals know the date of their 'execution' or release, skyjacked victims do not even know where they are or where the aircraft is going to land. Fear of the unknown and 'lack of power over one's fate' make things very difficult for the victims. Lack of power over one's fate makes prediction for the future uncertain and any feeling of security impossible. Knowledge of imminent death presents equally unbearable stress. They experience every day of life as a new gift.

In the initial stages the victim, stunned with shock

and exhaustion, loses all sense of time as if time has come to a standstill. Mental faculties cease working. Victims refuse to believe what is happening. Some count hours, others are in a trance looking everywhere, nowhere. Fear prevails and manifests itself in profuse sweating, shivering, shaking and cramp in the stomach. Victims sit and stare apathetically. The nights are endless and days restless. Occasionally somebody moans or cries quietly. In the state of shock as per the medical scientists, the heart beats faster and more strongly, blood is diverted from the skin to the muscles, the airways to lungs open more widely, and digestive activities are suspended. The people the eye is dilated The victim's ability to speak, think and act is nullified.

Certain disease symptoms, related to forced captivity, start surfacing. Clinically the following diseases, to varying degrees, are attributed to stress situation: "bronchial asthma, hypertension, ulcerative colitis, certain types of dermatitis, heumotoid arthritis, thyrotoxicosis, and peptic Ulcer. Certain general symptoms such as headache, menstrual disturbances, eating and sleeping disorders are also noticed. People get irritated more often, even by little things like talking, laughing or cigarette smoking". In certain cases loss of weight and appetite was reported. Vicious circle comes into being under captive situations. Emotional strains affect appetite, appetite affects nutrition, nutrition affects physical condition, which in turn affects appetite and emotions. Psychologically, a victim under forced detention starts with the feeling of fear and anxiety. As the time passes the victim becomes hopeful of getting released. He gains some confidence. When nothing happens he gets frustrated, impatient and intolerant. This is the most serious and dangerous stage because in a state of frustration a victim may start behaving irrationally. Despondency, dejection, resignation and remorse always lead to abnormal behaviour and action.

Another limitation is that victims of terrorism more often that not, do riot even know who the terrorists are, what their demands are and whether it will be, possible to appease them at all. Lack of information creates a syndrome of uncertainty. Victims experience a peculiar sense of insecurity which is often painful and intolerable. Under such conditions, where the hostages are cut off from any connection with the outside world and their families and are uncertain of their fate, they desperately want to make some sort of contact with their loved ones and tend to overreact thereby get themselves damaged partially or fully. This situation occurs frequently with victims, in a skyjacked plane, who know that their families are waiting at the airport.

Some unwelcome questions are put to the hijackers and in turn receive a rifle butt or bullet in the body. The desire for contact with the outside world is not just an expression of strong family ties, but also an intrinsic desire in human beings not to disappear without a trace. People who know that their chances of survival are nil have always been anxious to leave behind some trace, some report of what happened to them. This intense desire not to die without a trace has resulted in many hysterical fits among the victims of terrorism.

Wounds on the body are normally healed in a reasonable period of time if properly cared, but the injury inflicted on the mind takes time to heal. At times it may not heal at all, or if cured, leaves an everlasting impression on the mind which is not easy to erase. The injury on the mind is more agonising than the pain of the visible wound. The effect of captivity on the mind or attitude or outlook is far more damaging. It destroys the will to live, shatters faith in the living beings, in the surroundings and in humanity in general. There are certain visible long-term effects of captivity. When the initial shock and refusal to accept the reality is over the victim becomes frightened and the emotional shock and fear persist for a considerable period. "Disabling psychiatric symptoms, such as suspicion, anxiety, depression, change in character and life style and maladjustments and developmental problems in children are evidently observed in majority of cases, long after the episode is over". The victims show both difficult and prolonged struggles with powerful feelings and ideas aroused by the traumatic experience of the disaster and the survivors very often attempt to recognise themselves and rebuild their shattered will and faith. Victims have also been found nursing deep feelings of distress and hopelessness, of loss and isolation, much after the event is over.

Hostages, specially the rape victims, are isolated by their own feelings of guilt and shame; guilt over whether they perhaps could have taken some stand against the terrorists at the cost of their lives, and shame at having been taken, used, damaged and defiled. This makes it harder for victims to share their experiences with others and to work them through psychologically by themselves on a constructive conscious level.

Some of the guilt and shame has an unreal and unusual character when viewed by outsiders. Friends and relatives, who try to comfort victims, are often angered and saddened as they find out quickly that the guilt or shame does not go away as soon as the well-meaning helpers demonstrate that, from a rational point of view, it does not make sense. Even more agonizing in these situations is the possibility that the guilt may be genuine and justified.

Perhaps in situations like hostage-taking and rape, it is essential first to acknowledge the reality of guilt before we can expect real forgiveness from ourselves or from others, along with the possibility of effective atonement and healing. The need to consider guilt an emotion that is not always psychological may be applicable to situations less extreme than the international terrorism.

In terrorist incidents, realistic guilt becomes a problem when some hostages have been released before others or when persons having military or paramilitary backgrounds have not resisted the hostage takers with force. Such situations have occurred in many terrorist incidents. In the Tehran hostage situation, both factors were relevant to the marine embassy guards who were among those released by the terrorists early in the incident. The fact that they were released because they were black only added to their misery.

In addition to being isolated by his or her own psychological reactions, the victims of rape or terrorism faces a further and related process of isolation by others. These two processes often interact in a negative spiral with more social isolation leading to more unrealistic thinking and so on. Social isolation is particularly tragic, since friends and relatives sometimes pull away at the very time when they are most needed. This distraction is often a product of the discomfort caused by the issues of brute violence or sexuality that the incident itself raises, even if the victim tries to protect friends and relatives by not talking about it. Mixed with this is often a fear or suspicion that the victim has somehow been contaminated or changed irreversibly for the worse. The female victim of rape may be treated by a friend, lover or spouse, sometimes unconsciously, as "damaged good".

As a society, we must recognize the plight of the victims. Concern for the victims would definitely assist those who suffer the mental anguish and the humility of being held hostage or abused sexually. The distress and anguish and long-term emotional abnormalities as a result of captivity do not end with the release of the hostages, They persist much longer after the event is concluded. Public distrust and antipathy is not uncommon.

A greater degree of public understanding of the impact of the crisis on the hostage Would be an act of acceptance that would make the hostages assured. Sexuality and affection that greeted the hostages of the Indian Airlines hijacked plane was an important event in India. Like astronauts, the hostages had undergone a grave journey and come back alive. The heartfelt welcome to the hostages in India and other countries means that society has become mature enough to lavish positive feelings on people who have suffered rather than on those who have inflicted harm.

The description of the experiences of being captive provided by the surviving victims leaves no doubt that most hostages undergo physiological and psychological stress response of some kind. If such a response is intense enough and prolonged enough it can have important physical and mental consequences. Although the duration of captivity may only be a few hours, or a few days, the situation is much more threatening than most events in ordinary life and certainly much more so than any situation that has been orchestrated in laboratory research studies. It represents a very significant event for anyone who has experienced it. People's pattern of life reportedly changed significantly following captivity; such changes are known to have health implications, either through the mechanism of the primary psychological stress response or through secondary mechanism such as increased use of alcohol and other drugs, accident proneness, and other covert and overt self destructive behaviour.

On August 23, 1973, four employees of the Sveriges Kredit Bank, Stockholm, Sweden, were held hostage by a

32-year-old thief, burglar, and prison escapee named Jan-Erik-Olsson with the help of one more culprit. The siege, which continued for 131 hours, gave birth to a psychological phenomenon subsequently called the 'Stockholm Syndrome'. The particular hostage Situation gained popularity primarily because the media exploited the fears of the victims as well as the sequence of events.

Contrary to what had been expected, it was found that the victims identified themselves with the captors and feared the police more than they feared the captors. Even one young woman hostage allegedly initiated sexual relationship with her captor. Her response was neither out of fear nor coercion but resulted from a situation originated from the sharing of common fate in a situation of mutual crisis and the projected -dependence of the captive and the captor. For weeks after this incident some of the hostages felt no hatred for their captors. In fact, they magnified feelings that the captors had given them their lives back and they were emotionally indebted to their captors for their magnanimity.

Similar symptoms were observed by one of the hostages, Gerard Vaders, who along with others was held captive for twelve days in a train hijacked by seven Moluccans on December 2, 1975, near Amsterdam, Denmark. After the siege was over and postmortem of the event was carried out, Vaders confessed that he had to fight a certain feeling of compassion for the Moluccans. A feeling of pity did arise for the hijackers who, at the beginning, looked so strong, overdomineering, impregnable and invincible, ended up so small, broke and desperate. As envisaged by 'Stockholm Syndrome' the reaction formation and identification with the captors usually occurs over longer periods of time and thus it emerges in later phases of hostage incidents. Reaction formation may be described as an adaptive process in which an individual adopts attitudes and behaviour that are in fact opposite to the impulses he nurses either consciously or unconsciously. For example, fear of the terrorist is transformed into approval and admiration—a sort of identification with the terrorists. The victim unconsciously incorporates the characteristics of the feared person and becomes emotionally allied with him. By transforming himself from the person threatened into the person who makes the threat, the victim tries to reduce his anxiety.

This phenomenon has also been highlighted in the much publicised case of Patricea Hearst. Hearst then an 18-year-old newspaper heiress, was kidnapped from her Berkley apartment in February 1974 by the Symbionese Liberation Army gang. She was held hostage and subjected to severe stress for a prolonged period of time. Subsequently she appeared to have identified herself with her captors and joined them in the game of their violent activities by assuming the "revolutionary name" Tanya. Three months after her capture she carried a gun and even attempted to provide covering fire when her companions were challenged by a storekeeper for shoplifting. The "Stockholm Syndrome" seems to be an automatic, unconscious, emotional response to the trauma of becoming a victim. Although some victims may think this is not a rational choice by a victim who decides consciously that the most advantageous behaviour in this predicament is to befriend the captor. The phenomenon affects both the hostage and hostage-takers. The positive emotional bond in, or perhaps because of, the stress of the siege serves to unite its victims against all outsiders.

A philosophy of "its us" against "them" seems to develop. Like the automatic reflex action of the knee the bond seems to be beyond the control of the victim. The victim perceives the criminal as his protector and believes that his family and government, by their behaviour or refusal to accede to the demands of the captors, are the ones who are endangering his' life. Under such conditions, when anxiety and terror are overwhelming, the victim easily distorts reality and may actively view the terrorists as his mentors. The hostages visualise that the police weapons are pointed at them. The government's insistence on surrender of the terrorists is also-keeping them captive. Hostages begin to develop the idea that "if the police go away, we could go also. If they let the terrorists go, we would be free", and thus the bond begins. The captors and captives find a common enemy in law enforcing forces. They identify with each other in finding a common cause to the unfortunate situation.

In the beginning of the action, hostages experience the real danger of being killed. As the time passes and the threat of imminent death diminishes the hostages start gaining some confidence. Their mental equilibrium is gradually restored. The hostages feel a certain relief that opens the way for communication and usually some effort to understand the terrorists. Hostages start viewing a terrorist as a "poor guy" compelled to such extreme action because of political situation or because no other ways are open to him to put forward his grievances.

The victims thus unconsciously accept to a certain extent the hostage-taker's presentation of himself, viewing him as a human being with personal traits and problems deserving of sympathy. The terrorists reinforce this feeling when they stress that they have nothing against the hostages personally and treat them humanely. Further reconciliation comes when both view each other as individual human beings and members of a group. They no longer consider each other anonymous enemies. An unexplained understanding between the hostages and hostage-takers takes shape and develops into logical rapprochement. In spite of this apparent conciliation the deep-seated fear of death is constantly present in most hostages. When they are finally liberated, their immediate gratitude turns towards those who did not kill them, despite what the victims actually expected during their whole ordeal. This extreme feeling of relief will thus very often be expressed in the form of gratitude towards the captors because they did not implement the worst expectations of the victims, did not abuse them and kill them, but let them survive. The mere realisation that the terrorists did not pass the judgement of condemnation or annihilation will draw the victims towards the captors. In most cases the victims feel obliged to those who spared their lives.

In September 1976, when five Croatian hijackers took a Boeing 727 carrying ninetyfive people on a transatlantic flight from New York to Paris, another case of temporary surrender to the terrorists' cause occurred. The hostages were released at intervals. After flying over London, the aircraft landed in Paris, where it was surrounded by police and not allowed to depart. After thirteen hours the hijackers surrendered to the French police. The episode lasted a total of twentyfive hours for most of the passengers. Those victims who were released at Gander, Newfoundland, only after three hours of captivity did not express sympathy for the hijackers while those released later reacted positively towards them. Thus time played a significant role in the development of the identification process. If the hostage-takers do not abuse their victims, hours spent together will most likely produce 'positive' bonds with the captors. Time alone may not be the prime factor in the development of 'Stockholm Syndrome' but it definitely acts as a catalyst in nonabusive situations. Positive contact with the captors contributes beneficially to the generating of the 'Syndrome'. In the above hijacking case it was learnt that those victims who had negative contacts with the terrorists did not evidence concern for them regardless of time spent together. The victims who had positive contacts with the hijackers, which include discussing the hijackers cause and understanding their motivation and sufferings, took leave and attended the trials of their captors. A few began a defence fund. Some recommended a defence counsel to the terrorists. Importance of time and contact with the captors was duly appreciated by Col Charlie A. Beckwith who masterminded the Delta Force's abortive operation to free the American hostages from Tehran in April 1980. Writing about the American hostages in the book, 'Delta Force', he mentioned: "There is no way of knowing how they will behave. Will they try to protect their guards—that's a syndrome common to situations where hostages have been held a long time".

Not only the victims, but as the time passes the positive contact between the hostages and hostage-takers, the "identification" syndrome also begins to affect the terrorists. This was evident at Entebbe in July 1976. During this incident there were major variations in the quality of interaction between the hostage-takers and the hostages. These ranged from relatively friendly conversation to sadistic tauntings. During the final assault, one of the terrorists, who had engaged in conversation with the hostages from the Air France Flight 139, elected at the moment of attack to shoot at the Israeli commandos rather than to execute the hostages. The same process was probably at work in the decision of the south Moluccan terrorists not to execute Gerard Vaders, because he had narrated his not so happy marital relationship. The terrorists could no longer see him as a faceless symbol to be sacrificed. He was now a human being who might be spared.

Most people cannot inflict pain on another as long as their victim remains humanized. When the hostage-takers and hostages are locked together in a building, a train, or an airplane, a process of transference takes place and hostage-takers start understanding the hostages as human beings. When a person, a hostage, can build sympathy while maintaining dignity, he or she can lessen the aggression of a captor. On 5th September 1986 in the hijacking incident of Pan Am Aircraft at Karachi Airport, such a situation was evidenced. It took only three hours for the transference process to start. For three hours, from 5.30 to 8.30 a.m. passengers were forced to remain in their seats with their heads down and hands over the neck. Then the situation started easing. The hijackers started behaving in a courteous manner with the passengers. The children were shown affection and given some biscuits. The hijackers were suddenly in a playful mood. They listened to the people and let them have what they wanted. Hijackers took special care of women. The courage and mannerism of airhostesses and flight pursers (all of Indian origin) was duly appreciated by the hijackers. The hijackers were in no mood of harming the passengers till the light went out in the aircraft as also in the terminal building and drama came to a tragic end resulting in 22 dead and 139 injured. Whether the incident is a bank robbery in Stockholm, a hijacking of an American airplane, or a kidnapping in South America, there are behavioural similarities despite geographic and motivational differences. In each situation a relationship seems to develop within and between people caught in situations beyond their control and not of their making, This relationship seems to help victims cope with excessive stress and at the same time enable them to survive.

The 'Stockholm Syndrome' is not a magical relationship of blanket affection for the terrorists. This bond, although strong, does have its limits. Despite all the positive expressions, the feeling of affection seems to be a mask for great inner turmoil. Most victims, who felt considerable affection for the terrorists, reported night mares after the incident. These dreams expressed the fear that the captors would recapture them. Obviously the affection and positive feelings generated tend to be superficial, while in their subconscious mind, the terrorists were dreaded by the victims. 'Stockholm Syndrome' is a temporary phenomenon. It develops out of necessity rather than convenience. During the incident it is in the interest of the victims to develop profitable rapport with the terrorists by unconsciously identifying with them. Subconsciously and uncontrollably 'Stockholm Syndrome' is a defence mechanism to reduce stress in a hostage situation. It is the survival instinct which forces victims to develop intimate relations with the victimizer. After the incident, it is the gratitude that brings victims closer to the terrorists. Hostages owe their life to the terrorists and it is by showing some affection, a little consideration, that the survivors repay their debts.

There is a growing conviction that specific steps Must be taken to assess and deal with the unusual plight of the victims of terrorism. Those who have been made responsible for containing and resolving terrorist incidents as well as for protecting the victims are increasingly concerned with the development of a deep understanding of the psychological mechanism at work in the hostage as well as in the captor. Since both are likely to exhibit certain predictable behaviour under the stress and strain of a terrorist incident, an understanding of this behaviour and the mechanism underlying it is essential to any programme of intervention and control.

In addition, this understanding can be extended to the development of theories and techniques that may be applied by hostages to reduce anxiety and maximise the chances of survival. There are certain aspects involved in surviving victimization: face the threat, assess the threat and come out of the threat. Technically, defensive measures taken to cope with terrorist victimization are adaptation, defence mechanism, and coping.

Adjustment includes all responses and strategies a hostage may adopt or use in order to reduce stress and maximise his chances of survival. The inventory of adjustment or adaptive techniques is extensive and varies from individual to individual. Adaptive tactics also change with the passage of time and with circumstances. Mechanisms overlap and may even be contradictory. For instance, the victim may deny the reality of the situation and at the same time hope that things will come out all right. There are several factors which make it difficult to predict foolproof adaptive behaviour in a terrorist situation. These factors after the characteristics of the situation may have a profound influence on the outcome. The range of responsive measures available to an individual confronted with severe anxiety is determined to some extent by the duration as well as the intensity of the stress.

Victims of prolonged captivity will utilise means of adaptation different from those of the victims who face a violent, but relatively short, threat. Unless adaptive mechanism is adjusted to the temporal duration of the threat, an individual may not be able to withstand the physical and emotional stress. In the initial stages, stress usually inculcates sustained and guided activity. It has, however, been observed that individuals cannot maintain this response over a prolonged period of time. Unless he makes other adjustment, persistent threat will cause an individual's thought and judgement to deteriorate, somatic disturbances to appear, and often, an erratic and impulsive behaviour. An individual may become irrational and emotionally unstable. He may even develop symptoms of panic. Panic response, obviously, is not conducive to survival as it is followed by the collapse of mental faculties and mechanism that serve survival itself, including body control, attention and alertness.

Victims of terrorism vary both in their life experience before the incident and in the stock of behavioural response that they bring to it. Some individuals, with prior military or police training or experience, mobilise a wide range of conscious adaptive behaviour in addition to unconscious defence mechanism. Obviously, such personnel are better adjusted in a terrorist situation compared with individuals who have had little or no prior exposure to military or police experience. The latter are slow in generating unconscious adaptive behaviour.

Human nature and personality also help in determining survival behaviour. Certain persons with special characteristics adjust more successfully than others under identical situations. Those men who adjust poorly to the prolonged stress are frequently classified as being passive, dependent, and others who withstand well, are found to be healthy, physically and mentally. The personality and life experiences of the terrorists, their motives, and their objectives will also suggest which adaptive behaviour will be most useful in any given hostage situation. For example, most terrorists normally do not make women and children their immediate target. While executing the victims they always make sure that women and children, and at times old people, are spared. Such motives, expectations, and tactics of the terrorists may not be immediately available but as time passes they can be perceived and evaluated in order to institute adaptive behaviour. It has been observed that virtually in all hostage situations the motives of terrorists are not centred on simply killing the hostages but something more complex, which can be manipulated by psychological stimuli.

Denial mechanism is basically an unconscious psychological adjustment that the individual makes to control. A danger and its connected anxiety. When an individual is suddenly confronted with a severe threat he usually employs an initial mental defence of denial or a "counterphobic mechanism". Denial is said to occur when an individual partially or totally, deliberately or unconsciously refuses to accept the reality of an experience, the emotions attached to it or the memory of the experience. This common de fence mechanism helps the individual minimise the shock of the experience to a controllable level and may in some cases result in action such as excessive reflex 'heroism'. Denial can, however, be employed so long as it can coexist with reality testing. Too much and too long denial may lead to 'psychosis'.

As the stressful situation continues progressively, the individual starts realising the reality and it becomes increasingly difficult to reject the experience as not happening. Thus denial is a short-term defence. It generally loses its effectiveness after a period of time. Anxiety levels actually rise with sustained refusal to accept the perceived reality. The defensive denial gradually diminishes as the hostage assimilates the reality of the situation in emotionally acceptable degrees and adopts other adaptive behaviours. Thus the hostage's first reaction might be to outrightly reject what is happening. "I don't believe this", or "this might not be happening", may be the first outbursts of the hostage. For convenience sake he seems to assume that the real situation does not exist. The individual unconsciously and automatically refuses to comprehend the situation.

For brief periods denial helps. It permits time to lapse and protects the individual from physical collapse.

Panic reactions are checked and made less effective. Refusal to accept the reality gives the victim a chance to gradually assess the situation and formulate the coping devices. Extreme form of denials, however, may be dangerous and prove to be counterproductive. An individual might not give allowance to the captors' demand or might even try to push the gun away. Still, if the denial is not extreme, it can act as an unconsciously self-constructed better mechanism that protects the emotional balance of the individual and permits him to progressively and profitably assimilate a dangerous and threatening situation for evolving better strategies for his chances of survival.

The individual who utilizes counterphobic mechanism reduces anxiety and stress by excessive and sometimes precipitous behaviour that actually opposes his basic inclinations in threatening situations. Counterphobic psychological defence may, however, serve the individual well in some cases, but in violent circumstances, such as hostage incidents, counterphobic behaviour often, if not always, is counterproductive. In these situations counter-phobic response or false 'heroism' often increases the chances, in that the victim may be injured or killed. False heroism often leads to catastrophe, Counterphobic behaviour in potentially volatile situations is frequently futile and dangerous. For example, a robbery victim who, while the assailant is pointing a gun at him, reaches under the counter to get his own weapon. The assailant immediately shoots and kills him. In the Moluccan train hijacking, one hostage seemed a little too aggressive while putting tapes over the windows. He was segregated as one of the three hostages to be executed. The point, therefore, is that for a victim of terrorism to survive, the counterphobic mechanism though reduces some amount of tension, is not a good form of defence. Other forms of defence mechanism include "intellectualization", "creative elaboration" and humour. These devices are considered more creative and productive than the others. "Intellectualization" is a psychological process that reduces stress by taking the threatening situation into the sphere of intellect, thus divesting it of its emotional and personal meaning". The threat can be worked on as a cognitive problem with the conceptual tools of philosophy, religion, political theory and science. "Creative elaboration" is a related psychological process by which the victim elaborates on specific situations, sometimes in disguised forms—in dreams, stories, imagery, or fantasy. Like dreaming of sumptuous meal he would have when free, or designing and building a complex computer once out of the ordeal. Some scholars have listed fantasy as the most common coping device. The compensatory as well as distracting role these imaginations can play for people trapped in a hostage situation are self-explanatory. Humour as a defence mechanism can have an extreme adaptive function in reducing anxiety. These three defence mechanisms have been further elaborated in the following pages while discussing coping strategies.

A coping technique involves innovative rather than routine behaviour and differs from denial mechanism in that it is not restricted to unconscious psychological mechanism, but extends to conscious, deliberate behaviour as well. "Coping generally de notes creative as opposed to routine actions, and reflective as opposed to reflexive behaviour".

It has been discussed earlier that denial and counterphobic mechanism are the two techniques that many people initially use in frightening situations. Denial is usually limited to the initial stages of the unexpected threat and often dissipates as the individual gradually assimilates the reality of the experience. It has also been observed that continued denial often results in injury or death.

In other words, the refusal to relinquish control to a clearly dominated assailant increases the victim's danger. Thus the victim's most useful coping strategy in the initial stages of a terrorist episode has been to consciously accept that he must temporarily relinquish control to his captor. It serves two purposes: it emphasises the reality of situation for both the terrorist and the victim, and it reduces the possibility of a violent action on the part of the terrorists. It is important to note that terrorists are anxious, agitated and fearful too, especially in the initial phase of a terrorist incident and it is very likely that they will react sharply at the slightest provocation. This coping device was aptly applied by Gaby Dillmann, one of the hostesses of the ill-fated Boeing 737 when it was hijacked by four Palestinians and taken to Mogadishu, Somalia in October 1977, -where the hostages were finally rescued by a German counter-terrorist squad of GSG-9. Dillmann thought, "If they feel we are nice to them, it will be harder for them to kill us". Thus, the victims' most prudent initial strategy appears to be to leave resistance and intervention to law enforcement professionals who have been specially trained in appropriate strategies and tactics. Even if the terrorists are assaulted, victims are advised not to interfere, but instead seek cover and maintain a submissive posture as much as possible.

Victims must be aware of their own emotions in the situation. In addition to fear, victims of terrorism commonly experience rage, frustration and humiliation. Whereas it is counterproductive to act on These powerful feelings, it is essential that victims learn to control their emotions and actions. Some victims have found it useful to concentrate on their immediate environment, not letting their imagination wander through all the negative possibilities. Others have directed their thoughts towards neutral subjects or pondered comforting themes such as religion.

Assuming familiar roles and doing tasks that are easily mastered have also helped victims reduce anxiety and maintain self-control. It is important to understand that calm and composed action in the face of grave threat is in fact "doing something". Inactivity can help victims to maintain self-esteem, a crucial component in reducing immediate stress and facilitating successful adjustment after the terrorist episode.

Following the initial coping strategies of consciously relinquishing control to the terrorists and then maintaining passive emotional self-control, victims can begin to use adaptive measures that are more appropriate for long-term captivity. Some of these tactics include gathering information, establishing affiliations with other victims, focusing attention on survival for some purpose and maintaining the will to survive. Gathering information about the environment, physical layout, situation of fellow victims and most importantly about the group of terrorists can substantially reduce stress and tension. In the case Hanafi siege in Washington, DC., the women hostages were treated more gently than men. This attempt may be the outcome of religious belief of Hanafi Muslims. This assessment boosted the morale of the captives as it was suggestive that execution was not the paramount interest of the terrorists. In the Pueblo incident it was observed that although the guard beat the captives brutally, they were careful to avoid visible disfigurement. This gave hope to the victims. As in the case of counterphobic mechanism so in the case of collecting information care must be taken that receiving too much or too little information can often increase rather decrease stress and its symptoms. It is thus imperative that the individual should adjust his interaction with the terrorists or with other sources of information according to his ability to control his emotions.

It is beneficial to establish positive bonds with the terrorists. This, however, is a double-edged weapon—a controversial proposition. There are two schools of thought on the issue of establishing a purposeful contact with the terrorists. One recommends that victims may attempt to establish dialogue with the terrorists, taking care not to expressly and seriously interfere in their personal and political beliefs. In contrast, others recommend that victims should not attempt to establish any contact with the captors unless and until the captors initiate dialogue.

A viable solution would be that victims should grab whatever opportunities the terrorists off er for contact. Without taking any apparent initiative it should be the endeavour of victims to look for any opening that the terrorists offer for conversation. The aim of the contact is to induce the terrorists to develop positive emotional bonds with their captives. Hostages should vigilantly seek such bonds and respond quickly and earnestly, since greater human awareness of each other generally reduces possibility of violence.

An example is the experience of Betty Neal, who acted as secretary to the Hanafi leader and assisted him in handling phone calls. The leader, in return, gave her advice as to where to hide and how to protect her life should violence errupt. The Moluccan leader's decision not to execute Gerard Vaders was prompted only after hearing detailed account of Vaders' family problems.

Another extremely profitable strategy to reduce tension is for victims to establish personal and friendly relations with other captives. The feeling of common adversity, of "all being in the same boat", has been authentically evidenced as a stress-reducing psychological process. Victims should take every safe opportunity to discuss and evaluate their situation with an emphasis on what they can do to help each other, Group interaction also provides an atmosphere to boost morale and reduce fear. Humour plays a pivotal role in such situations. Humorous remarks and anecdotes minimise tension and fear of likely death.

In the Mogadishu hijack incident, the terrorists fixed plastic charges inside the cabin and then sprinkled seats and hostages with liquor, presumably to make even a bigger bang. In such a tense situation a remark by a stewardess to a fellow passenger: "It will be very quick. We won't feel a thing", did initiate a surging smile on the faces of hostages in the face of imminent death.

Similarly, in the case of Moluccans' hijacking of train, when the terrorists announced that in the event of an attack by the anti-terrorist squad every body should lie down, one old woman remarked, "I am not going to do that my dress will get dirty". In the face of a grave danger such light-hearted remarks reduce the anxiety and give strength to cope with stress.

The ability to concentrate on survival for a cause or for some purpose in life allows the victims to successfully fight fear and thereby reduce tension. Some hostages have reported that they were determined to live through the incident because they felt they were desperately needed by other members of their families. This strategy of survival for purpose may take the form of faith in something bigger, something that transcends the human conditions. This sublime view evidently has great positive values for anxiety reduction and survival, whether it be commitment to religious faith, devotion to a cause or the positive value of carrying on certain interests to which one is deeply attached. Many hostages have reported that religious faith was helpful.

A deep and abounding faith in mankind or in one's colleagues may also serve as a positive focus. Under prolonged captivity, like the Americans held captive in Tehran, many sustained themselves with the firm conviction that the bulk of humanity would not tolerate such actions. Love also plays an important role in focusing attention on somebody. Many victims have survived with the firm belief that their love for near and dear ones will give them strength to face the ordeal against great odds.

The will to live is yet another factor that helps the victims to overcome grief in a hostage situation. The will to live refers to a more primitive commitment to life. It may occasionally take the form of a deep and total conviction to live no matter what and on any term to choose life for its own sake. Among hostages the will to live often becomes the entire motivation of the individual, bypassing all others.

On the other hand, lack of it is one of the causes of non-deliberate death. Although most terrorist incidents have been mostly time-bound, the basic urge to survive has been a focal point around which hostages can organise their coping strategies. If a person has something to live for, the amount of sufferings he can endure is practically without limit. The Pueblo Commander Bucher's report that "at one specific time repeated beating, exhaustion and pain had made him contemplate suicide, but instead, as the next beating approached he stood up drawing upon a fundamental will to live and prevail over the odds", is to the point.

Countries have since prepared themselves against terrorists and funnelled their own strategies. It is, however, very clear that terrorism is going to stay and humanity has to endure it for quite some time. It is true that no major government has fallen, nor is likely to fall in the world, yet this form of conflict will be with us for a very long time. Preparation against terrorists can be dealt with under two heads: primary and, secondary prevention. Primary prevention reduces the incidence of terrorism in the country, and the secondary prevention reduces the duration of significant events that occur. Stated in simple terms primary prevention of terrorism consists of withdrawing its rewards and punishing its perpetrators promptly. Rewards may be withdrawn by refusing to pay or to publicise the demands of terrorists and by attempting to explore and undermine the emotional wellsprings that feed movements based on revenge. Punishment in the behavioural sense works best when it is applied quickly and when it is not relied upon too heavily.

All primary preparations for potential victims of terrorism start with the assumption that incidents will occur. If such preparations are to yield results they should probably be applied initially to those whose geographic or occupational situations put them at high risk for becoming hostages. In order to prepare for possible captivity by potential terrorists it is important to formulate strategies which have twin goals, willingness to suffer injury and death and supreme purpose that can match the dedication and fervour of religious and political extremists.

Some experts have suggested that military training may help in this area. It may be possible that this type of training may prepare people to face issues of sacrifice, obedience and violence; that it will make people face the ordeals of captivity is a questionable proposition. The concept of courage, therefore, needs to be broadened to include the physical and mental endurance that helps people successfully tackle prolonged captivity as well as the concentrated discipline that is so vital in brief violent encounters.

Traditionally, religious systems have provided some sustaining relief in threatening situations. Our antipathy to religion should not blind us to the resources that these traditional systems offer to potential victims of terrorism. Under difficult situations man has remembered God. Recent hostages have testified to the usefulness of those resources. It is felt that any person who thinks he might possibly become a victim would do well to examine his personal and family's religious belief and find out what his religion or faith says in explanation and support of victims' experiences. Some people will be able to see hostage experiences as a time of testing, others will see them as a time of punishment for past misdeeds, and a few others will more or less accept God's will or their destiny. More often than not hostages are isolated or confined in small groups for enhanced period of time, This concept of isolation makes it more important for potential victims to set their religious and ethical houses in order. Effort for personal preparation may also include understanding that depending upon past experiences, different people react differently to highly stressful events. These experiences give a meaning and purpose to an event, such as terrorist captivity, that may interact with areas of vulnerability or conflict in the particular victim. The ultimate reaction of the victim, to a hostage situation, is thus a function of his own personality.

Preparation of the potential victim's inner turmoil should be accompanied by a thorough familiarization with the physical and cultural environment in which he or she will work, and with what knowledge is available about potential terrorist captors. This kind of specific, detailed preparation may go a long way towards helping a hostage make realistic and logical decision about chances for escape, areas of personal vulnerability and strength of commitment in various dimensions. In addition, this kind of acquaintance can help diminish the sense of bewilderment and of dealing with the unknown that seems to have aggravated stress in hostage experience. In order to achieve the above dimensions it would be advantageous if former hostages are associated in planning and executing primary prevention programmes relating to the minimization of hostage related anxieties. A lot about coping devices that work well in hostages Situations can be learnt from hostages who have coped well as hostages and captives. Their experiences can be fruitfully utilised in future planning processes. Contemporary hostages are a storehouse of unpleasant experiences from which all types of help may be derived.

Humour as an effective method of overcoming monotony and fear of captivity has been discussed earlier. Humour has helped many people overcome extremely difficult situations. It is, however, unfortunate that this aspect of humour, as a coping technique, has neither been properly understood, nor has it been effectively explained by providing concrete examples. In this respect former hostages can also provide valuable advice. Humour works better, where other techniques fail, and should be ideally tried out before a probable incident occurs'.

One helpful technique for mastering coping skills and evaluating individual vulnerability during captivity is the use of simulations or meaningful exercise. Such mock exercises have been used successfully to train for hostage negotiations and may play a major role in reducing the shock of actual terror incident. It is important to have these exercises or manipulations as realistic as possible so that potential hostages can experience at least some of the emotions they will have to deal with during an actual incident.

Hostage situations can be created and techniques

like evaluation of escape possibilities, collection of information about surroundings and captors and the use of communication system mastered in a training programme. It may be impracticable to run such training programmes for majority of population but the vulnerable few may be taught some of the coping devices that have proved extremely useful to hostages in captive situations. It may also be difficult to present a realistic panorama of events, but examples may still be given to the potential hostages.

Media can help the programmes in dissemination to the general public of some of the positive coping techniques. Several television programmes portraying prisoners of war have been televised and focused successfully depicting the coping method used by the prisoners, reaction of their families and the problem of readjustment.

Terrorism is by nature coercive, dehumanising, a theatre of the absurd, and designed to manipulate its victims, and through them, a larger audience. Definitions of terrorism are notoriously difficult and imprecise. A nosology includes (a) non-political terrorism, defined as the deliberate creation of fear for coercive purposes with an end goal of collective or individual gain, or terrorism engendered by seriously mentally disturbed individuals; (b) quasi-terrorism, defined as the application of terroristic techniques in situations that do not involve terroristic crimes as such. Examples of this type abound and include the taking of hostages in derailed bank robberies or prison riots as bargaining leverage to secure freedom or concessions; (c) limited political terrorism, which involves ideologically or politically motivated terroristic acts, such as assassinations or the bombing of public buildings, but which fall short of seeking to overthrow established governments; (d) official or state, terrorism, defined as governmental rule-based on fear, oppression and persecution, and finally; (e) political terrorism, defined as violent, criminal behaviour designed to create fear in a society—or in a substantial segment of it—for political purposes. When fully developed, political terrorism is revolutionary in character and seeks to subvert or overthrow an existing government. Even though the data on the incidence and severity of terrorism, in all its forms, are sketchy, fragmented and therefore suspect, it appears that terrorist activity is rising the world over, that there is a trend towards more lethal incidents and injuries compared to years past and that US citizens (diplomats, the military and business personnel) and US property are being increasingly targeted.

The October 1983 suicide bomb attack that killed two hundred and forty-one US marines is but an example of the growing risk of terrorism and its increasing costs. Given these trends, an increasing number of officials and private citizens will find themselves involved in terroristic crime, as victims of abductions and hostage-holding incidents or as targets for destruction. Some victims are deliberately targeted on the basis of their personal or professional characteristics or because they symbolise whatever has become the object of terrorist hate and annihilation. Other victims are chosen randomly and become victims strictly by chance.

There is a growing body of literature on the subject of terrorism and its victims, but it is scattered and reflects many points of view, as well as many disciplines.[1] The diversity of research methodologies used, such as retrospective studies of hostage experiences or laboratory studies of stress and sensory deprivation, presents major problems for generalising from the information we do have. In the absence of epidemiological studies and base line data, it is difficult to chart psychological, social or physiological changes, much less predict future effects of terrorisation on the victims of these crimes. Given the complexity of the issues, starting with the acute trauma surrounding the terrorist event, the peculiar interrelationship that may develop between the terrorist and his victim, the variety of psychological and physiological response mechanisms that are involved, it is obvious that any holistic understanding of the victim experience can only be derived from an interdisciplinary perspective.

Any examination of recent history clearly shows democracy's peculiar vulnerability to terrorism. Bound by the rule of law and due process, a democratic regime cannot resort to the same bloody methods used against it in combating terrorist crime. It is surely no accident that we do not hear much of revolutionary violence in totalitarian countries, where autocracies with limitless powers terrorise ethnic, religious or racial groups, and sometimes brutally subject entire populations.

Terrorism is by definition anti-democratic for at least two reasons. First, sustained incidents of terrorism will inevitably produce governmental counter-measures for the purpose of self-defence. These in turn, can also become oppressive, thereby alienating the population from their government. Second, terrorist movements are clearly elitist, in spite of their alleged glorification of and identification with the masses. By seeking to coerce duly elected governments into concessions or even abdication, terrorists exert great stress on a country's institutionalised legal mechanisms and wholly circumvent the democratic process established to bring about orderly social and/or political change. While there are no systematic studies of the effect of terrorism on the quality of life in nations experiencing sustained and serious assaults, there is growing evidence of encroachments of the civil liberties in such nations.

Great Britian, for example, one of the oldest and more stable democracies in the world, in its struggle with sectarianism and periodic armed insurrection in Northern Ireland, has instituted such basically undemocratic measures as internment, in-depth interrogation, as well as arrests, searches and seizures without the benefit of warrants. There is also censorship. There has even been a relaxation of the rules of criminal procedure, such as trials without juries, the admission of hearsay evidence, a shift in the burden of proof from government to defendant, as well as an increase in penalties for activities classified as terrorism. West Germany and Italy, under sustained assault, have made comparatively benign procedural changes but have also significantly increased the penalties for terrorist-related crimes.

Governmental countermeasures such as these are not only understandable as mechanisms for self-defence, but are also demanded by the public. No form of political authority can long expect to survive continued, serious assaults on its institutions, and people, under the long-recognised concept of 'social contract' do have a right to protection. Public outrage and demand for harsh action against terrorists seems to be the norm in nations experiencing serious problems with terrorism. Jenkins, commenting on public opinion polls conducted in Western Europe during the 1970s, notes that a majority of people polled supported military reprisals, the killing of terrorist leaders, capital punishment for offenders and summary executions, even if these measures seriously violated civil liberties or endangered innocent civilians.' European nations are not alone in terms of public resentment of terrorism and in succumbing to questionable control mechanisms.

When in the early 1970s the city of San Francisco experienced the so-called 'Zebra' killings, in which White persons were randomly shot on the streets by a small band of profoundly disturbed Blacks, public fear led to public approval of search and seizure tactics that were clearly in violation of the probable cause requirements of the US Constitution. In addition, states and federal governments perennially resort to military force to quell domestic violence, whenever they deem it necessary. These and similar developments justifiably raise serious questions as to the future of democracies as democracies. How does one properly balance the protection of the public with the requirements of constitutionally guaranteed civil liberties? The collective evidence clearly points to an erosion of these liberties, whenever counter-terrorist controls are applied, and to a public only too willing to trade its freedom for a modicum of law and order. It can therefore be stated that to the degree that terrorism succeeds in changing a democracy into a facsimile of a garrison state and thereby into a totalitarian regime, the foremost victim of terrorism is democracy itself.

Looking at the impact of terrorism on individual citizens in countries that have consistently borne the brunt of terrorism, such as Italy, Northern Ireland, Spain and West Germany in Europe; Egypt, Israel and Lebanon in the Middle East; Turkey; and Argentina, El Salvador, Nicaragua and Uruguay in Latin America, one notes a serious erosion in the quality of life of those affected. Terrorism is exacting a heavy toll on international diplomacy and on the life styles and work habits of political leaders, diplomats and business executives the world over.

Political assassinations disrupt the conduct of governmental affairs and can overthrow existing state authorities; international relations are strained when diplomats are killed or imprisoned and their embassies sacked; officials and representatives of criminal justice systems must carry out their work under well-advertised death threats; and corporate executives cannot operate their businesses without persistent threats of kidnappings, bomb threats, extortion attempts and similar terrorist activities. Concerns for personal safety are affecting a widening circle of people the world over. For example, air travel is encumbered through the scanning and frisking procedures for travellers who must endure a serious invasion of their privacy. Sally-ports and waiting areas separate passengers from family and friends. The transport and storing of luggage is increasingly difficult. Airports, banks, industrial complexes, private and public institutions and even penitentiaries have been affected by terroristic actions. The fear generated by terrorism and by the possibility of victimisation in an ever-widening arena is raising the social costs of the problem, in addition to the economic costs. They do so by weakening the social and political fabric of affected countries and by diverting scarce economic and criminal justice resources from other vital areas.

The circumstances under which individuals may become victims of terrorist acts are as varied as the causes of terrorism and depend upon the particular objectives and targeting tactics of the terrorists. Victims may be chosen selectively or at random. In selective terrorism, specific groups, such as police, judges, soldiers or prison personnel are targeted. In randomised terrorism, victims are chosen indiscriminately, a method guaranteed to instil maximum fear among the public.

Variations in the objectives of terrorists affect the degree of threat posed to the victim. As a result, victims may be killed, maimed or injured. They may also be taken prisoner or hostage. Further, the specific form of terrorist victimisation also varies widely. There may be face to face contact, such as during state-sanctioned torturing of prisoners or concentration camp inmates, the brainwashing of prisoners of war, skyjackings or other hostage-taking events. There may also be anonymity between victims and terrorists. Letter bombings, car bombings or similar explosive devices, randomly or purposively placed, fall into this category. Some incidents may be brief ranging from minutes to a few hours, while others may be of long duration, lasting weeks, months and sometimes years.

As seen earlier, some incidents may involve political hostage takings and others may be instigated by criminal or mentally deranged persons. Yet, in spite of the formidable diversity of the circumstances and form terrorist incidents can take, there is evidence of similarities in the effect of victimisation.

These similarities persist to a considerable degree, even when unexpected terrorist captivity is compared with victim experience of natural disasters.Given this evidence, exploration of that experience is warranted, independent of its causes and forms. The exclusive focus on victims is merited, both for its own sake, and because a cumulative systematic assessment and evaluation of the victim's knowledge and experience can increase the effectiveness of treatment, improve society's responses and thereby reduce the harm to victims of future events, and finally, to the small degree that it may be possible, facilitate prevention.

Before, proceeding with the detailed analysis of the victim experience, it is useful to note that our knowledge of this subject is based on a gradually accumulating body of information about the pathology connected with trauma-induced stress. It includes retrospective studies of torture victims and concentration camp survivors, and information on such psychologically coercive techniques as the 'brainwashing' of prisoners of war in North Korea, first collected during the 1950s and 1960s Szu-hsiang kai-tsao, also known as Chinese thought reform or ideological remoulding is also included in this genre, since it exploits so-called brainwashing techniques on a mass scale.

Since these earlier years, more data have been added from studies of former prisoners of war in Viet Nam and from the examination of torture and other abusive treatment of political prisoners in Northern Ireland, Portugal, Greece, South Africa and several Latin American nations, to name a few.

The most recent efforts have examined hostage experiences in Ireland, Iran, Canada and the United States. While much empirical research remains to be done, the cumulative effect of this knowledge base is helpful in defining the parameters of the issue and in pinpointing critical areas where more data will be needed.

Regardless of the objectives and format of terrorisation, its basic process involves an unpredictable, powerful force, threatening the victim with annihilation. The experience is immensely stressful and generates in the victim feelings of anomia, total helplessness and powerlessness.

Terrorisation denies the victim's ability to control his behaviour. Psychological and physical shock, characteristic of any severe trauma, follow. The degree of horror involved is perhaps best described by Weiss, who coined the term idiocide. It means 'death of self, and constitutes an almost universal crime characterised by many degrees. Weiss defines the term as a crime, committed against an individual, which 'reduces, extinguishes, or precludes the presence or exercise of vital human powers'.

Since the choice of victims in many terrorist attacks (as well as in most criminal assaults) is determined by chance, they can neither anticipate nor control the event. The victim's experiential repertoire contains little, if anything, to prepare him for such an incident, on the basis of which he can try to predict what may happen next or how he should best conduct himself. The multiple threats to life, security, bodily integrity and self-esteem precipitate in most victims a crisis reaction in which the emotions and behaviour of the threatened person are significantly disrupted.

A victim suddenly faced with the very real possibility of imminent death, finds himself unable to muster the necessary physical and mental resources to rise against the assault on his person. Such feelings of impotence shatter the self-image, dissolve the self-confidence and set in motion sequelae of complex and interrelated social psychological and physiological response mechanisms.

Symonds identifies four distinct phases of psychological responses of victims to violent crimes, in his informative work on victimisation. While the duration and intensity of each phase varies according to the nature and quality of contact between the criminal and his victim, the responses seem to hold for such diverse victimisations as kidnapping, hostage takings, rape, robbery and even burglary, where there is no contact with the criminal at all. The first two phases constitute the acute victim response, the last two the delayed victim response.

The first phase of the victim response to terrorisation

is concerned with the immediate situation and its experience. It consists of shock, disbelief, denial and delusion. It is characterised by a paralysis of action and the denial of sensory impressions. Only when the victim begins to perceive the reality of the situation and feels hopelessly entrapped, the second phase begins. It is characterised by a paralysis of affect. Symonds calls this terror-induced, pseudo-calm, noticeably detached behaviour 'frozen fright'. Trapped in a life threatening situation, the victim feels isolated and powerless. After denial of the situation, there is often a brief period of a delusion of imminent reprieve.

Unrealistically, victims expect that authorities will rescue them within minutes or at least within a few hours. While such imaginings are usually not grounded in facts, this phase is generally thought to reflect a growing acceptance by the victim of his or her predicament. If unresolved, a period of adaptation sets in, which the literature invariably describes as 'coping'. It includes such activities as writing, reading, counting, handcrafts (if possible) or similar 'busy work', and for most victims, an embarking on a review and reflection upon one's past life. Strentz, after interviewing many former hostages of skyjacking events, notes that he has never interviewed anyone who did not take stock of his life, or vowed to change for the better, should he be given a second chance after the horrifying experience.

If victims are not rescued during this period of initial adaptation—a period that can last from a few hours to one or two days—the pressures of the situation and terror combine to overwhelm most victims and produce a state of traurnatic psychological infantilism in the majority of the victims. Individuals in this condition lose their ability to function as adults and begin to respond instead with adaptive behaviour first learned in early childhood.

Thus, behaviour exhibited under the phenomenon of traumatic psychological infantilism includes appeasement, compliance, submission and ingratiation. Even cooperative and wholly voluntary acts are often noted, which tend to confound rescuing authorities, the public and even the victims themselves.

Persons experiencing this syndrome will empathise and sympathise with their victimiser. They may even come to his aid and contravene the efforts of their rescuers. If the situation is not resolved within a relatively short period of time and the terror continues unabated, the traumatised victim tends to attribute his continuing survival to the good will of the offender.

At this point, many victims experience profound and lasting attitudinal as well as behavioural changes. Symonds calls this latest development pathological transference. It tends to occur when a victim's life has initially been threatened by someone who later decides (perhaps only temporarily) not to kill. Given these conditions, victims no longer focus on the actual death threat but begin to feel that they have been given their very lives by the offender. These changes in victim perceptions are particularly acute and reinforced in criminal or political terrorist hostage takings, where their instrumentality is obvious to all concerned. Victims will quickly delude themselves that their captors will not harm them, if only the intended victim—the one who has the power to meet the demands of the terrorists—acceded to their demands.

Police guns and other weapons are trained on terrorists and victims alike, is not lost on the latter. It further reinforces their delusions that if the terrorists got what they wanted, and the police retreated, the matter would be resolved with no one being hurt. Pathological transference is said to be complete when the victims begin to perceive their release as being contingent upon the offender's realisation of his goals. This perceptual merging of the victim's hopes for freedom with the purposes of the terrorists has led some to speculate that we may be dealing with a variant of yet another psychological phenomenon, the identification of the victim with the aggressor.

It is a psychoanalytic concept and refers to the well-known socialisation processes of early childhood, during which children learn to identify with their parental role models. In normal childhood situations, this process describes a positive development. If, on the other hand, the parent figure is excessively punitive and inconsistent, the child may incorporate the parent's punitive and aggressive traits, in an effort to adapt to highly stressful and often intolerable situations.

The concept of identification with the aggressor is related to the notion of conversion and has been useful in explaining instances where prisoners of concentration or similar death camps assume the character of their keepers and begin to torture fellow prisoners, in an unconscious, last ditch effort to save themselves. The chief motivational factors in these instances are hate (not love) for their enemy and the primordial desire to survive. As helpful as this concept has been in explaining the otherwise unexplainable, it is of doubtful theoretical value in illuminating the psychodynamics of most terroristic episodes. The literature records no recent event during which victims of terrorism either abused or tortured their fellow victims. The few instances where at least some elements of conversion may apply, are those where a victim, after being subjected to traumatic stress, joins the cause of the captors and actively participates in subsequent terrorist operations.

A highly dramatic case in the recent past fitting this

category involves the kidnapping of Patricia Hearst in 1974. Donald 'Cinque' DeFreeze, self-proclaimed leader of the 'Symbionese Liberation Army (SLA) a small pseudo-revolutionary band of former prisoners and radicalised youths from the University of California at Berkeley, had been an inmate at the California Medical Facility at Vacavillie from 1968 to 1972.

At Vacaville, DeFreeze underwent chemotherapy, aversive conditioning and similar experimental treatment techniques designed to rehabilitate or 'convert' seriously disturbed criminal offenders. If appears that DeFreeze subjected Patricia Hearst to a mixture of violence and drugs, as well as to variations of the same conversion techniques that had been applied to him. The rest is history. Patty joined the gang, denounced her parents, posed in a fetching battle dress complete with submachine gun in front of the seven headed Cobra symbol of the SLA, assisted in a bank robbery in San Francisco, robbed a store and went on the lam. Until her capture in September 1975, she managed to lead the nation's law-enforcement apparatus on an embarrassingly fruitless chase. When the government finally did catch up with her and tried her, she took the Fifth Amendment to the Constitution to avoid self-incrimination no less than forty-two times. Field, analysing the case, likens Hearst's experience to those of adolescents in Northern Ireland, who, when subjected to traumatic stress, are less able than adults to withstand assaults on their ego and notes:

> She was terrorized, and she converted to terrorism. Had she been less isolated from the support systems of the larger society, and had she experienced a shorter captivity, it is probable that she would never have assumed the role of a fugitive bank robber. The case of Patty Hearst epitomizes the dynamic relationship between victim and terrorist because of its singularity in combining the features evident in

> other cases: *i.e.*, psychological and psycho technological forces operating in a social context that exacerbates stress through denial of institutional supports, prolonged threat to life, identity, and bodily integrity, occurring in a circumstance of powerlessness, helplessness, and unpredictability.

While the Hearst kidnapping appears to be a classic example of the phenomena of identification with the aggressor and conversion, we must look elsewhere to explain what has fittingly been described as an 'unholy alliance between terrorist and captive, involving fear, distrust or anger toward the authorities on the outside'.

Traumatic psychological infantilism and pathological transference are two critical components of what has come to be recognised as the Stockholm Syndrome. It is named for the unexpected positive feelings developed by captives for their captors, during a prolonged hostage taking at the Sveriges Kreditbank in Stockholm, Sweden, in 1973. During the incident, four bank employees were held hostage in the bank's vault for one hundred and thirty-one hours by an escaped prisoner. The group was-later joined by another convict and former cellmate of the would be bank robber, who had demanded his release from prison. Once the Syndrome is manifest, it tends to last for the duration of the crisis and beyond. In fact, it may continue for years. Strenz reports that positive or negative bonds tend to develop between captors and captives with the passage of time. In essence, if perpetrators do not abuse their victims, that is, if there is no serious physical abuse, assault, battery or rape, a positive bond (the Stockholm Syndrome) is likely to develop between them. However, if victims are seriously and persistently abused, the Syndrome is not likely to develop. But even in situations of abuse, exceptions are noted, as when victims, injured or assaulted during the initial rush of capture, come to identify with the offender and his cause during subsequent phases of their captivity. In these cases, victims rationalise initial abuse and/or injury as having been necessary for the offenders to gain control, and more often than not, blame themselves for their victimisation. Only when victims closely identify with their government, or when there has been at least some training or preparation for the ordeal of captivity, does the Stockholm Syndrome not tend to develop. The annals of terrorism reflect some outstanding examples of such instances.

In the 1970s, British Ambassador to Uruguay Geoffry Jackson was captured and held hostage by Tupamaro terrorists for two hundred and forty-four days. Maintaining his distance and dignity under the most difficult of circumstances, he won the grudging admiration of his captors without ever succumbing to the Stockholm Syndrome. The same applies to American agronomist Claude Fly, also held by the Tupamaros for two hundred and eight days.

Similarly, military records bear witness to many instances where American prisoners of war in Korea and Viet Nam survived unspeakable horrors of captivity without ever approaching an alliance or identification with the captors. While the Stockholm Syndrome is a relatively new phenomenon for law enforcement and the public, the fields of psychology, psychophysiology and psychosomatic medicine have long recognised its basic element of 'regression' as one of several defence mechanisms available to victims of inordinate psychosocial stress.

Next to regression, the remaining defence mechanisms include the previously discussed conversion syndrome, repression, rationalisation and sublimation. Even though these concepts are well-accepted by researchers and theorists of stress disorders, they leave us with many unanswered questions. For example, we know little about the processes involved in selecting and elaborating a particular defence mechanism. Also, what is the nature of interaction between unconscious cognitive activity of victims and their conscious awareness of the situation? What internal factors are at work that enable the unconscious to accept the success or failure of a particular defence strategy? In the absence of answers and unifying concepts in this area (and pending future research), we must be content with the conjecture that the processes of regression and the Stockholm Syndrome are probably functional for most victims of terrorist attacks.

Given the trauma of sudden life-threatening events that characterise most incidents, the alternative ego defence mechanisms would hardly do. Thus, the victim's return to the adaptive patterns of infancy has substantial surface validity, since it provides him with behavioural modes that have worked before, when he was totally dependent upon a caring adult in terms of sustenance and life. As such, this adaptation speaks volumes not just about the horror of the terroristic victimisation but also about the apparent terror inherent in the ordinary childhood experience.

It is important to note that the Stockholm Syndrome goes beyond victim identification with and sympathy for the offender, which may last far beyond the actual period of captivity. It also involves the development of the captive's negative feelings and distrust towards police in particular and governmental authorities in general. These feelings are exacerbated the longer captivity and/or negotiations last. After all, the victim wants to survive. And survival is tied to release. Therefore, anything that delays his release will be interpreted as a rejection of the captive's needs, as cold-blooded indifference to his plight and as an outright expression of hostility towards the hostage who is facing a life-threatening situation.

The final component of the Stockholm Syndrome often involves the development of reciprocal positive feelings on the part of the terrorists towards their captives. It is this aspect of the Syndrome that is of major significance to law enforcement, since it can aid immeasurably in the successful resolution of the situation. Beyond these basic elements of the Stockholm Syndrome, it is best understood as an automatic, at least partly unconscious adaptation mechanism for the survival of exceedingly traumatic and highly lethal situations.

Factors which seem to promote the Syndrome are: (a) the quality and intensity of the victimisation experience, (b) the passage of time, (c) the degree of dependence of the captive on the captor for survival and (d) the psychological distance of the captive from his or her government. It seems that no particular age group is exempt from the Syndrome. Males and females succumb to it equally. As noted before, this remarkable phenomenon does not develop immediately upon seizure but requires time to evolve. But if it takes hold at all, it will be well-established by the third day.

The Stockholm Syndrome occurs with sufficient frequency during kidnappings, hostage takings and similar victimisation that the highly organised terrorist groups have begun to apply tactics to prevent its occurrence. For example, hostages may be kept in total isolation. They may have hoods placed over their heads to prevent any contact whatsoever with their captors. They may be bound and forced to lie face down to prevent eye contact with anyone. They may be permitted to have only one spokesman and guards may be changed frequently during prolonged captivity to interdict the development of any relationships between hostages and terrorists.

Any such development, if known to law enforcement, adds special urgency to rescue efforts because of the added risks to the lives of the hostages. Given the obvious advantages to the hostages of a fully developed Stockholm Syndrome, law-enforcement agents should foster its growth to the degree that it may be possible. As a result, any activity which may require captor and captives to work together for the common good should be encouraged. For example, food preparation, distribution of blankets or clothing *etc.*, are ways in which joint activity and cooperation can be engendered.

Finally, given any extended exposure of captives to hostage takers, law enforcement should never count on the assistance of the victims, when they communicate and deal with them during rescue efforts. Otherwise, police may find, much to their dismay, some of the victims counteracting their rescue efforts. Similarly, prosecutors should expect considerable difficulty in gaining victim cooperation during subsequent prosecution of the offenders. The star witness for the prosecution too frequently turns into the star witness for the defence. And governmental authorities should prepare to hear bitter complaints from released hostages who tend to judge official responses to their plight as inadequate, bungling and grossly inept. Up to this point, this analysis of the sequelae of victim responses to terrorism has been limited to the psychodynamics of the acute victim response. As important as these responses are to our understanding of the victim experience, the picture remains incomplete.

The physiological response of victims to highly threatening situations is best understood by examining stress and stress reactions. Stress, in the words of its foremost researcher Hans Selye is the 'nonspecific response of the body to any demand made upon it'. Of importance is that stress is not the 'precipitating incident', but rather the condition of the human organism as it responds to the event. Recent researchers have modified Selye's definition by emphasising that stress results from three interrelated elements: (a) stimulus, (b) response and (c) a combination of stimulus- -response reactions. Thus, stress is seen as disrupting a person's psychological and physiological condition such that he or she is forced to deviate from normal functioning. Even though the timing of the stress response varies considerably from person to person, the response does involve three distinct stages: the initial stage involves alarm, followed by resistance. If stress continues unabated, the body's resources become exhausted and the victim's defence mechanisms will break down. Selye labelled this adaptation pattern GAS or *General Adaptation Syndrome*. The alarm stage consists of two phases: during the 'shock' phase the body's resistance is lowered, while physiological defences are mobilised during the 'counter-shock' phase. Surging adrenaline triggers the release of glycogen from the liver, increases the rate of respiration and heart and shifts the blood flow away from the skin and digestive tract towards the muscles and brain. All this leads to the resistance stage, during which the body will show maximum adaptation to stress.

An individual faced with a terrifying situation will now be able to, perform at peak output, and, if possible, will either fight or engage in flight. If stress continues, the body's reserves will be depleted. The third stage involving exhaustion will last until the body's resources have been replenished. Unalleviated stress is increasingly tied to symptoms of physical and mental illness. As such, stress will interact with the individual to disrupt psychophysiological homeostasis and may lead to psychosomatic disorders.

Recent research findings in such diverse disciplines as psycho-neuro-endocrinology and psychoneuroimmunology on the subject of stress add special poignancy to victimisation by terror. It is not the stress itself that is dangerous to individuals but rather their inability to cope with it that is significant. Whether a person eventually succumbs to physical or mental illness, and whether that illness will be serious or fatal, seems to revolve around the individual's ability to do something about the situation and proactively change his or her predicament. And since the essence of terrorisation involves the negation of the victim's capacity for willing his behaviour, it must be seen as one of the most damaging stressors that can be inflicted on humans.

It is now known that prolonged stress affects at least five basic response systems: (a) the skeletal-muscular system, leading to muscular pain and tension headaches; (b) the parasympathetic nervous system, leading to gastrointestinal distress, such as ulcerative colitis or ulcers; (c) the sympathetic nervous system, leading to hypertension, arrhythmia, palpitation, sodium and fluid retention; (d) the endocrine system, responsible for the overall integration of skeletal muscular, parasympathetic and sympathetic nervous systems; and (e) the immune system, responsible for the body's complex infection-fighting mechanisms. Current research has begun to tease out the exact processes of stress responses. Upon perception of a serious threat, neurons in the brain tissue stimulate the hypothalamus which regulates all essential life-support systems. The hypothalamus then stimulates the pituitary gland of the endocrine system and triggers the sympathetic branch of the autonomic nervous system. The pituitary gland, in turn, releases a series of hormones: Beta-endorphin and adrenocorticotropin (ACTH), the most important and best-known hormones in the stress response. The ACTH travels to the adrenal glands (located near the anterior medial border of the kidney), which in turn release corticosteroids. The latter chemicals exert positive as well as negative effects on the body. While corticosteroids function to reduce inflammation in the body, they can also depress the body's immune system, when stress continues unresolved. The adrenal glands also secrete epinephrine and norepinephrine (better known as adrenaline and noradrenaline), which are substances designed to serve the goal of preparing the organism to meet threatening situations involving fear, rage or pain.

Epidemiological research on stress has come to recognise that hormonal secretions accompanying the stress response not only assist the body in coping with stress, but also can cause direct and indirect damage. Direct damage can occur during the alarm stage of the General Adaptation Syndrome through ulceration of the gastrointestinal tract, and indirect damage can occur through the shrinkage of the thymus gland and the reduction in the number of lymphocytes in the blood. The latter phenomenon weakens the immune system's capacity to resist infection, and thereby increases the likelihood of illness. These findings, coupled with a growing body of research analysing the long-term effects of highly stressful situations on humans (and animals), all point to far-reaching consequences for the victim's state of health. As a result, the psychological shocks and trauma of the terroristic incident pall when compared with the long-range damage inflicted on victims.

A final aspect of the stress response to be discussed here has major significance for law enforcement. Judging from the results of physiological and psychological measurements of stress reactions, mind and body are not activated simul-taneously as has previously been thought. Rather, a victim's ability to think and act is not only modified under stress, but mind and body are also activated separately. First, the relationship between activation and performance under stress is best described by an inverted 'U', where perfor-mance is optimal for many activities at an intermediate level of activation, and where either too much or too little activation produces a decrease in performance. Second, mind and body are activated independently of each other.

Under the concept of dissociation of arousal, a victim's (or terrorist's) ability to think clearly and rationally may be at maximum output, while the autonomic system may be on low, or vice versa. The relevance of these findings for hostage management situations is clear. A highly aroused victim may bungle a rescue operation, if complex tasks are expected of him. Nor is it prudent or productive to withhold food and/or water, if the result is a reduction of the terrorist's or hostage's capacity to think rationally, while disinhibiting their visceral and autonomic nervous systems. The result of such action could easily be a finely tuned animal, unfettered by reason [and] dangerously coiled and ready to spring.

There is considerable and growing evidence from long-range case studies and laboratory research that victims of terrorism suffer serious and long-lasting damage to their physical, mental and emotional health. Even brief events can produce major problems, years after they have occurred. In this respect, these victims are not very different from any other victims of trauma and violence. Unfortunately, these findings have yet to enter the public's mind. Nor are they reflected in the criminal justice system in terms of compensatory and punitive damages awarded to victims. The same is applicable to sentencing practices because punishment, in most instances, is not commensurate with the harm done to victims. The last two phases of victim responses to terror tend to occur long after the horrific incident has passed. Phase three consists of an array of psychophysiological reactions. Phase four involves victim adaptation and formulation of new resolve. Both are the subject of the ensuing discussion.

Post-traumatic psychological reactions tend to involve the following response patterns. Closely following an incident, victims tend to exhibit a wide variety of anxiety syndromes, ranging from intense anxiety to free-floating anxiety, to phobias. Victims will report insomnia, startle reactions, nightmares and nightsweats, inability to concentrate, memory lapses, sexual problems and interpersonal difficulties with spouses or significant others. Obsessive reviews of the terroristic incident lead to much self-recrimination, self-blame and circular spells of anger, apathy, depression, hostility, rage, reclusiveness, resentment and resignation.

The motivation for these alternating responses is based on the absolutely devastating effects of depersonalisation, helplessness, powerlessness and humiliation that victims experience during the incidents. Depression, a mental state characterised by feelings of dejection, lack of hope and alienation, may last long after the traumatic event. Less frequent reactions include feelings of paranoia, with victims exhibiting abnormal sensitivity, suspicion, brooding, excessive self-consciousness and fixed ideas that may include systematised delusions of persecution.

A reinforcing circle between psychological and physiological effects of terror emerges when insomnia, dietary changes and self-imposed restrictions affect the victim's gastrointestinal and circulatory systems which in turn can lead to further mental and physical impairments. Still longer after the incident, physical and psycho-physiological damage can bring about significant pathological changes in victims.

Hypertension, for example, has consistently been identified as a major contributing factor in the development of cerebral vascular accidents, the genesis of congestive heart failure, coronary thrombosis, atherosclerosis and kidney failure. The previously discussed suppression of the body's immune system may lead to a plethora of illness, including cancer.

Even though victim response patterns reflect remarkable similarity, it should be clear that stress responses do not produce identical psychophysiological reactions in everyone. Roth identifies at least five sources of variability in stress responses:(a) stimulus response specificity, referring to specific kinds of stressors eliciting specific kinds of physiological responses; (b) response specificity, reflecting idiosyncratic differences in patterns of reactivity based on genetic and learned response differences; (c) personality specificity, attributable to differences in personality characteristics leading to differences in response patterns; (d) emotional specificity, assignable to differences in victim reactions to stressors; and (e) conflict specificity, traceable to differences in intrapsychic impedimenta victims bring into a stress situation.

Assessing delayed victim responses, differences emerge among a number of variables. Availability of treatment to the victim and his or her family appears to be a major factor affecting the extent of trauma and damage. System response can greatly ameliorate or aggravate the victim's feelings.

In addition, after-effects of traumatic experiences are inversely related to (a) previous experiences of a similar nature, (b) the age of the victim (maturity and a well-developed sense of identity lessen the traumatic effect); (c) the degree of humiliation and ego threat experienced by the victim; and (d) the degree of psychological and social isolation experienced by the victim.

During the final phase of the victim response, a resolution of sorts is worked out, which integrates the victim's experiences into a new set of behavioural patterns. This involves regaining some feelings of control over his or her life, shoring up of self-respect and the development of new patterns of alertness and defence mechanisms. Those looking for encouraging evidence of victims returning to a state of normalcy will not find it in the literature. Even though there are many degrees of adjustment, the accumulated evidence suggests that the scarring of the experience of terror is so damaging to mind and body that victims will never be as they were before. With time, most arrive at a modus vivendi, characterised by revised values and attitudes towards life, government, faith, criminal justice, people *etc*.

The trauma sustained by victims of terrorism appears to be of such magnitude that it is not an exaggeration to analogise the experience to an interstellar catastrophe during which planets are forever forced off their trajectory. The foregoing sections have analysed the victim experience using a multidisciplinary perspective.

The analysis of a wide variety of victim experiences of stressful situations reveals a number of coping strategies, all of them geared towards (a) bringing the crisis situation to a quick resolution with a minimum of loss in terms of life and limb; (b) keeping one's anxiety level within tolerable limits to remain alert and functional; (c) maintaining one's self-esteem in spite of frequently dehumanising and degrading experiences; (d) preservation of one's relationships with fellow victims;

and (e) establishing some linkage with the terrorists without ingratiation. Once caught up in the crisis situation, the following repertoire of coping mechanisms appears to produce positive results: (a) assuming a familiar role, if possible, by engaging in such varied activities as writing, handcraft, counting *etc*; (b) adjusting one's expectations to the reality of the situation; (c) learning from successful coping behaviour of fellow victims; and (d) accepting constructive criticism without losing one's sense of self-worth and self-esteem.

Given the documented deleterious effects of terrorism on its victims and the fact that the United States is now at a greater risk of terrorism than ever before, it is critically important to develop effective strategies for counteracting acts of terrorism and for assisting its victims. There is an urgent need to develop a thoroughly coordinated national policy to fight terrorism. Given the peculiar and inefficient structure of law enforcement in this country, most terrorist incidents come under the control of local law-enforcement agencies, with national organisations standing by or offering assistance. The net result is a veritable maze of too many agencies with little or no coordination between them. It' terrorism is to be effectively controlled, we will have to have a totally integrated command, control, communications and intelligence system.

Looking at institutional support systems for victims, there is an equally critical need to develop an integrated and comprehensive system response. Embassy personnel, members of the military, airline staff, business executives (including mid-level managers) abroad and at home are fast becoming attractive potential victims. As a result, compre-hensive security measures, defensive strategies and tactics, as well as training for seizure and captivity are urgently required. While some hostage training has been undertaken for embassy staff since the Iranian Embassy debacle, such efforts need to be systematised and extended to all persons at risk. At a minimum, business executives of US multinatinal firms overseas should be provided such training.

In addition, the scores of private firms offering an array of protection services, which have mushroomed in the face of rising anti-American terrorism the world over, should be scrutinised by government agencies to protect the consumers. The uncontrolled growth of these businesses cries out for objective evaluation of services and the development of at least some guiding principles and regulations. On the individual level, law enforcement agencies and emergency personnel responding to victims of terrorism need to make sure they do not inflict secondary damage to the victims. Given their experience of dehumanisation and feelings of helplessness, care needs to be taken to act in a nurturing and patient manner. Symonds writes of the victims' 'silent expectations' that rescuers will help restore their self-esteem and injured pride. If victims are met with indifference, detachment, emotional insulation so characteristic of professionals, their silent expectations will go unmet. Their feelings of helplessness and rejection will be reinforced and a 'second injury' will have been inflicted by the system. In sum, victims of terrorism require much reassurance, comfort, a willingness to listen and much support, not only from law enforcement and emergency personnel, but from the entire criminal justice system, friends, family, the community and society as a whole.

In a relatively short period of time, both the frequency and the number of people taking hostage rose dramatically. The initial efforts of psychologists and government were aimed at incident resolution, primarily in the development of hostage negotiation techniques. Part of this effort was directed towards studying, primarily, hostage behaviour within the incident, and, secondarily, after-incident behaviour by the exhostage. The study of within-incident behaviour produced information which has contributed significantly to the successful resolution of many subsequent hostage-takings. The study of after-incident behaviour began to show that even relatively brief hostage periods produced a range of short- and long-term reactions in a large percentage of the victims.

Natural violences are exemplified by fires, earthquakes, floods *etc*. Although one may later argue that design improvements or adequate maintenance may have prevented a building fire, such an event would be generally classed as natural violence. However, a major fire planned and deliberately started by an arsonist would not be included in this group even though the fact of arson may not be discovered until after the fire has been contained, as the victims are then aware of the wilful nature of the act. The states during natural violence/major disaster have been well chronicled elsewhere and will be only briefly highlighted here. The initial impact is usually characterised by simple appropriate movement, panic or physical immmobilisation. Mass initial hysteria is relatively rare in natural disasters. If a simple, direct movement will permit an escape, most victims will appropriately use it. If such a movement does not permit an escape, panic or immobilisation responses appear rapidly in the victim group.

Panic is an often illogical attempt to flee the area: pushing, shoving, fighting through various exits or jumping from heights at which the possibilities of surviving are small. Attempts by others to physically move the person are frequently rejected. The presence of a firm, directive authority figure has been shown to have a significant impact in many cases upon the extent of such reactions. In fact, most disaster planning is based upon pro viding simple, direct information about what to do initially. The heroic stage does not occur for all, but many individuals, usually without a previous history of such behaviour, will place themselves at great risk to help other unknown victims. For some, the situation is so far out of their ordinary life that they are able to play out a fantasy role. For others, it is a way to keep reality out for a short period of time. In a major disaster over a large area, police and fire personnel will often state that they do not wish to know of their own family's condition until the disaster situation has been stabilised. The next state is characterised by a great deal of community spirit, sharing of experience and influx of public aid. The idealistic theme is that like the mythical phoenix bird rising from its own ashes, 'We will rebuild it better than it was before'. Disillusionment follows as the extent of effort needed to rebuild becomes apparent, government assistance becomes slow and bureaucratic and individual problems become dominant.

The initial impact human-induced violence is marked by a thought that this is not real, it cannot be happening to me. This is quickly followed by selecting one of the freeze, flee or fight alternatives. The freeze response is by far the most common. Acceptance or respect for the dominance of the perpetrators is quickly established: 'I didn't want them to get nervous or have an excuse to shoot me. I just wanted to get through it.' In the third stage, interaction between victim and perpetrator begins to take place, as the victim develops a survival strategy. The survival strategies are almost always relatively straightforward, ranging from a simple, proposed bargain ('I'll do anything you want, just don't hurt me', or 'You haven't done anything wrong yet, why don't you just leave') to an attempted diversion ('My husband is coming back soon', or 'Just give me a minute, I'm hurrying as fast as I can') to letting the fear response dominate 'Maybe if he sees how truly frightened I am, he won't hurt me').

Disintegration or termination of perpetrator's control is usually by the perpetrator himself or by other external factors, seldom by the victim alone. The last stage may occur simultaneously with the rescue, or if the victim is left at the scene of the crime may wait until security is re-established at a police station, friend's residence *etc*. As this security is re-established, a second wave of fear and anxiety over the risk just experienced frequently occurs, accompanied by expressions of embarrassment over this behaviour ('I don't know why I'm acting this way now, it's all over', or 'I'm sorry, I just can't stop shaking').

Although physical security has been re-established, emotional security is still obviously absent. The continued fear and feeling of vulnerability is accentuated by what Symonds' has labelled the 'second injury'. The recent victim wants emergency personnel and family members to feel a part of their pain and help them emotionally. However, to survive themselves, emergency personnel have often learned to distance themselves from victims. Family members, unless they have been a previous victim themselves, simply do not have an experience base with which to relate to the victim.

The thoughts and emotional processes of adult hostage begin in a similar way to those of the general human-induced violence victim. The hostage does not believe this is happening, but the anxiety and fear is rising within him despite this belief. At the same time, behaviourally, he seems to select from one of three response patterns: freeze, protect self or protect others.

The hostage freeze response appears to be quite similar to the freeze response of the general victim. The protect self response is characterised by quick attempts to hide under cover or run from the scene. In contrast to natural disaster victims, there is very little panic movement. The protect self response constitutes a high risk-high gain action. Although it is not widely known to the public sector, such attempts have been successful in a number of incidents. However, if serious injuries or deaths are to occur, they are most likely to occur in the initial moments when the captors may see any action as a challenge to their control.

Civilian hostages very rarely protect themselves through an initial aggressive act towards the captors. In the protect others response, the hostage will stand in front of someone else to shield them, stand in front of a doorway to try and block someone else's entrance into the situation, talk loudly ('don't shoot') in the hope of alerting someone or directly request protection of another hostage of high vulnerability ('Just don't hurt or scare the children'). Interestingly, the initial responses are reported as semiautomatic, without deliberation or extended conscious thought.

The second state is labelled as acceptance/respect for the captors. The dominance and control of the situation by the captors has been firmly established. The hostage responds with 'frozen fright' versus heroic action plans. Frozen fright, also present in victims of other terrorism, is manifested by outwardly cooperative and compliant behaviour while inwardly the fright is terrifying the individual. Such a hostage does as he is told while his mind races with the various possibilities of his death. Other hostages are less fearful. Instead, the situation offers a potential opportunity for heroic action: 'It was just like a real life movie. I started looking for ways that I could get the gun away.' The key phrase here is potential opportunity. The thoughts and fantasies represent a frequent defence mechanism, but the thoughts are almost never translated into action. Time and time again, exhostages will connect this part of the experience to a television programme or a movie, and experience a sense of excitement about that. It would appear that the visual media has not only influenced captors, but has also touched a vicarious responsive cord in the general public as well.

The third stage of increased interaction between victims and captors begins. The initial rush of commands and threats has slowed. The captors have become less concerned with internal security and more concerned with external security, plus the process of negotiating itself. Sitting or lying down, the hostage has nothing to do except think. His mind turns to the development of a survival strategy. Some strategies are simple, but others are often very complex and closely adhered to. William Niehous, kidnapped from his Caracas, Venezuela, home on 27 February 1976, and escaped on 29 June 1979, described his strategy in five points: (a) be human (b) communicate, (c) set individual goals, (d) eat and exercise and (e) have faith.

Niehous' points parallel those of other successful exhostages, as well as POWs and other captivity survivors. Being human means communicating to establish yourself as an individual, with distinguishing and interesting characteristics. If killing does take place, captors have demonstrated a strong preference for troublesome, annoying hostages, or dehumanised 'objects', mere symbols instead of lives with families, likes, dislikes *etc.* Further, an object can be manipulated according to desire; a human being will resist sometimes on some issues.

Selective resistance on small issues has been quite important in many hostage survivors. Setting individual goals, plus eating and exercising, become a part of the strategy only when the situation extends beyond several days. Niehous would set a goal of living until next Wednesday, then the next, then the next. He thereby made daily survival a source of some self-esteem. Eating and exercising provided some structure to the long days and kept him healthy. Niehous states that he was not a religious zealot before his captivity, but that the experience increased his faith 'a Hell of a lot'. The primary component appears to be faith in a positive outcome, a focus upon positive aspects of one's past life.

A third recurrent, complex strategy is to go along with the captors, while attempting to make fools of them to the outside world or other captors. Some Vietnam POWs allowed pictures, but made small obscene gestures, or allowed filmed interviews, but blinked messages in morse code. The mass media has widely educated a large portion of the general public about these strategies.

The general public, in turn, has responded favourably, accepting the need of the captive to cooperate, as long as it is only partial cooperation. Frequently, however, the hostage creates strategies that are so obscure or complex that others cannot read them during the incident, and, after the incident, even this hostage finds it difficult to point out the coded resistance. At least one soldier in the American-Iranian hostage crisis found himself in this position.

Another recurrent, complex strategy is to attempt to assume a known role. Gerard Vaders, a newspaper editor held for thirteen days by Moluccan terrorists in a Dutch train in December 1975, almost immediately began taking notes for future writing. On the same train, another hostage who was not a doctor but knew something of medical care, assumed the role of doctor. In the Japanese Red Army hijacking of a JAL aircraft to Bangladesh in 1975, a US movie starlet used her acting skills to fake a nervous breakdown and gain her escape. The most frequent role assumption, however, is that of kind parent, employing warmth plus mild guilt and disapproval over the captor's behaviour.

Sometimes a hostage's previous behaviour appears to heavily influence his strategy development. Vaders reported guilt for not having taken more risks to help the Jews in the Second World War. A state probation officer always held a strong belief that by not physically abusing others, he would not be severely physically abused himself. When he was held hostage by one of his probationers, he consistently referred back to this belief as part of his strategy, recalling his captor's words: 'I like you. You're a good guy. You've treated me fairly. I don't want to see you dead.' Overall, then, the hostage who develops a strategy often creates a complex one based on partial cooperation with his captors. However, these strategies can become so complex as to be obscure, and are only partially employed. It is the process of a 'good' (e.g., complex and crafty) plan that is important to the hostage. This seems to renew his determination and self-esteem, even if the plan exists only in his mind.

The third stage also includes increased interaction among victims. The survival strategy discussed previously must make a practical decision about self versus group survival. The most common early decision is that no one must act to make the captors angry. Strong group pressure is exerted on anyone who acts out of turn or draws attention to himself. Gradually, however, the hostage selects one of four basic strategies:

(a) protect self first,

(b) construct plan of action with others,

(c) support fellow hostages,

(d) assume a protector/primary care-giver role to others.

In the first strategy, the hostage has a range of behaviour. He may attempt to isolate himself from interaction with others, or to willingly assist his captors in hopes they will favour him. Or he may become involved in the well-known Stockholm Syndrome.

As defined by Ochberg, three conditions characterise this syndrome. First, positive feelings are felt by the hostage towards the hostage taker. Second, negative feelings are felt by the hostage towards the authorities responsible for rescue. Third, positive feelings are reciprocated by the hostage-taker. Thus, in Ochberg's formulation, the genesis of the positive feelings on the part of the hostage is not identification with the aggressor, nor is it a conscious attempt to gain mercy. It is, rather, a result of infantilisation, denial of the fact that the hostage-taker is responsible for terror and confinement, and a primitive gratitude similar to the feeling of a oneyear-old towards a parent.

The second group strategy usually begins with one hostage sharing an observation with another: 'I've been noticing the right door isn't guarded well', or 'The younger terrorist doesn't seem very bright'. If the other hostage is responsive, more conversation takes place, and plans of potential action are reviewed. The original planners are quite cautious about new members in their subgroup, making strong value judgements about trustworthiness and courage of the others.

As is true in the individual survival strategy, the process of making the plans seems to be more important than their actual implementation. Relatively few of these plans are successfully carried out. An exception to this is noted in the experience of the People's Republic of

China. In their only two recorded incidents, Chinese passengers and employees overpowered the hijackers with exceptional physical force. Interestingly, the bus was filled mostly with Western tourists who remained quietly in their seats. This certainly raises interesting issues about the cultural conditioning of hostage behaviour. The decision to support fellow hostages is the most frequently selected option in a group situation. This may take the form of assurances, holding hands or doing small things to make another more comfortable. This fits well into the individual strategy of assuming a known role, taking care of others without assuming group leadership. For others, it has a more childlike quality of drawing together into a protective group. This subgroup's need to see themselves as equal and the same is very intense. Again, from the Hanafi Muslim takeover, one hostage states: 'We identified with the people we were lying on the floor with, whether black or white, Christian or Jewish.' Any individual member of this subgroup who asks for more food, or appears to be selfish in some other behaviour is sharply censured.

The fourth group strategy is to assume a protector/ primary care-giver role to others. This is more than offering support to others, but involves trying to become known to captors and fellow hostages alike as a primary figure, who utilises active mediation rather than confrontation. This is the doctor-like or priest-like role, and is almost universally allowed by captors. The motivation for such a strategy may vary, of course, from assuming a known role such as parent, to avoidance of survivor guilt. Baders, held by Moluccan terrorists, wished himself, rather than another, to be taken out and shot. Once again we see a blurring between actual behaviour and the way a hostage wants to perceive himself. If the incident is lengthy and hostage strategies have been relatively unsuccessful, many hostages will experience periods of wanting an assault or acting defiantly, even if it means the risk of their death. After the long American-Iranian hostage crisis, several exhostages publicly discussed times 'when we wanted to hear the planes', and know that the assault was beginning.

Feelings of anger towards captors, frustrating boredom and increasing difficulty in tolerating anxiety all contribute to these periods of' strong feelings. These feelings are often discussed among subgroups, with a concurrent increase in small expressions of defiance towards the captors. Retaliation by captors for these small expressions ranges from nonexistent to minimal. The recorded incidence of highly provocative behaviour resulting from these feelings is extremely low.

The fourth stage is labelled disintegration or termination of captors' control. The relationship between captors, hostages and negotiators has reached a kind of balance. There exists a pattern of give and take. Basic needs of the hostages have been attended to. As termination becomes a possibility, many hostages experience extreme fear and anxiety, They have become accustomed to the stability, and fear 'something would go wrong in the surrender. The police would start shooting. It was too quick. I was very frightened'. Thus, the attitude is partially attributed to a desire to maintain stability and partially to a lack of trust in the police response.

In the last stage, the adult hostage is freed or rescued. Tension relief is dramatic, both verbally and non-verbally. Nonverbally, handshakes, hugs and arms around the shoulder are exchanged between hostages and police officers. The previous ambivalent attitude is sharply reversed: 'I was worried, but they really came through for me.' Verbally, the focus is upon one or two aspects of risk in the situation. The freed hostage, using short comments, will go over and over these points of risk: 'I didn't know if I was going to make it when....' These comments are made repetitively to everybody. As in the general violence pattern, apologies are also made for continuing to shake or show other outward signs of anxiety. After this cathartic expression, the freed hostage will begin to ask about relatives or family, presenting the possibility of Symond's second injury. This first contact between family and freed hostage can be quite significant.

In looking at the stages of the adult hostage situation, several items stand out. The basic pattern is indeed similar to that produced by general human-induced violence. However, the development of both individual and group survival strategies is often more complex, with the individual strategy being created first. Further, the hostage appears to highly value his development of such strategies, whether or not he is able to implement them. Finally, he has become exposed to a range of very new feelings and behaviours in a short period of time, including wanting to die, wanting to support his captors, extended vulnerability, fear of the police *etc*.

During the first moments of child hostage stage, the child's reactions are more primitve. Behaviourally, the child hostage seems to select from one of three response patterns: freeze, panic with crying and screaming or making jokes. In contrast to the adult patterns, attempts to immediately flee or fight are rare. The freeze response is accompanied by internal fear, anxiety and thoughts of being hurt. Panic with crying and screaming is an especially high frequency choice if the child is physically seized, or if one child in the group begins crying. Some children will first attempt to make jokes. These children appear to be assuming a known role, the comedian. The comedian is one of the few roles the young child has learned will gain acceptance from most adults and peers. In each of these response choices, the child's conception of what is about to happen is variable. He may see the captor(s) as 'bad', 'robbers' or 'bad people Mummy told me to stay away from'. He fears that something very bad is going to happen, but he is not very sure what that is going to be. One important exception should be noted. Police hostage negotiators are often faced with dealing with the parent or relative who has seized their own child. These adults express a wish to 'save' the child from other family members, or to save the child from the pain the adult has experienced in his life. If the child resembles or is the favourite of a hated family member, the adult relative captor has the potential to emotionally injure the hated family member through the child. These children tend to see the adult relative captor as 'crazy', or 'acting funny'. They know that the adult relative 'acts funny' only a small percentage of the time. Amidst the fear, their thoughts and wishes are for the adult to return to his normal behaviour pattern. The child's later reporting of the sequence of events during the takeover is generally better than the adult's. However, some children display a tendency to add an event, or misidentify a captor.

In the Chowchilla bus kidnapping of twenty-six children in 1976, six of the children either described a nonexistent kidnapper or created characteristics: 'a man with one leg who used his shotgun as a cane', or 'a fat chubby man when they took our names'. The kidnappers were subsequently captured and convicted. They did not have such characteristics. Police detectives have long known about the unreliable nature of suspect descriptions from children. Confabulation in child play and parent-child interaction is also well known.

In the second child stage of acceptance/respect for captors, the choice is similar to that of the adult hostage: frozen fright versus heroic action thoughts. The primary difference seems to be in heroic action plans for adults versus heroic action thoughts for children. The child, in wishing to be a hero, has brief thoughts or ideas of taking action. As one might anticipate, these are not formulated into a heroic action plan in the way that the adult does. As with the adults, action is rarely taken, but the fantasy of action shows up once again as an important defence mechanism.

The third child stage of increased interaction between victims and captors is characterised by the development of simple survival strategies, as opposed to the complex strategies of the adult. Both physically and mentally, the adult captor is able to exert such extensive control over the child that it is not surprising that the child's response is submissive and cooperative. While some children engage in searching behaviour for means of escape, the most striking observation is the failure to utilise opportunities for escape. Even after the incident is over, the child experiences difficulty in explaining why he did not use such opportunities or why he picked the opportunity that he did, Whether such a degree of control is induced by the adult captor, or is attributed to the adult captor by the child hostage is an issue worthy of further investigation. Increased interaction among victims does occur during the third stage, but to a lesser degree than with adults. Obtaining food, water and privacy during body eliminations become priority items involving limited group interaction. Subgroups form based on two principal characteristics: age and aggressiveness. Younger children and less aggressive children form one cluster, with older and more aggressive children in another cluster. Such sub-grouping is consistent with normal play patterns. The more aggressive children do internally experience doubts and fears, and have shown a willingness to reveal them after the incident is over. One does not see the highly differentiated role assumptions that occur in this same stage among adults. As disintegration or termination of captor's control begins, the child does not tend to show the adult's fear of loss of stability. Fear of death or injury during surrender or police assault appears to be largely an adult attitude. As a child, admiration for or trust of the police officers remains relatively high.

In the final stage, the rescue is accomplished. Supportive physical exchanges between the child hostage and police officers are even more pronounced than with adults. The number of police officers involved is more limited, with the verbal exchanges being lower in audio level. The child usually has a lot to say, and is quite willing to talk at length about the incident. A much greater willingness is demonstrated to talk openly and at length with unknown police officers than with parents. The reasons for this remain speculative, and centre around a child's fear that he has not lived up to parental expectations.

In most victims, the reactions are transitory, alternate with performing everyday tasks in a routine manner and decline over time. If the victim isolates himself or is rejected by his social support systems, the probability of successful functioning is greatly reduced. In addition to the commonly shared reactions, the disaster victim shows little guilt about the problems of other victims and little guilt about not having prevented the event. It was a natural disaster, an act -of God, so the victim feels legitimately excused from responsibility. At the same time, he resents those who suffered fewer losses, and does not feel the government is responsive and sensitive enough. The desire for reprisal is expressed in anger against God or Fate: 'Why me, why me The disaster has so disrupted established social control rules, that he will often loot, vandalise or act aggressively in a manner that he would not ordinarily do. There I is a strong desire to return to the scene, to salvage items from the rubble, to compare recollections with others on the scene. The amount of energy expended in salvaging and planning for rebuilding cannot last, and 'burnout' occurs rapidly.

The adult victim of natural violence/major disaster has his status accepted by both his community and the larger society. There is little humiliation as the event is seen as an act of God or Fate. The victim did not cause or precipitate the disaster. Because of this and the graphic nature of a major disaster, others tend to accept the genuineness of victim complaints. In contrast, the victim of human-induced violence is frequently seen as having done something to cause or precipitate the event. This rejection and censure is frequently accompanied by doubts by others of the genuineness of victim complaints. If these social processes are pronounced, even the individual with exceptional ego strength will begin to feel humiliated and isolated.

The adult exhostage experiences considerable guilt and feelings of responsibility about his behaviour. Part of this is survivor guilt, but a major part is guilt for not having acted as a 'stronger individual', the John Wayne Syndrome. The exhostage feels better that he at least planned some heroic actions, but wishes that he could have at least resisted his captors more. In his dreams, the event may be frequently repeated with a heroic action added. If the Stockholm Syndrome or identification with the aggressor manifested itself in behaviour during the incident, the exhostage will experience difficulty rationalising his actions. This often leads to unsuccessful attempts to explain the captors' cause to others.

Both Western and Eastern cultures strongly sanction loyalty to values and non-submissive behaviour under stress. There are few internal rationales available for the exhostage who failed to exhibit such behaviour under stress. The return to work is a critical point. Almost all adult hostages report 'startle reactions', and watching for signs of another takeover to occur. This lasts from several days to several months. Embarrassed apologies are offered for such behaviour.

Attitudes towards work authority and governmental authority can be quite resentful. A typical scenario involves the exhostage experiencing concentration difficulties in doing routine paperwork. The supervisor expresses the need to get back to work as usual. The hostage reacts angrily at the perceived insensitivity of the supervisor. Part of the reaction may indeed be due to a supervisor's insensitivity, but part is due to the exhostage's remaining resentment of the way he was dominated by his captors.

Intrusive waking images are undesired mental pictures of the hostage event. Adult hostages rate this as a major problem, and will use it as an index of their overall readjustment. The frequency of the images declines with time; some continue to appear irregularly over a period of many years. Among the psychophysiological reactions of adult hostage victims, gastrointestinal problems are the most commonly reported. Research has yet to be conducted to determine whether this can be explained by the possible internalisation versus externalisation of anger, or predisposing factors in the hostage population, or some other variable. The desire for revenge is initially reluctant, then moderate to occasionally severe in strength. This may be attributed to the process of identification with the aggressor which lessens upon return to the usual social relationships.

Adult exhostages commonly state an interest in returning to the scene, provided they are given a waiting period of several days to several weeks. The initial return to scene is emotional. Stories are retold. Small items become stimuli to images and memories. Considerable relief is expressed afterwards: 'I knew I needed to do it. I'm glad I did it.' Once again, primary value is placed upon the 'strong' response to stress. Burnout' does indeed occur, but in a delayed pattern. After several months, the exhostage wants to move on from the experience. He wants the return of his ability to concentrate and work, unhampered by intrusive images and thoughts. A great deal of effort is made to suppress these. This, of course, works for a period of several weeks to several months, then rails. Often feeling tired and defeated, the exhostage begins to accept the periodic coming and going of the images and thoughts. In both work and personal obligations, smooth functioning alternates with immobilisation. Employers will report that the exhostage's work is back at his usual high level of quality. Then days will begin to appear where his productivity is extremely low. This frustrates employers and friends more than continuous difficulty in getting up to a productive level again.

Rejection by others can take a number of forms, in addition to the previously described Symonds' 'second injury'. The most common form described by exhostages is the rejection of their need to retell the story. After the first couple of times, family and friends do not want to hear it again. It is old news. However, for the exhostage, the retelling is an important way of ordering the experience and regaining a sense of mastery over it: 'I needed to go over and over it, but I felt I was boring people. I stopped talking and the feelings got worse.' Immediately after an incident, this author routinely tells exhostages to tell the story as frequently as the they want to when they want to. They are further told that if no one wants to listen: 'Call me and I'll listen, even if it's the exact same story. Exhostages find this amusing at the time, but later report that this very early permission giving was very meaningful to them. If newspaper and television coverage is quite extensive, a special type of situation is created for some hostage victims. In effect, this mass, detailed coverage 'steals the victim's story', so that the victim is often not the most complete source on the incident. This reduces the opportunities to master the experience through retelling. The victim as well as his story soon become yesterday's news, and he is left with a feeling of incompleteness and depression.

Envy is another form of rejection. Attention is so valued by so many that envy can occur even when the attention is the result of tragedy or life risk. After the Hanafi Muslim takeover incident, a B'nai B'rith employee joked that his tombstone would be engraved: 'Here lies Sol Goldberg, who was not there. He had a stomach ache that day. On the one hand it was a joke. On the other hand it was a profound insight into the behaviour going on around him. Family members can be the object of envy also. During the American-Iranian hostage crisis, the family of one hostage soldier received a great deal of press attention. The family lived in an economically less advantaged area. When one small sister began to receive rides to school in a television network's 'limousine', the neighbourhood reaction was clearly critical and envious. Often the curiosity of others takes the form of the Monday morning quarterback: 'Why didn't you try this' or, I would have tried to jump him when These comments feed into the exhostage's internal John Wayne Syndrome, triggering feelings of humiliation and inadequacy. Others continue to enhance the John Wayne Syndrome by doubting the genuineness of complaints: 'She is just being a baby. She should quit trying for so much attention.' Following the rescue, short-term anger and rejection occur among the exhostages. Anyone who did not seem to behave in the manner favoured by the group becomes the target of the anger. When the American exhostages were moved from Tehran to Wiesbaden, several were actively shunned by the others for several days. When ex-President Carter first met with them in Wiesbaden, a few exhostages angrily lashed out at him. A split developed later between those with remaining anger and those who did not feel this was the time or place to deal with it. As time passes, such differences seem to lessen with the profound nature of the event providing long-term felt cohesion, felt cohesion because group contact is relatively rare and usually brief when it does occur.

The child is logically far more vulnerable than the adult. Accordingly, wishes to see the captors punished conflict with fears of reprisal. These fears, that the original captors or friends of theirs will return, are quite consistent across different victims. An adult has the ability to move away, invest faith in the police or rationalise away a possible second incident. The child has limited access to such sophisticated defences, being primarily dependent upon adults for assurances, adults who 'falled' to protect him from the first incident. Both the feelings of loss related to the incident and fear of future loss are attached to adults/parents. This shows up in anxiety if a parent is late coming home or is away on a long trip. Most child exhostages display little interest in returning to the scene. Even given the fact that parents are routinely reluctant for the child to return, the child does not seem to carry an imperative to return for incident mastery in the way the adult does. 'Burnout' is considerably less delayed than with adult exhostages. After a few days, the child wants to return to normal play and activities: 'I don't want to talk about it any more. I want things to go back to the way they were.'

Terr, in her study of the Chowchilla school bus kidnapping, noted that the children seemed to have no intrusive, waking images. The children stated that they thought about the event as they wanted, although the occurrence of their dreams was not under similar control. It may be that this is the result of a semantic or interpretative difference over the intrusive phenomena. If not, it may represent a major clue as to how children process trauma. Survivor guilt shows up in a special childlike manner.

In a well-known Israeli terrorist incident, a booby-trapped refrigerator exploded on a crowded street killing several people. The surviving ten-year-old daughter of one of the victims developed very strong guilt feelings. These were based upon a fight she had with her father in which she wished he would die. Although this example is a terrorist, not hostage, incident, it illustrates well the combination of anger and magical thinking that induces what is labelled childlike survivor guilt. Even older children who rationally know that such thoughts did not cause an incident may still hold emotionally to this special type of guilt.

Jealousy is a very real social process for the child as well as the adult, with the child often wishing to conceal the event to avoid such attention. David, age eleven, and Eric age nine, saw both their parents killed when Arab terrorists took over a passenger bus in Israel in 1978. David escaped during the attack and Eric escaped later after witnessing his mother being shot in the chest.

A few moments later, the bus blew up with both parents inside. Within the range of reactions one might anticipate from such a tragedy, both boys developed strong feelings about wanting to be treated like others, not in a special way. Conversely, this envy may extend into doubt in some of those who do express complaints. The child can be labelled as an attention seeker, or manipulator. In contrast to adults, there is little humiliation by others or belief that the victim could have done more.

3

Target India

Head West out of Amritsar and keep going. The drive may not be very comfortable but at least finding the route is straightforward. It'll take you a few hours to Lahore and then it is a fast three-hour run along the new motorway to Islamabad. Go on up to Peshawar, the bustling and violent Pakistani frontier town, through the Khyber Pass, across the border into Afghanistan and then, keeping the Kabul river on your right, drive for another three hours. After a 100 more miles and a dozen checkposts you'll be threading a way through the bazaars of Jalalabad. Turn left at the main intersection and aim for the dusty hills on the southern horizon. Cross a bridge and drive up to the two Taliban tanks dug in on the crest of the ridge. If you're sensible, you'll stop here. If you are not then keep going along a straight flat road with lines of tall cypress-like trees on either side. After about five miles you'll see the overgrown orchards and dilapidated huts of Farmihadda, once a Soviet-style collective farm and now the place where Osama bin Laden—the world's most wanted terrorist—has built his new home. It is from here that bin Laden is believed to have issued his threat of September 16, which appeared in *Jang,* the mass circulated Urdu daily published from Pakistan. Calling for an all out jehad against India for the first time, bin Laden declared: "India and America are now our biggest enemies ... all mujahideen groups in

Pakistan should come together now to target India ... we are always ready to help the Kashmiri mujahideen."

Even before the chilling statement came from Farmihadda-where bin Laden has established a new communications, training and logistics centre—senior Indian officials had been concerned that a dangerous nexus may be building up between Pakistan's Inter Services Intelligence (ISI) and the Saudi terrorist.

During the Kargil war, there were rumours that bin Laden's fighters were among those pouring fire down from the heights of Tololing and Batalik.

One Indian intelligence report claimed that bin Laden's personal bodyguards were at the forefront, helping keep the supply routes open. And also that the Stinger missiles used to bring down two Indian aircraft may have come from his armoury.

Now a senior official in the Ministry of External Affairs (MEA) says, "We don't need to hear from Farmihadda to know that a lethal cocktail is being brewed. We already knew. The coming together of the isi, bin Laden and his hosts, the Taliban, is serious." Their worst fears are, in fact, coming true.

India appears to have become a target of the man the Americans, and now ironically the Russians too, see as their single biggest security problem since the end of the Cold War.

Bin Laden's sudden declaration of jehad against India is not being viewed as an emotional outburst. It was delivered at a point when India and the US are adding a new dimension to their relationship through cooperation on counter-terrorism. Bin Laden's statement came shortly before Ambassador Michael Sheehan, coordinator in the US Department for Counter-terrorism, held senior-level talks in Delhi. Sheehan came to Delhi as a follow-up to the visit of two senior mm officials to the US a fortnight ago to discuss the new threat emanating from Afghanistan.

Bin Laden's threat also has a direct co-relation to India's new Afghan policy. India had always supported the former regime headed by Burhanuddin Rabbani and Ahmed Shah Masood and of late it has been extremely vocal in its criticism of the Taliban.

At a press briefing recently, External Affairs Minister Jaswant Singh had even gone to the extent of stating that India would no longer "supinely" accept what was happening in Afghanistan but pursue a "proactive" policy.

There were indications that India, along with possibly Russia and Iran, had supported Masood and Rabbani in their spirited fight-back against the Taliban's summer offensive to dislodge them from the Panjsher Valley. The Taliban and bin Laden are furious over the reversals and believe that India had a hand in it. The revenge for the Kargil debacle is believed to be another major reason. Pakistan and the so-called mujahideen, many of them Afghan mercenaries, are still smarting under the humiliating retreat.

Post-Kargil, the ISI has already upgraded its proxy war in Jammu and Kashmir. The militants coming in are better trained, equipped with deadlier arms and strike in much larger groups than ever before.

The majority of the militants sneaking in are said to be non-Kashmiris who now dominate organised terrorism in the Valley. Many are believed to be battle-hardened Afghan mercenaries who may have links with bin Laden. So concerned has been the Research and Analysis Wing (RAW), the country's external intelligence agency, over the growing threat posed by Islamic fundamentalists, including bin Laden, that it recently revised its six-year-old doctrine on threat perception. The analysis of Indian intelligence agencies shows:

— A large number of Arab mujahideen involved in Afghanistan have found it difficult to return to their own countries and consequently a nucleus of pan-Islamic mercenary forces has come into existence. Their presence and acts of terror are increasingly becoming evident in Jammu and Kashmir, apart from other trouble-spots in the world.

— Bin Laden is proving to be a rallying point for militants operating in India and his photographs are reported to have been found in the possession of slain militants in Kashmir.

— There is a growing nexus between Islamic fundamentalists and the criminal fringe elements in various countries. They include the underworld dons of Mumbai, the smugglers of Nepal and the drug mafia in Pakistan.

— Large quantities of sophisticated arms and explosives which have entered the country are yet to be recovered. With reports of their dispersal to various cities, the threat is said to be serious.

— The list of the suspected targets of militant groups is growing: It is not just in Jammu and Kashmir but also in Assam, Andhra Pradesh, Maharashtra and Gujarat where the communal cauldron can be stirred.

That bin Laden is lethal as a foe has never been in doubt. It is just over a year since two massive blasts demolished the American embassies in Dar-es-Salaam and Nairobi. The bombs killed more than 200 people, injured 5,000 and catapulted bin Laden into the front rank of global criminals. The retaliatory US missile strikes on his suspected hideouts established him as a hero of sorts among millions of Muslims. Now bin Laden's dark eyes stare out of posters displayed proudly in thousands of Pakistani and Afghan shops and tea kiosks. Son of a Saudi construction millionaire, bin Laden, 45, became a key player in the jehad against the Soviet-occupation of Afghanistan in the '80s. The former civil engineer-turned militant not only organised the flow of funds, munitions and men to the mujahideen groups and built a number of training camps and depots, but was also in the thick of action.

In the early '90s he was in Sudan fomenting violence. By 1994 he was stripped of his Saudi citizenship for dissident political activities against the royal family. He came to Afghanistan in May 1996 with about 100 followers and is believed to have funded the campaign that led the Taliban successfully into Kabul. Bin Laden's relationship with the Taliban—a key strength—remains good.

Many of the militia's senior commanders are old comrades. He saved their lives, they saved his. On Fridays—after prayers—he goes fishing with Mullah Omar, the reclusive, one-eyed cleric who is the spiritual leader of the Taliban and a good friend. Bin Laden is also a devout Muslim and is said to be prepared to make extreme sacrifices to achieve his aims. Today, apart from money—the CIA estimates his funds total almost $ 350 million (Rs 1,505 crore)—bin Laden has a network of contacts in key Islamic fundamentalist groups across the globe.

Says a senior Indian intelligence officer: "He continues to stay in constant touch with important Islamic militant organisations like the Islamic Jehad in Palestine and the National Islamic Front in Sudan." In the subcontinent he is suspected to have strong links with two militant groups—the Harkat-ul-Mujahideen and the Lashkar-e-Toiba—that have been at the centre of militant activity in Kashmir. Many of these militants are believed to be trained in Khost in Afghanistan in camps that are run by bin Laden in collaboration with the Taliban.

The years of jehad have prepared him well for his present life. Bin Laden's domestic arrangements are modest. Farmihadda is a dilapidated collection of outhouses, barns, sheds and residential blocks with debris-filled canals on two sides. The living quarters are sparsely furnished.

Bin Laden shuns even rugs and carpets, preferring to squat on the floor or on a small stool. His daily life reflects the rigours of his surroundings. He gets up at dawn to pray and then studies the Koran or other Islamic texts until a light breakfast of dates, yoghurt, flat Afghan bread and black tea. Until recently, he followed a tough physical-training regime, with a daily ride and exercises, but now a bad back—possibly a result of shrapnel wound sustained while fighting the Russians—has mad anything strenuous impossible

Married with three wives and 13 children who, like him, divide their time between Farmihadda and his home in a disused barrack at the airport near the southern desert city of Kandahar—the headquarters of the Taliban—security concerns seem to dominate his life. He travels constantly and rarely spends two nights at the same place.

Roads in Afghanistan are appalling and a 200-mile journey can take days. Bin Laden frequently drives for a while in one convoy and then walks or rides for a distance before switching to a second set of vehicles. His satellite phones are often carried in a third convoy. Instead of using them personally—he believes that the Americans tracked signals from his phone to pinpoint his location for their missiles last year—bin Laden usually dictates his message to an aide who relays it over telephone from a separate location.

There have been two reviews of his security in the last 10 months—both prompted by fears of betrayal. Soon after the US attack, he sacked almost two-thirds of his 200-strong bodyguards

Many of those who survived the first purge were Afghans, former comrades from his days with the mujahideen. But recently most of them were fired too and bin Laden now relies on a select group of mainly Arab fighters to protect him. And his eldest son, Mohammed, who is believed to be around 16.

Bin Laden's Organisation is now known as the "International Islamic Front for jehad against Jews and Crusaders" and is effectively an umbrella group for all the terrorists currently holed up in Afghanistan. Experts believe that in the absence of the means to genuinely control a vast web of inter-linked terrorist cells, bin Laden's strategy may be to create the leadership and motivation that might galvanise individual, independent units into action. If they then claim to be part of bin Laden's Organisation it's good for him. More publicity means more recruits. The major input that bin Laden may make to Kashmir militancy is through funding fundamentalist groups operating in Pakistan, which in turn patronise militant outfits in the Valley.

The role of Pakistan in all this is unclear. There is a strong body of bin Laden supporters among the army and the intelligence services and also, obviously, among the increasingly powerful clergy. However, there are also many moderate politicians who realise that Pakistan cannot jeopardise its relationship with the US, and the continuing drip-feed of IMF and World Bank loans, by overtly obstructing their efforts to capture the man.

Caught in the middle, as ever, is Prime Minister Nawaz Sharif who is trying to tread a careful path among domestic opinion, political lobbies and the demands of the West.

In Kashmir, bin Laden's jehad call has received a mixed response. Wary of offending the US, the All-Party Hurriyat Conference is downplaying any links its supporters have with bin Laden. "What can Laden do for us when he himself is in hiding?" asks Hurriyat chairman Syed Ali Shah Geelani. Adds senior leader Professor Abdul Ghani: "Kashmiris don't need Ladens. We can sustain the struggle on our own. It is a bogey raised by India to win the US support on Kashmir." There may be some element of truth in that. Also a certain amount of hype by the ruling BJP to keep security at the forefront since the Kargil war has been a major factor in the parliamentary elections. But there is no doubting the threat bin Laden poses.

Especially in Kashmir where there is growing disenchantment with the Farooq Abdullah Government. Says state police chief Gurbachan Jagat: "Kashmir is now the theatre to whip up the Pan-Islamic fervour that Laden is funding." Bin Laden's jehad may revive the ideological basis of Kashmiri militancy that had been on the wane.

The Indian government is beefing up security measures, including bringing the army back into the counter-offensive grid. Security experts expect Pakistan to soon make Kashmir a flashpoint again, especially with reports that over 2,000 well-trained militants have sneaked into the Valley in the past three months. India just cannot afford to ignore the threat from the world's most infamous terrorist holed up in Farmihadda, Jalalabad.

Trimors in Kashmir

It could be India's worst nightmare—the breakaway of a restive, culturally distinct and strategically significant part of the Union. The scenes of chaos beamed nightly on television may belong to East Timor, but their parallel with Kashmir are giving South Block mandarins hot flushes.

A small speck on the Indonesian archipelago, Catholic East Timor is about to succeed in its 23-year struggle to break away from one of the world's largest Muslim countries.

On August 30, the territory's people voted for independence under a United Nations-supervised referendum. However, it's the imminent arrival of the Australia-led UN peacekeepers to quell the ensuing violence by pro-Jakarta militia that poses a dilemma for India—whether to join the force and risk endorsing a precedent for Kashmir, or to stay out and turn a blind eye to the militia's attempt at genocide. Former foreign secretary J.N. Dixit is adamant that India should not send its peacekeepers to Dili, capital of East Timor, and the centre of the violence. "If we send in peacekeepers to East Timor, we'll have to face questions about why UN peacekeepers can't come to Kashmir—and of course we are not going to allow them into Kashmir. So why do we want to face such a problem and open ourselves to needless criticism?" Kashmiri intellectual Dr Nusrat Andrabi agrees that such a decision would indeed amount to rank discrimination against the people of Kashmir who've been clamouring for self-determination for 50 years. Consultations meanwhile are on in the UN in New York on the final composition of the peacekeeping force.

So far, specific offers of personnel have come from Australia, New Zealand, the US, Canada, Portugal,

England, France, Sweden, Thailand, the Philippines, South Korea, Italy, Singapore and Brazil. Non-specific offers have come from Bangladesh, Pakistan, Argentina, China, Russia, Malaysia and Fiji.

Events have moved fast since President Habibie announced a referendum for East Timor on May 5, even though he's in little more than a caretaker position since President Suharto stepped down in '98.

Indonesia expert Ganganath Jha at the Jawaharlal Nehru University in Delhi, says that "none of the western powers were pushing for a referendum at this time, nor were any of the Asian countries; it's taken everyone by surprise." Although the West and many of the Asian countries have come to grips with the situation, it appears South Block mandarins are still floundering in a sea of uncertainty. "India's always accepted East Timor as a part of Indonesia ... the new situation's thrown up new questions and to be very frank I do not have the answers," says one MEA official, a few days after the referendum. But South Block is clear on one issue—that of sovereignty. As one official put it: "No one pressured Indonesia into taking the decision to hold a referendum, it was purely their own." His implication: none can pressure India into holding a similar referendum in Kashmir.

South Block officials are also quick to deny any link between the decision to send peacekeepers to the former Portuguese outpost, and implications of that decision for Kashmir. "After all, we've sent peacekeepers to other places too, like the former Yugoslavia and Kosovo, so why should we not send peacekeepers to East Timor?" Jha, however, dismisses the comparison as naive. "We have close connections with Indonesia in trade, we've had cooperation in fighting drug smuggling as well as strategic cooperation... Indonesia has the power to destabilise us if they want to. Kosovo is insignificant in that respect. These officials are living in some sort of fairyland."

They're merely trying to take comfort in the fact that India will send in troops only if invited to do so by Indonesia—thus avoiding the risk of angering a worthy Muslim ally which has been giving much-needed support to India's stand on Kashmir. But critics say Indonesia does not have a veto on the force composition, and that such statements by the MEA are just another attempt to duck and dive from the crisis at hand. In fact, it has been observed that whether it is the Moscow coup, or the invasion of Kuwait, the world's largest democracy ends up as a friend of the oppressor.

And while policymakers in New Delhi may rest content in the knowledge that events in East Timor can't touch India, little do they realise that local Kashmiris have been drawing inspiration from TV images flashing in recent weeks.

Says Omar Farooq, Mirwaiz-e-Kashmir: "I feel there's a striking resemblance between the two situations, East Timor has shown the world that complex issues can also be resolved." He is in fact planning a trip to New York to emphasise his point at the UN General Assembly. And India will risk international criticism if it tries to block his visit. The Mirwaiz-e-Kashmir detects a new enthusiasm and optimism among intellectuals in Kashmir. But what he disagrees with is their viewing the violence in East Timor as an unfortunate but necessary pain that must be gone through to attain freedom. "We must take time to come to an agreement, even if it takes us another 15 years ... we do not want to descend into anarchy." East Timor is in fact an example of botched integration by force compared with India's successful integration of the former Portuguese colony of Goa in

December '61. Parallels between Kashmir and East Timor are being drawn by analysts in Delhi as well.

According to Jha, Portugal had referred East Timor for a referendum to the UN just before its aggressive takeover by Indonesian forces in December '75.

Nehru had likewise referred Kashmir to the UN for a plebiscite that never took place, And just as the West did not accept East Timor's annexation, so also countries in the European Union, the US, China, *et al* believe Kashmir to be a disputed area. The difference between the Indian and East Timor situation, however, is that while Kashmir became the battleground for an Indo-Pak war, no third party has been involved in East Timor. Also, while the population in East Timor is overwhelmingly Roman Catholic, apart from the Indonesian army, the population in Kashmir is heterogenous—comprising Sunnis, Shias, Bakerwals, Gujjars, Paharis as also a substantial number of non-Muslims.

Kashmir analyst Amitabh Mattoo believes the two situations are fundamentally dissimilar. "The East Timorese movement had tremendous leadership ... it did not get criminalised, instead, it threw up Nobel peace prize winners. Can you imagine any Kashmiri leader winning one?" The awards given to Jose Ramos Horta and Bishop Carlos Belo in '96 raised the profile of the struggle; world attention had been focused on it ever since the '91 Santa Cruz cemetery massacre in Dili. Former coloniser Portugal, accused of doing little for the people of East Timor, had used the opportunity to lobby for self-determination for the territory within the EU. Also, for its part, the Clinton administration has taken more interest in the situation than any prior administration. It was this international pressure, combined with Indonesia's economic collapse and its subsequent dependence on the IMF for a $11.3 bn bailout package, that finally forced Indonesia's hand. "India has no such impending crisis," says Mattoo. And Kashmir is safe, for the time being. Mattoo says East Timor is nothing more than a symbol for the Kashmiris, which may encourage popular resistance. But if asked to be a part of the peacekeeping force in East Timor, he thinks India shouldn't refuse, "It would just attract international attention." Onward, Indian peacekeepers then?

Nobody would have ever known who the five men killed by the security forces at Panchaltran, 13 kilometres east of Chittisinghpora were, but for the uncle of Zahoor Ahmad Dalal, 28, of Anantnag. Zahoor was one of three men picked up late on the evening of March 24. When news of the encounter deaths of militants behind the

Sikh massacre broke out, Zahoor's uncle went to the cemetery where the five were buried and someone who had helped with the burial gave him a ring and piece of vest of one of the buried men. He instantly recognised it as that of Zahoor, whose body along with that of 60-year-old Jumma Khan was exhumed and identified by relatives on April 6. Jumma's widow Roshan Jan could never mistake the chin and nose of her husband.

Even as people waited with a sense of victory for the exhumation of the remaining three bodies the following day, the government's response was characteristic: "We Will take action against the culprits once they are identified by the independent probe ordered by the Anantnag Chief Judicial Magistrate Abdul Waheed." The probe had been ordered on a petition filed by 14 residents of Brariaangan village from where some men went missing after the Chittisinghpora incident.

Zahoor's uncle, according to a resident of Anantnag, approached deputy commissioner Pawan Kotwal, since replaced, for the bodies, but his request was turned down. Then began the petition and public demonstrations, one of which saw seven civilians falling to police bullets.

Minister of State for Home Mushtaq Ahmad Lone said that the four policemen involved in the shooting have been suspended and arrested. "We know that the people are suspecting that the killed militants were actually missing villagers," he said. "All this is to be probed. The state government will do everything to the satisfaction of the people."

While 17 men from Anantnag are alleged to have been picked up by the security forces since the killing of the 36 Sikhs, the killing of the seven civilians is threatening to push Kashmir into another bout of communal frenzy. Sections of the majority community have alleged that a Sikh member of the Special Operations Group fired the first shot that led to the killings, "to avenge the Chittisinghpora massacre".

Aprehensions about those who were behind the Chittisinghpora massacre.

Some of them believe that the rogue group behind the massacre had targeted the Sikhs of Chittisinghpora to hurt the visiting Clintons, who are close to the Sikhs in the US. Sikhs form a significant portion of the fund-raisers and campaign managers, besides voters, of Hillary Clinton who is seeking election from New York. The American President's delegation to India included Chehal, an NRI Sikh and owner of the Bombay Palace chain of hotels.

A Sikh leader says that Naresh Chandra, the Governor's brother and Indian envoy in Washington, knows of this affinity between the Clintons and the Sikhs. He also points out how Farooq said one day that he would resign if any Indian agency was found to be involved in the massacre and kept mum on the inquiry he promised for many days thereafter.

According to this leader, their fears were confirmed when the chief minister ordered an inquiry into the police firing on protesters in Anantnag after seven civilians were killed. "We all saw the genuine anger and shock of the majority community at the Chittisinghpora massacre. That was not there when the Pandits were killed. Then we made inquiries at different levels, and what we learnt was shocking. Apparently, Dr Abdullah was as shocked as we were," he said.

Traditionally brave, the Sikh community is staying put in the Valley. The community's mature leadership, including Punjab Chief Minister Prakash Singh Badal, Gurcharan Singh Tohra and Simranjit Singh Mann, has helped. "If the Sikhs migrate from here it will have repercussions all over the country, and create a I communal divide between Sikhs and Muslims," said the Jammu and Kashmir Shiromani Gurdwara Prabandhak Board president Sudarshan Singh Wazir. "It'll have its impact in Uttar Pradesh and Maharashtra... so Badal agreed to convene a meeting. But he will simply say' you stay back and whatever steps you want the Centre and the state government to take, well take up these issues at the appropriate forum'. But the decision to stay has been that of the people."

Some people in the Valley interpret the initial reluctance to exhume the bodies of the five people killed by the police at Panchaltran near Chittisinghpora as proof of the "hollow claims" of the security forces. "Whenever a major incident happens, they pick up somebody from somewhere, kill them in such a way that the bodies cannot be recognised, and then claim that the terrorists behind that incident have been killed. The

Special Operation Group is desperate to show results," said a retired government official.

He pointed out that various security agencies had claimed to have killed the same prominent militants at different times, at different places.

For instance, within a month of the Badami Bagh cantonment incident, Abutulla, Hazarvi, chief of Lashkar-e-Toiba in J&K was reported killed five times in as many locations. Similarly, Abu Muza of the same outfit was declared killed three times by different agencies. The security forces have been maintaining that the five killed in Panchaltran were armed and in army fatigues, reason enough for the forces to engage them in conflict. But off the record, each government agency is blaming the other for the goof-up, and many are waiting anxiously, hoping that the DNA tests will vindicate their stand. "Even if that does not happen, the government will say that there is an inquiry anyway. So nothing will come out of this," said an advocate.

During the recent phase of militancy, the public may not have supported the forces in their battle with the *fidayeens* (foreign militants) but they also did not display any sympathy for the militants or take to the streets when many of them were killed.

But after the Panchaltran killings by the security forces, people of the Valley have once again taken to the streets. "It can become explosive and worse than the early 90s," warned a high school teacher. "All these years we quietly stomached the alienation caused by the forces."

This is not the first time that use of force by security forces is creating public discontent. In 1992, when people took to the streets against the killing of Molvi Muhammad Farooq, they were shouting slogans against a pro-Pakistan militant outfit but after the police fired at the mob and killed 40 civilians, their wrath changed direction towards the forces.

During the Hazratbal shrine incident, many demonstrated their anger against the militants for occupying a holy place, but the mood got reversed after the forces fired at a procession in Bijbehara killing 60 civilians.

The roses and butterflies are all that 16-year-old Raza can make out on the colourful card that came inside a soiled envelope bearing Pakistani postage stamps. At her remote village in Kupwara's Lolab valley close to the Line of Control (LoC), she wistfully holds the Eid-ul-Fitr greeting card sent by her brother Abdul Rashid from across the border. As a member of the Tehrik-ul-Jehad Islamia (TUJI) militant outfit, Rashid—code-named Mushtaq—is now a resident of Manshehra town in Pakistan. "*Agar khuda ne chaha to mulaqat hogi* (God willing, we will meet again)," says the brief handwritten message in Urdu, moving Raza and her ageing father Habib to tears.

Many more Kashmiri families are reposing this faith in their maker. The number of such families has only increased dramatically in the past one year because the ISI, which trains militants in numerous camps in POK, has decided to recruit more and more local Kashmiris. And schools have now become the new hunting grounds for recruits because the ISI seems to believe that the younger they are, the easier it is to train and indoctrinate them. The Indian Army made an alarming discovery this year. In north Kashmir alone, at least 150 boys didn't return to their schools after the winter break.

Khalid Var, a 14-year-old student of Class IX, for instance, did not rejoin the Government High School in Devar, a remote village nestling in the Lolab valley.

Instead, he disappeared into the nearby forested mountains, graduating into the ranks of the dreaded Lashkar-e-Toiba (LET) group. As the only male member left in the family after his father and uncle, both top LET militants, were killed in encounters with security forces, Var hardly needed any motivation to throw away the satchel and pick up the gun.

In the frontier land of Kupwara, notorious as the gateway of militancy in the Valley, Khalid is only one of the recent entrants into the militant fold. The teenager represents the new crop of recruits—school-goers and drop-outs who are easy to motivate and easier to train. Reference to *"nayee kitabein* (new books)" is frequently popping up in wireless intercepts in Kashmir. *"Nayee kitabein jaldi bhejo ... padhi-likhi honee chahiye* (Send the new books immediately ... should be educated)," said a wireless message flashed on April 9 by the POK-based militant outfit Al Badr to its Valley-based calling station. In militants parlance, *"nayee kitabein"* is the code word for fresh recruits.

With the jehad fervour not holding much appeal, militant outfits are combining money with motivation to lure new recruits. Foreign mercenaries flush with funds are spending liberally not only to buy logistical support from the locals but also for enticing recruits. The financial inducements work well in the impoverished areas of rural Kashmir.

The huge financial transactions noted in the diaries recovered from Manzoor Ali, the north Kashmir chief of the Harkat-ul-Mujahideen who was killed on April 13 in an encounter with the security forces, reveal the money power being employed to sustain militancy in the Valley. In the past one year, Ali had disbursed Rs 48 lakh as inducements.

In fact, isi funds are helping the Kashmiri militants to portray themselves as modern-day Robin Hoods among the locals and revive the glamour of the gun to attract new recruits.

Hamid Gaddah, one of the longest-surviving top guns of the Hizbul Mujahideen who was killed last month, managed to elude the security dragnet all along because he had learnt the art of mixing terror with financial doles for the families of slain or detained militants in the Ganderbal area.

Similarly, much of the public outpouring of grief at the recent killing of Maqbool Shah, district commander of TUJI, was on account of the monetary assistance to the militant families and the poor locals. Militants are using a mix of cash and coercion to attract a new lot," says Brigadier Noble Thamburaj of the Rashtriya Rifles in the Lolab valley That holds good for new recruits like 16-year-old Manzoor Ahmed Wani.

A student of Class IX and son of a willow basket weaver of Kanchen village in Ganderbal, Wani drifted towards the Hizbul Mujahideen after his peer, Sajjad, a militant, promised him Rs 10, 000 for a training stint in POK. "The offer of gun and money was too tempting," says Wani matter-of-factly. But 10 gruelling days with militants, during which he lived under the constant fear of an encounter with security forces, led to a change of heart.

Before he could wade in deeper, Wani and three other teenaged fellow travellers slipped away from the militants' hideout and reported to the army camp. Among them was Abdul Razak. His mother Taj is relieved to have her son back. "My son is not made for the gun. His escape is a new birth," she says. Many parents of youths who have already crossed over to the

POK try to negotiate a surrender with the army or advise their sons to settle down there. The security forces are not always averse to a surrender but as a senior officer pointed out, "The ISI would not induct these boys if it were not sure of their high motivation levels."

It is tough for the parents as they wait for their sons to return. Begum Badida, mother of Ghulam Ali who is currently in a training camp in POK, is one such hapless mother. "He was taken away at gun point. He is too young to hold the gun. Toys are what he should be playing with at his age," she says plaintively.

But then, the perspective of the boys is different. Money is an important factor and the lack of employment opportunities in the Valley and an indifferent administration only make the offer more tempting.

A catalyst in the ISI's recruitment drive is the cadres of the pro-militant Jamait-e-Islami. "The militant ideologues are using the clergy to inject jehad into the young minds," says Major-General Nirbhay Sharma, GOC, Kilo Force, an anti-militancy army formation in north Kashmir.

A recent intelligence report talks about the Hizbul Mujahideen issuing instructions to its cadres in the Kandi areas of the Valley to motivate more local youth for jehad.

The militants are succeeding to the extent that the past few months witnessed a significant increase in the recruitment and exfiltration of Kashmiri youth. At least 600 locals are reported to have crossed the borders and entered the POK last year against 285 in 1998. Once in the POK, jehad becomes a fait accompli for the new recruits. They undergo a three-month basic course that trains them in handling weapons and negotiating difficult terrain. The brighter ones in the lot are given specialised training in handling advanced communication equipment and sophisticated weapons and explosives. "Training in POK camps follows an army-type regimen," says Javed Ahmed, a former militant who received training in Pakistan.

Security officials discern a change of tack in the renewed efforts by the militants to draft Kashmiri recruits. Implicit in the overdrive to recruit these Kashmiri youths is Pakistan's attempt to portray the decade-long secessionism in the Valley as a locally inspired movement.

The waning of local militancy in Kashmir had forced the ISI to infiltrate more and more foreign mercenaries into the valley. For the past two years or so, foreigners—mostly Pakistanis and a sprinkling of battle—hardened Afghans—have been calling the shots in Kashmir militancy.

Pakistan's concerted efforts to play down the foreign mercenaries angle in Kashmir militancy have been evident especially after US President Bill Clinton did some plain speaking in Islamabad last month. "Providing local impetus to militancy forms the key element of the ISI's new game plan on Kashmir," says state DGP Gurbachan Jagat.

The Indian Army interprets the trend as part of Pakistan's strategy to balance out militant groups under its wings and prevent them from becoming too powerful. Says Major-General Sharma: "The militants' mentors are making an extra endeavour to impart an indigenous thrust to the militancy."

Intelligence inputs and militants intercepts are awash with reports on how various outfits have been tasked to reactivate new cadres, recycle surrendered militants, and send Kashmiri youth to POK for training.

After his recent meeting with General Pervez Musharraf and isi chief Lt-General Mehmood Ahmed, the Rawalpindi-based chairman of the pro-independence Jammu and Kashmir Liberation Front (JKLF) Amanullah Khan is keen to resuscitate its dormant cadres. Khan has sent clandestine messages to his supporters in the Valley to arrange the exfiltration of five JKLF leaders to POK in April. Reports say that Khan has been offered financial help and armaments as an incentive to reactivate his JKLF cadres in the Valley.

What has added to the militant outfits' desperation to have more Kashmiris in their ranks is the security forces' new strategy to target local militants, so crucial for the logistic support to foreign mercenaries.

Since January this year, when security agencies categorised 170-odd local militants and put hefty reward tags on their heads, a majority of the militants killed in Kashmir were locals, many of them veteran top guns. Of the 210 militants killed in the troubled valley this year, only 65 were foreign mercenaries.

Security officials say that the foreign mercenaries, while confining themselves to certain pockets of tough terrain in the region, are now giving a bigger role to the locals. Adds DIG (Kashmir) K. Rajendra Kumar: "The ISI would push in more Kashmiri militants than foreign mercenaries in the summer infiltration." Even the Pakistan-based militant outfits have lately been attempting a mix-and-match strategy by roping in locals in their ranks for better logistical support.

This summer, officials reckon, could well be a turning point for militancy in the valley. Unlike the summer of 1999, when militant outfits swelled with fresh inductees from Pakistan in the wake of the Kargil war, much would now depend on the quantum of infiltration and exfiltration of freshly recruited militants in the winter months. Recent intelligence reports speak of roughly 2,000 trained militants strung out at different launching pads along the LoC, waiting to infiltrate into Indian territory once the passes open. This year perhaps another indicator will have to be closely scrutinised: how many schoolchildren bunk classes to cross the border for armed lessons in jehad.

4

US Interest on Bilateral Issues

The first official-level contact between India and the U.S. since Bill Clinton's triumphal presidential tour, provides important clues to newly evolving priorities in bilateral relations. Louis Freeh, Director of the top U.S. law enforcement agency, the Federal Bureau of Investigation (FBI), spent three days in India in the first week of April. His major engagements included discussions with top officials of India's enforcement and intelligence agencies.

Freeh met with the Director of the Central Bureau of Investigation, R.K. Raghavan, the Director of the Intelligence Bureau, Shyamal Datta, and the Special Secretary in the Ministry of Home Affairs, M.B. Kaushal. Arrangements for the FBI to set up an outpost in the premises of the American embassy in Delhi were reportedly finalised. And for its part, the CBI will establish a counterpart institution in the Indian embassy in Washington. The FBI also promised assistance in the pursuit of the hijackers of the Indian Airlines flight IC-814 in December 1999.

A growing convergence between Indian and American perceptions of terrorism has been a much celebrated event in recent times. But in the past the divergences have been so sharp that there is much scepticism about the depth of this supposed new understanding. India sees the problem in terms of the events in Jammu and Kashmir. In contrast, the U.S. has a much wider perception, beginning with West Asia, taking in parts of North Africa, and now seemingly centred on Afghanistan and the wider Central Asian region. India tends to see the West Asian theatre in a different light. And for the U.S., the problem in Kashmir is the deep-seated legacy of a historical dispute that is not amenable to any simple characterisation.

Freeh's visit came as a minor surprise to many observers, since the protocol on "institutionalised dialogue" that was appended to the Vision Statement signed by President Clinton and Prime Minister Atal Behari Vajpayee did not specifically mention law enforcement as an area of cooperation. Evidently, the schedule for the FBI chief's visit was agreed at the first meeting of the newly constituted Indo-U.S. Joint Working Group on Terrorism in February. That meeting also decided to work on a mutual legal assistance treaty, which is now reportedly in the early stages of negotiation.

While the broader framework is being worked out, it is learnt that India and the U.S. have decided to step up cooperation in surveillance in two areas of concern—terrorism and drug trafficking. It is unclear, though, whether that any agreed basis exists for coordinated action in these areas.

The immediate difficulty would be for the U.S. to rid itself of the legacy of Cold War entanglements with Islamic militant groups. Much of the problem of insurgency in Kashmir today owes its origins to the quixotically tided jehad that the U.S. and Pakistan waged jointly in Afghanistan through the 1980s. When that struggle was consummated in the medievalist regime of the Taliban, the holy warriors who risked redundancy seemingly turned their attention to the Kashmir theatre.

Beginning in a series of minor incursions around 1994, the Afghan element in Kashmir is believed now to be the main force fighting Indian rule.

The Taliban in Afghanistan and the military junta in Pakistan insist that the Kashmir insurgency is a spontaneous and wholly indigenous movement. In identifying "elements" of the Pakistan military as sponsors of the insurgency, Clinton indicated during his visit to the subcontinent that the U.S. has finally decided that these alibis were worthless. This has enthused Indian security and intelligence agencies to propose a whole new beginning in cooperation with their U.S. counterparts. How far, if at all these new initiatives will be able to overcome the legacy of past disagreements remains to be seen.

The terrorist threat in Afghanistan and the neighbourhood of India emanates from former clients of the U.S. who have now escaped their control. But the situation remains anomalous, since of the three countries that have recognised the Taliban regime in Afghanistan, two—Saudi Arabia and the United Arab Emirates—are the closest allies of the U.S. in the Islamic world. And in a further twist to this rather tortuous plot, the countries that the U.S. is most wary of in the West Asian and North African regions—Sudan, Iraq and Libya—are in the Arab context adversaries of the Saudi-UAE axis.

The U.S. evidently believes that the Sudanese regime, the Taliban and the Kashmir insurgency are all similar in origins and inspirations. Some of the possible tensions that can arise from such an over-simplified reading of a complex ground situation were evident when the U.S. launched its last major strike against global terrorism in August 1998. While privately applauding the strike against militant camps in Afghanistan, India in public expressed alarm at the arbitrary and unilateral nature of the U.S. action. And indeed, sufficient evidence has since emerged to prove that the missile strikes against a pharmaceutical factory in Sudan were grossly misdirected. The U.S. has been unable to prove any complicity with militant activity on the part of the factory owners. It quietly decided last year that it would not contest a claim for compensation they have filed.

In the heated aftermath of the August 1998 missile strikes, India sought to appropriate for itself the mandate for unilateral action that the U.S. had applied. Union Home Minister L.K. Advani, for instance, proclaimed that the Indian security forces would actively consider the option of "hot pursuit" into Pakistani territory in order to neutralise militant camps. However, senior officials of the U.S. State Department pointedly warned against such a course.

Evidently the U.S. has different compulsions shaped by contingent circumstances that prevail in the arc from Pakistan to North Africa. In an earlier phase, they actively patronised the Taliban in the belief that stability in the strategic crossroads of Central Asia was a crucial geopolitical imperative. They are now more ambivalent, though nowhere being as unequivocally committed to neutralising Islamic militancy as India is.

The situation is different in West Asia, where the U.S. resolve is very much more unambiguous. But Islamic militancy here has a very different origin, being in most cases an outgrowth of long suppressed Arab nationalist movements. And since India has traditionally had a more congenial relationship with Arab nationalism, it may be a difficult proposition for it to go along with hardline American sensibilities in this region. Celebrations of a new concord between India and the U.S. in the enforcement of law and order in the regional context may, for these reasons, prove grossly premature.

William Jefferson Clinton's visit to India was good. It was made even better by the contrast with what happened in Pakistan. But there might be snakes and ladders ahead. India must be ready to side-step the former and climb up the latter. The Indo-American future may then be better than it has ever been. So also the world's understanding of India's case of the Line of Control (LoC) in Kashmir.

Clinton did not sign, seal and deliver much that was both specific and significant. What was specific was not great. The agreements signed and deals struck were modest. Of course there was the "Vision Statement". But apart from being flawed in some respects as critics have pointed out, it was more a promissory note than a commitment, a cocktail of good intentions distilled out of the unprecedented "feel good factor" which Clinton unleashed with the triumph of his diplomacy through personality and turn of phrase.

But the immediate result was remarkable. Prospects that had seemed very unlikely in the past few years began to look very probable in the next few. The ground got ploughed with goodwill as it has never been before, More seeds got sown than in any earlier season. The climate changed as with a wand. Indian public opinion was purged of its habitual mistrust of the United States and the U.S. purged of the once infamous "tilt" towards Pakistan.

The transformation was at least as remarkable as in Indian feelings for Britain during the late 1940s and early 1950s. Or even for Pakistan during Rajiv Gandhi's brief duet with Benazir Bhutto or Atal Behari Vajpayee's bus *yatra* to Lahore. These comparisons may seem ominous, because they show how hopes based on moods can perish. But it seems more likely that they will bear some fruit this time, though the Clinton presidency might miss them. Take a few probabilities:

— The U.S. may reject India's "nuclear doctrine" in its fullness but a more "minimum" Indian deterrent will no longer provoke the "roll back and eliminate" hectoring in which Madeleine Albright indulged even a few days ago before Clinton began his discovery of India.

— The painstaking, gentlemanly labours of External Affairs Minister Jaswant Singh and Deputy Secretary of State Strobe Talbott will remain a persuasive precedent for the Indo-U.S. dialogue which, commendably, the "Vision Statement" has written into the joint agenda of the two countries.

— India and the U.S. may (one hopes) never become strategic partners, but Indian interests have become and will remain a factor in U.S. (as indeed in Russian and Chinese) calculations about security dynamics in Asia, not only in South Asia.

— Future pictures of South Asian geopolitics, even if drawn in the U.S., will no longer mistake the Pakistani scale for the Indian scale.

— The image of a cerebral India will stand alongside, and perhaps taller than, the (somewhat unrealistic) image of an India full of a vast consumerist middle class.

Some changes have occurred in the more limited South Asian picture as well, and they are likely to endure into the post-Clinton U.S. as well if India continues to abjure obduracy. For instance:

— The ghost of the U.N. resolutions on Kashmir, which were killed by Pakistan, not India (a fact admitted by the U.N. also before its brain was frozen by the Cold War) will never hover over an Indo-U.S. banquet even if Pakistan sneaked in.

— On the other hand, bilateral Indo-Pakistan talks will remain the first option for any significant third country which may choose to advise either country, or both, on this matter.

— The Lahore initiative, which means both the Declaration and the joint statement signed by the Foreign Secretaries of the two countries, can no longer be brushed aside unilaterally by Pakistan because of General Musharraf's allergy to them.

— There will be wider acceptance in India now of Clinton's position that while the U.S. "will not and cannot mediate it could help to "restore the promise and process of Lahore".

— Pakistan will now find it very difficult to trigger direct mediation by any major third party by threatening that otherwise it will ignite nuclear fires in South Asia. The world will accept it from the U.S. President, if it did not from India, that Pakistan is using the threat to blackmail third countries into intervening in Kashmir on its behalf

— Whether India and Pakistan like it or not, the LoC has become the first choice of most third countries as the basis for a settlement unless the two countries can bilaterally come up with an alternative.

In his broadcast to the people, not the government, of Pakistan, Clinton warned Musharraf against trying to "redraw borders with blood". Thus he further elevated the status of the LoC. In his tight-faced reply on television Musharraf tried to bypass this warning by claiming that the LoC was only a line, not a border.

The world will not believe this now, nor should Pakistan forget what happened to it when it tried to change the "line" with blood.

Echoing the words India has used often, Clinton said Pakistan too "must create conditions that will allow the dialogue to succeed". That hurt, and Musharraf claimed India had "de-educared" Clinton. But the Clinton visit, the "vision", and their fallout also have traps which India must negotiate with the greatest care. They are the "snakes".

First, Clinton, the U.S., and the world in general will judge India adversely if it is seen to be dragging its feet on the road back to Lahore. India should therefore not impose any undefinable or unverifiable "conditions" for the restoration of "the promise and process of Lahore".

Such as the condition that "jehad" and "violence" must stop. What is "jehad", by whose definition, and whose violence against whom? Such terms are a minefield of definitional problems and should not be used as "conditions".

The two Lahore documents are on the table, and both countries stand committed to them. If either country wants to discuss what they entail or wants any changes in them it must come to the table. But the agreed texts must be the starting point of what may follow. They cannot be rubbished, as the Pakistan Foreign Minister once tried to do. That must remain India's only and consistent "condition".

Second, New Delhi's—and Srinagar's—handling of the situation within Jammu and Kashmir continues to be deplorable, and very damaging for its case both at bilateral and international fora. This situation must improve, and as soon as possible. Otherwise it will undermine all the potential that awaits India in all arenas—bilateral, regional, Asian, global—in terms of the "Vision Statement".

Third, there are phrases, concepts and suggestions in

the statement itself which must be unpacked with the greatest care. Otherwise they may spring very inconvenient surprises upon us later on, as India undertakes the burdens of "partnership"—strategic, economic, or diplomatic—before it gains the strength to reap its benefits.

5

International Terrorism

During the age of imperialism the rulers used terrorism against those who resisted colonial exploitation and struggled to assert the right to national self-determination. Militancy was resorted to only when the imperialist rulers stubbornly refused to respond to the demand for national independence.

Violence in those cases was not the first choice of the freedom fighters; it was usually the last resort. What is being witnessed today is something different. It has come to be the instrument of governments to score over other nations. It has become a major threat to stability of international order. The UN has taken note of the challenge and called upon member states to cooperate in putting an end to the menace. No global challenge however can be met without comprehensive understanding of its genesis and character.

It is therefore necessary to go into the origins and motivations of contemporary terrorism, its modus operandi, and its support base. It is significant that threat of what is, called Islamic terrorism has come into the reckoning of international community after the end of Cold War or the collapse of the Soviet Union and the disintegration of the international socialist network. Is there a relationship between the two phenomenon? To understand this it is rewarding to have a look at the process that led to the fall of the regime established in Afghanistan as a result of the *putsh* known as the Saur Revolution of 1978. Erstwhile Soviet Union has come to the aid of the forces that had ousted the Daud government.

The new government was perceived by the United States as a cat's paw of Moscow and therefore an adversary. A proxy war was unleashed against the Kabul regime which proved Afghanistan for Moscow what Vietnam had earlier been for Washington. Indeed it proved to be a fatal blow for the very system that the Soviet Union represented. The instruments, that Washington used towards that end developed its own dynamics and is strutting about the world stage as crusaders for Islam.

Revolutions are known to eat their own children and the instruments of Washington-style assault on world Communism have turned out to be a Frankenstein as the blowing up of New York's World Trade Centre and the bombing of US Embassies in Dar-es-Slaam and Nairobi showed.

It is no coincidence that, Harkat-e-Jehad-i-Islami, the parent organisation of all the groups operating as Islamic crusaders was launched in 1980 with headquarters in Pakistan by bringing together various Afghan dissidents. That was the time when the struggle against the new pro-Soviet dispensation in Kabul was integrated.

In later years rivalry between the leaders led to a group parting company and starting operations under the name of Harkat-ul-Mujahedeen. The two were brought together under a new banner Harkat-ul-Ansar. When the Ansar was declared illegal by the US Government it reverted, to its original name. The role of United States in this development is no longer a secret. It has been disclosed by a high ranking US official Yossef Bodansky.

He was part of a bipartisan Congressional team, Task Force on Terrorism and Unconventional Warfare. He had the opportunity to see Afghan operations at close quarters from inside Pakistan. What he told an Indian correspondent, Indranil Banerjee throws a flood of light on the US involvement and deserves quoting at length. He had pointed out earlier in his report to the Congress that "the very same Afghans trained by the Pakistanis during the Soviet occupation of Afghanistan are being used in international terrorist operations". On being questioned why the US government had connived at the operation, he replied: "By and large we went into Afghanistan because it had to be done—there were strategic threats to vital American interests in the Persian Gulf.. Number two: Zia-ul-Haq, though far from being perfect, had very, very strong pro-West inclinations. He believed that the future of Pakistan, Islamic or otherwise, was with the West. Number three:, During the days of Mrs. Indira Gandhi, India increasingly sank into being an active participant in the Soviet "grand design" which was essentially anti-West. Given 'all that Zia's policies, including his nuclear -policy, were seen to make perfect sense. "We found ourselves going with the ISI, accepting the ISI's responsibility in training and running the Mujahideen. As it was, the ISI ran its own show and lied and cheated to us. However, we were intimately involved with the situation and knew what was going on. But the powers that be decided that higher interests—that for us to get the Soviets out of Afghanistan and remove the threat to the Persian Gulf-were of far greater importance to the USA than the abuse of American help, the ISI support of Gulbuddin Hekmatyar and the diversion of a little bit of arms to Jammu & Kashmir. Especially in the early 1980s we could live with all this."

He further pointed out how the US perception changed:

"Till the collapse of the Communist regime of Najibullah in Afghanistan there were a lot of things we were willing to swallow and tolerate but then things started changing. Nuclear weapons instead of being seen as instruments of the last resort were transformed into hegemonial instruments for the Islamic bloc. The training system that the ISI had created for liberating Afghanistan and bleeding the Soviets, moved into involvement in Thailand, Central Asia, not to speak of the Islamist terrorist systems which tried to blow up the World Trade Centre. It is no longer an issue that is okay, so we gave them a hundred rifles, they took five and gave it to some Sikhs. Big deal. Now it is a question of regional instability, of global instability. It is a whole new ball game."

Pakistan's interest in building up a terrorist organisation in the name of Islam goes *further into* the past, before the Soviet intervention in Afghanistan, particularly after the defeat in Bangladesh. Though Z.A. Bhutto had signed the Simla agreement he had started moving towards making Pakistan a power superior to India. With that aim in view he began to mobilise support by projecting Islamabad as the spearhead of Pan-Islamism. With help from China he began to equip Pakistan with nuclear weapon which he called 'Islamic Bomb' to enlist the support of oil rich Gulf countries and Libya. On Afghanistan he had an eye to give Pakistan a strategic depth in the event of any conflict with India. Bhutto's strategy came handy to General Zia-ul-Haq who legitimised his usurper regime by adopting the cause of Afghan opponents to the pro-Soviet regime. Those who left Afghanistan were welcomed as brothers in faith to be given not only shelter but also facilities for military training to carry on *jihad* against their 'Godless' adversaries.

Recruits from, the Afghan migrant camps were

provided training and weapons. Pakistan was declared a 'front-line state' in the anti-Soviet crusade so that finance and weapon support began to pour in from the US and its allies in West Asia.

It was a boon for Pakistan's ISI which diverted part of this support to spur anti-Indian terrorism. Islamist organisations like Janunat-e-Islami and Jamait Ulema-e-Islam were encouraged to set-up a chain of madrassas which imparted ideas of religious fanaticism to young men drawn not only from Pakistan but also from other countries like Algeria; Tunisia, Saudi Arabia, Jordan, Egypt and Sudan. Their agents went to the oil rich countries of the Gulf to mobilise funds for advancing the cause of Islam.

Pakistan's army personnel were deployed for military training in these camps. Jammat preachers went to army units to impart ideological education. That brought the Pakistan army and jihadis closer together.

Common interest in smuggling of arms and narcotics further cemented this relationship. How adversely it affected the Pakistani society was reflected in the early eighties by a Karachi Urdu weekly *Meyaar* which cried out 'Revolution for Afghanistan and Narcotics for Pakistan' (Afghanistan ke liye Inquilab aur Pakistan ke liye Manashiyat). Border areas between Pakistan and Afghanistan developed into a vast manufacturing complex for illicit arms. Narcotics trade became a major source and partner in arms trade. This collaboration has further flourished after Afghanistan came under control of the Taliban, an outfit of madrassa-trained terrorists which was created to, oust the Rabbani government when the latter showed-reluctance to serve Islamabad's interests. Osama bin Laden has emerged as the main patron of the Taliban after the US lost interest in Afghan operations. A Yemeni Arab Osama had started his *jihad* operations from Saudi Arabia during the conflict in Afghanistan. When Jeddah became lukewarm, like the US, he shifted his headquarters first to Sudan and then to Afghanistan.

Afghanistan under Taliban has become the largest producer of heroine in the world. According to reports out of its 31 provinces, 18 are under illicit cultivation of opium.

During 1998-99 Osama was in control of 64,000 hectares of land for opium cultivation. The area has been further expanded to 91,000 hectares from which was recovered 4,600 metric tons of the drug, more than 60 per cent of the total world production. The total accrual from drug trade in the world is estimated to be of the order of $500 billion. From this can be guessed the financial strength of the promoters of terrorism.

Terrorism could not have sustained itself just on money and weapons. Only fire of idealism, genuine or fake, is necessary to sustain the morale of those who have to risk their lives and separation from near and dear ones. That is provided by appeal to Islam which was connived at by powers interested in defeating the USSR. The militants operating in Afghanistan had started consolidating their position even before the fall of Najibullah and ascendance of the Taliban. Way back in 1988 a Tablighi Jammat convention was held in Illinois which attracted over 6000 Muslims from around the world. They spread out into various countries of North Africa and Europe and recruited volunteers for *fihad* from countries life Algeria, Tunisia, Egypt, Sudan, and Saudi Arabia. These volunteers were trained in Lahore arid have been seen, in operation in J&K, Chechnya, Bosnia, Kosovo, Sudan and Egypt, besides their own countries. Now that the magnitude of the menace has been internationally realised the world community has to devise a comprehensive strategy to rid itself of the terrorist threat. The problem no longer concerns any particular nation. It has assumed world-wide sweep and with vast resources at their command terrorist outfits can Jay hands on nuclear and chemical weapons. They can cause serious misunderstandings between nations which may trigger major armed conflicts in various hot spots scattered around the world.

The UN has taken cognisance of the problem but it has to bend its efforts towards saving world peace and progress even as it has been pursuing its resolve to save humanity from the scourge of war.

The member nations of the UN must be made to realise that conduct of international politics through this means shall not be accepted. Secondly, every nation-state must see to it that they do not allow alienation of segments of their societies to reach a point where they provide congenial conditions for these criminal operations. Thirdly, and that is important, terrorism should not be allowed to use the respectable veneer of religion. No religion permits murder and mayhem. And each religious group has its extremist fringe. Conflict theories like that of Huntington must be universally rejected. During the last two centuries, once in every four-five decades, Russians either fought a war against the Chechens or deported them.

New generations grew up which seemed unmindful about the past relationship. At one time it even appeared the Marxist-Leninist system had solved the nationalities problem in the Soviet Union for ever and the Chechens, too, got used to 'the Soviet mode of life'. But the events of the last fifteen years demonstrated that old feelings and distrust die hard. The much vaunted Marxism-Leninism had actually no prophylactic, no answer at all for the rancorous nationality problems. It never appeared on the surface—thanks to the Comlnunist Party monopoly on the press—but Georgia, Azerbaizan, Armenia, Chechnya and several others remained hostile to each other and to Russia even in the Marxist era.

Now for the last several months Russia is grappling with the hostile nationality feelings combined with deadly terrorism in the North Caucasus, especially Chechnya. Terrorism was never heard before in Russia, but in October last year it arrived with a bang when several bombs exploded in residential buildings in Moscow and other cities.

More than 300 innocent people were killed in these explosions which, it was widely believed, had direct links with the terrorists and extremists entrenched in the Caucasus region. Just before it happened a notorious Chechen commander Shamil Basayev had openly threatened with terrorist attacks in Russian cities in a television interview. Since then Russia is fighting a grim battle to clear out the terrorists from the North Caucasus. The result, so far, is not yet clear even as the Chechen capital continues to be under seize. In fact the trouble began in August last year when some terrorist-extremist squads, based in Chechnya, tried to capture some territory in the Southern Russian province, Dagestan.

Apparently they had been making preparations for a very long time. Nearly two years ago some Wahhabi (an Islamic sect from Iran) extremists drove out the local authorities in Dagestan. They dislodged the civil administration, the militia and the public prosecutor's officers from two villages named Karamakhi and Chabanmakhı, established *Sharia* and proclaimed the formation of an "independent Islamic territory". No actions followed by the state to restore the civil, constitutional rule iii the villages. It naturally encouraged the extremists.

Moscow got alarmed Only in the August when armed squads of Shamil Basayev and Hattab, terrorist commanders from Chechnya, captured two whole districts, Botlikh and Tsumada in Dagestan.

A swift military action then followed and at first it seemed the incursion was repulsed. Later events showed it was not. The terrorist forces did not withdraw, even though they had got a safe passage. Instead they again attacked with added force.

The invasion in Dagestan was, obviously was not to seek Chechnya's independence from Russia. The very act indicated it was a pursuit of a terrorist-expansionist agenda. The aggressors coming from Chechnya wanted first to overthrow the local regime and, then using it as a bridgehead spread further in the North Caucasus. They wanted to 'liberate the ethnic Muslim population from the 'Russian colonial pressure and create, ultimately, an Islamic state on the territory of Chechnya and Dagestan including some other areas of North Caucasus, if possible. For this essential cause radical Wahhabism was used as the ideological platform. The operation had also apparent support from some influential quarters of the Middle and Near East. The terrorists and Chechen warlords have been receiving logistical and financial support from external sources: some Western countries, the Saudi millionaire and super-terrorist Osama bin Laden and other Arab quarters. President Yeltsin Was not off the mark when he underlined, in a meeting of the Russian Security Council, that the "external military, financial and moral aid" are the mainstay of the terrorists in the region. According to Russian security agencies and the press bin Laden alone had spent millions of dollars on arming and training Chechen rebels.

Chechnya has had no such impressive means as displayed in the ongoing hostilities with the Russian army. Caucasian newspapers repeatedly mentioned a former Jordanian Colonel Amir Al Hattab with many Jordanians, and a Pakistani unit headed by a Pakistani, Abu Abdullah Jafar, who are fighting from the Chechen side.

According to Vladimir Rushailo, the Interior Minister of Russia, foreign mercenaries from some Mid-eastern and South-west Asian countries are also taking part in the conflict. As usually happens, the terrorists entrenched in North Caucasus pin their hope on exploiting various unsettled ethnic, social, economic, political, territorial and even criminal problems of the region. They are not all Chechens, nor are controlled by the Chechen President Aslan Maskhadov or other official Chechen authorities. Among the mercenaries there are a number of Islamic *jihadis* from Afghanistan, Tajikistan, Pakistan, Turkey and Middle Eastern countries who act largely independent, even though camping in Chechnya.

Before the invasion of Dagestan the terrorists made numerous raids for quite some time on the border of Chechnya, Ingushetia and Stavropol territory. It indicates the escalation of conflicts is a planned one, using the pathological militancy of the local youth who chose the "ray of violence in desperation, for money or faith.

The rebels have been trying to force the Russian troops to spread along the mountains, involving them into a drawn-out fighting against a large number of small terrorist groups in the ideal conditions of mountains and forests that would be most suitable to the Islamic guerrillas. The prevalent apprehension among the Russians is that terrorist attacks will not subside in the region in the near future. Even if the Wahhabi militants and terrorists stationed in Chechnya fail this time, they may not budge from their course and would choose some other target nearby. The growing area of provocations and terrorist acts in central Asian states like Kyrghizia, Tajikistan and Uzbekistan is a pointer to this apprehension.

The terrorists and rebels in Chechnya claim they are guided by purely religious motives in the ongoing hostilities, that they want to purge Islam of all alien and superficial aspects. They draw inspiration from the cause of 'pure Islam', for which death in a battle against the 'infidels' is a way to the Allah. They openly propagate an Islamic Communism, suggesting killing off rich people for the sake of better life.

According to such propaganda everything will be perfect if infideis are killed. Such statements are not the usual, age-old Chechen pronouncements against the Russians, which give credence to the belief that the forces of Hattab, Basayev and other commanders are being guided by some Islamic countries' political circles and international terrorist groups led by bin Laden. By all indications their central motive is to destabilise the entire North Caucasus, and to sever this region from Russia. That is a territory which smells oil and boasts vital oil-transportation routes. The current trouble in Chechnya, however, was facilitated also by the unique political situation of Chechnya after the Soviet disintegration.

After the stalemate in war with Russia in 1994-96 Chechnya's relation with Moscow became peculiar and vague. After signing the Khasavyurt statement in 1996 the war ended, but no side fulfilled its promises. Chechnya: remained a part of the Russian Federation and independent at the same time. During the last three years the issue itself faded into background. Meanwhile, all kind of Islamic mercenaries, terrorists and fundamentalists armed with foreign arms, funding and backing have made it their, home. Chechnya proved to be an ideal, strategic place for them. This produced a mass of Chechen recruits who find it more lucrative to fight than toil for a living.

A large number of local youth now hold guns, instead of going to work in fields. The Chechen people and President Maskhadov could hardly be comfortable with the situation. But they were more helpless than unwilling to change it. Dagestan is a different case. Dagestanis do not prefer separation from Russia. So many small ethnic groups live there, and once separated from Russia they understand the separatist virus will eat up the land itself and Dagestan might disappear by successive disintegration. Secondly, they are essentially a peace-loving people. Chechens, on the other hand, are by nature a warrior, even bandit kind, and their relation with -Russia is historically marked by incessant fights. Perhaps Chechens never accepted -wholeheartedly to be a part of Russia. There have always been mutinies, they have been exiled and then allowed to come back. Dagestan has known nothing of the kind.

Chechens generally never recognise any authority above them. When they do, it is for a period or a purpose only. Since the last war with the Russians in 1994-96 the Chechens are now each man for himself and nobody tells him who to shoot at and who to abduct.

In contrast, the Dagestanis are different. They understand an elder should be respected, even though he is not so good a person. Most of them also don't like Chechens because, historically, they have often been the losers in their interactions with the neighbouring Chechens.

Generally the relations between them have been those of a farmer and a mounted highway robber. Another important differentiating factor is the *Sufi* system of monasticism which is followed by a large number of Dagestani population. It is a tradition of disciples' subordination to the liberal teacher.

Orthodox Islamic extremists, agitators and Wahhabists reject such *Sufism*, or mystics of any sort, the role of the teacher as a go-between the God and the common man. Instead they aggressively demand that the Koran be followed to the dot as they see, it. That is what happening in Chechnya and Afghanistan arid being asked for in Pakistan. However, even in Chechnya separatism is thriving on outside incitement and financial help.

The training camps in Chechnya have been paid for by mostly Arab money. Rich extremist organisations from Arab states have been supporting the terrorist activities in the North Caucasus. Mercenaries from Afghanistan and Pakistan, trained by Laden, are directly involved in the hostilities. They all have their eyes fixed on not only the land itself but also the large storage of natural resources, including oil, between the territory of the Black Sea and the Caspian Sea. The Chechen situation was initially seen in the West through the glass of Western geo-political interests, to take advantage of Russia's weakness and undermine her position in the region.

At the Istambul summit of the Organisation for Security and Co-operation in Europe (OSCE) held in Nov.'99 US President Bill Clinton accepted that Russia is confronted with international terrorism in the North Caucasus. He also noted that any country would have to solve this kind of problem and Russia has every right to resolve it. Yet he criticised Russia, mildly in Istambul and very severely after wards, on the issue of 'ends and means' to solve the ticklish issue in Chechnya. Clinton later said in a statement from Washington that Russia will have to pay a high price for its campaign in

Chechnya. Russia is already paying a heavy price, but such criticism seems quite unfair. Usually if the terrorists attack some Western territory or people the Western public condemn terrorists severely, and demand harshest action against them. But when the sufferers of terrorism are lesser mortals such as Serbs, Russian or Indians they become all restraint.

Disregarding all international norms, they hurled missiles in Afghanistan to destroy just one terrorist, Osama bin Laden, though instead it only killed others. Is not something perverted about the Western approach, which in turn asks countries like Russia or India to be ever restraint even though hundreds and thousands of innocents of these countries have been killed by terrorists? Other Western critics say Russia is concealing 'the true situation' regarding the humanitarian disaster. But the representatives of several international organisations—the OSCE, the UN and the Council of Europe, for instance—themselves observed the ground realities of Chechnya. Not long ago the OSCE had to close its office in the region for fear of life.

The bandits in Chechnya killed the Red Cross staff, including some women from Norway. A French group went to Chechnya and one of them was taken hostage. He is not yet released and the French President Jacques Chirac called then President Yeltsin several times for him. The problem is also that many people in the West do not believe that a small mountainous province, Chechnya, can pose a strategic threat to big Russia.

In Istambul summit country after country called on Russia to negotiate a settlement. Ironically, no one knows better than the Russians that as far as Chechens are concerned, military solution alone would not work-it never did. However, this time it is not just Chechnya which is at war with Russia.

The threat to Russia in the entire North Caucasus came more from international terrorism, it is a real strategic threat with far-reaching geo-political consequences. Not only for Russia but others as well. This has to be understood. It was quite natural if the Russian government feared a 'domino' effect from the Dagestan invasion.

It was an open challenge and a success for the invaders could have blown up the situation in adjacent Tatarstan, Bashkortostan and Volga regions. By the method and determination of the invaders the Russians could not shut their eyes that it was indeed a part of a strategic endeavour.

It was especially threatening and had a chance of success, because, in the words of the acting Russian President Vladimir Putin, "Centrifugal trends in relation to federal [Russian] authorities and separate regions of the country are still strong in Russia." International terrorist brigades wanted to use this situation for their expansionist designs. Hence Russia was forced to act, to defend her territorial integrity. This, too, has to be understood. It is beyond doubt that the Western leaders would not have behaved differently, had they found themselves in a similar situation. The political solution of Chechnya is of course necessary-there is indeed no substitute for that-but there must be circumstances to achieve it. Moscow rightly argues that for a lasting peace in the entire region the terrorist bases must be eradicated first in and around the Chechen territory. Because since 1991 Chechnya has gradually turned into a centre of international terrorism. It became infested with all kind of murderers, kidnappers, drug dealers, terrorists, Islamic mercenaries and *jehadis*. They took over trampling all norms of morality and law.

It is difficult to disagree with the Russians that such

forces have neither the locus nor reason to strive for a peaceful settlement, nor they wish to respect the integrity of Russia. Which is why the peaceful, if primitive civilians living in the North Caucasus are suffering for years in the first place.

The heavy concentration of terrorists, arms and drug dealers in Chechnya for the last four-five years created a difficult situation in The whole region. They frequently attacked neighbouring regions, kidnapped people and sold them into slavery, or demanded heavy ransom if the captured were Europeans.

As Russia is grappling with a grim scenario in Chechnya, the West is trying to enforce a double standard as to how Moscow should deal with the terrorists in Chechnya.

Bill Clinton said he has "no sympathy with terrorists in Chechnya, nor the invasion of Dagestan, but it is a question of ends and means". The same Clinton led the NATO last summer to indiscriminate bombing in Yugoslavia, a sovereign country, for seventy-eight days for 'solving' the Kosovo problem—without taking any mandate from the UN. It killed thousands of innocent civilians, including ethnic Albanians whom they supposedly came to help. In the wake it created a much bigger refugee problem than existed earlier, and increased mutual hatred among the Serbs and the ethnic Albanians.

Chechnya, on the other hand, is a Russian region where for several years local and international terrorists *de facto* rule. The West is fully aware of this situation. According to a recent *Newsweek* report, "the main source of foreign exchange in the [Chechen] region has—quite literally—become kidnapping. Hundreds of Russians and Westerners have been grabbed in Chechnya during the past three years." They are exchanged at the rate of $1 million or more for one hostage, the report said. According to the Russian Interior Ministry at least 506 confirmed hostages, Russian and foreigners, are in terrorist captivity in Chechnya.

In such a situation the acting Russian President rightly asks, "with whom and about what should we negotiate?" More than the conflict being religious, or ethnic, it is a fight between terrorism and counter-terrorism.

President Putin's explanation for the Russian campaign is noteworthy: "The bandits attacked once, we repelled them. They attacked again, and we again repelled them. They attacked again and again... We saw this would never end, unless we destroy them in their bases." It is not without reason that the world-famous Russian writer Alexander Solzhenitsyn, himself a great champion of freedom and human rights, supported the Russian position saying it is Russia which has always been at the receiving end—so far as Chechnya is concerned.

According to Moscow, before trying a political solution it is necessary to create ;a vital pre-condition: the political leadership of Chechnya must influence forces inside Chechnya to release hostages, and extradite international terrorists operating from there and guilty of killing civilians in Dagestan and in major Russian cities. But the Chechen Presidents is hardly in control and no reliable political forces are visible inside Chechnya who would be able to help create the pre-condition.

Even though a political solution takes place, no one can take responsibility for peace in Chechnya. As long as such a situation continues any political solution would hardly be viable. Besides, Russia cannot negotiate with

Basayev and Hattab for a 'solution'—just as the United States would not negotiate with Osama bin Laden for a solution.

The Chechen government has been clearly unable to check the terrorists living in Chechnya, to curb the export of terrorism, or keep the province from sliding into anarchy. It has distressed the Chechen civilians as badly as it did to others.

For the last four years schools, hospitals and shops are not working in Chechnya. Wages and pensions to ordinary citizens have not been paid for a long time. The local government, for all practical purposes, hardly exists in Chechnya today—thanks to the terrorist regime. The Russian campaign against the terrorists in Chechnya have undoubtedly caused civilian casualties. The refugee problems have also come up, though it already arose due to terrorist activities even before the Russian campaign began. Such unfortunate problems occur everywhere despite the most carefully, planned military operations. Were the NATO forces immune to such incidents in Kosovo? Did the US missiles, aimed at Osama bin Laden, not kill others in Afghanistan? If those incidents could not be avoided, the West should not adopt a double-standard for Russia, or for that matter any other country. They describe the Russian action an act of rage and vengeance. Should Russia watch it helplessly, arid allow herself to shrink further and further? And, should Russia fail, what will be the result?

Terrorism, wherever its breeding ground, cannot limit itself to one region or one country. From Tanzania, to Afghanistan, to Kashmir, to Dagestan it is just a matter of time before it targets the West again.

It must be recognised that the Chechen region today is contaminated with an infectious disease, Islamic terrorism to call broadly, and the North Caucasian and

Russian people have fallen victim to it. The human disaster in Kosovo (for which NATO bombed Yugoslavia) was far less than what have been committed in and around Chechnya for several years.

Terrorism is a policy which is carried out through the revolutionary process in order to maintain control over the population and also to gain necessary support of the people who may not be very keen to support the guerrillas under normal circumstances. Such set of people are terrorised in order to gain their support, passive or active.

Terrorism is a very good weapon in the armoury of guerrillas if it remains confined to limited or selective killings. It can be dangerous if used without any rhyme or reason or used without control and coordination. Illogical killing is dangerous. It is a double-edged weapon which if not used properly can cut the hands of the user.

Terrorism has great potential of misfires or backfires. If fear becomes the main reliance of control the machinery would weaken when government becomes able to exercise its strength. One has to be very discreet and careful in the application of terrorism. Thus a good organization will refrain from using general terror against the population.

Use of terror is at its best when it is selective; if continued beyond a certain point it may rebound and may drive the people away from the fold of revolutionaries.

Retribution against a traitor is definitely an effective way of winning the support of the people but not random killing. When people are overcome with terror, they act in a predictable way. Some go into catatonic trance, some continue to go about their affairs as though nothing was happening, some are so wounded, so hurt, so frightened that they will do anything to escape from terror oven to the extent of doing whatever was demanded of them by the power that wields the weapon of terror; but there are some who fight back. Terror is a complex proposition; there are many variables. Mindless stupidity affects people in a state of terror. It is this mindless stupidity that allows quite a few to retaliate. If a man is blindfolded, handcuffed and bound to a stake, with a firing squad of ten men standing in front of him and an officer at their side ready to deliver the 'coup de grace', he has the right, even at this last stage, to rid himself of his blindfold, the handcuffs, the ropes, the firing squad and if he can achieve one or all of these acts, he has manifested to some degree his human dignity against the forces of terror. One in ten thousand times such person may succeed. He will accomplish the impossible because he believes in the impossible.

The intention of the terrorists is to terrorise the entire population to submission. But is it possible? Is it not possible that they overstretch themselves and fail precisely -because the weapon of terror can be bent back and turned against the user. A regime of terror, shattering noises, huge fires, random shooting, destruction of intellectuals, economic disruption, cultural annihilation can only bring chaos with no material gain for the terrorists. Communist insurgents in Malaya were very ruthless in their acts. Indiscriminate murders were committed, buses were bombed, grenades were thrown in cinema houses and in one case the whole village was destroyed. Communist terrorists concentrated all their efforts on terrorising the people into supporting them and this they did with utmost ruthlessness. Terror was planned and executed coldly and brutally. If a family opposed communists' demands one or two of the leading members would be dismembered in front of their family members or pegged out in the sun for ants to eat. Even women were not spared.

Mau Mau terrorists in Kenya also indulged in indiscriminate murders. People were mercilessly butchered only on suspicion. Use of terror on a very large scale was a blunder on the part of the Malayan and Kenyan terrorists for which they had to pay heavily. Instead of gaining support of the masses, terrorism went against the terrorists and population started doubting the very foundation of the movement. In both Malayan and Kenyan counterinsurgency operations terrorism was one single factor which turned the tide in favour of the ruling government. Extremists in Punjab have also resorted to random killing of both Hindus and Sikhs. On some days as many as 49 hits have been made, family members butchered and bus passengers brutally murdered. Time will tell that terrorism contributed significantly to the breakdown of the nerve centre of Sikh extremism in Punjab.

As against Communist terrorists in Malaya and Mau Mau terrorists in Kenya or for that matter Sikh terrorism in Punjab the use of terror by the Vietcongs in Vietnam was better controlled. The Vietcongs also made use of terror on a large scale but it was more systematic and well coordinated and thus played a significant role in building the strength of the Vietcongs. The value and result of terrorism was duly realised by the Vietcongs both as a strategy and tactics and it was assigned to a specific organisational wing which ensured elaborate curriculum for assuring precision and control. Individuals were marked after great deliberations, defamed after much thinking and then annihilated with great pomp and show. The purpose was to undermine and bring down the government by systematic elimination of its elites.

Terrorism also served to enhance the prestige of the Vietcongs by demonstrating its capability and its superiority to the existing government. Unlike the Malayan terrorists, the Vietcongs were more rational in selecting the potential targets of annihilation and considerable gains were achieved in inducement of defections and recruitment into the Vietcong fold. Terrorist activities caused serious drain on the government strength without antagonising the masses in general. The terror was not indiscriminate and was carried out as a punishment and was some times preceded by public trials. Terrorism assisted the Vietcongs in maintaining its dominance by intimidating the enemy, by the impression of fear and the respect it made on the neutrals and by confirming the wisdom of their decision among the supporters.

History of terrorism is full of instances where indiscriminate and ill-planned use of terror made the people hostile to the terrorists; in certain cases they even helped the government in apprehending the terrorists. Abraham Stern organised and carried out terrorist activities against the British and the Arabs during 1940 in Israel. A number of lives were lost and much property damaged or destroyed. The majority of Jewish population became hostile to the ruthless acts of terror used by Stern. The Jewish community turned completely against him and helped the government in hunting him down. As a result, lie was located in a hideout and shot dead while attempting to escape. The Naxalite movement in Bengal was contained primarily because the Naxalites made very liberal use of terror. Burning alive a village moneylender along with his moneylending papers and other sadistic acts of Naxalites created doubts in the minds of the people about the validity of the movement. As the public support was withdrawn the government was able to crush the movement without much opposition.

Propaganda by deed has been very meaningful and did arouse public sympathy in many cases. Heroic acts committed by Madan Lal Dhingra, Bhagat Singh and others played a vital role in making the image of Indian revolutionaries and very many people were drawn into their fold. Still, however, Indian terrorists could not gain much ground because the selection of targets was not very well planned and coordinated. Individual acts of heroism did draw the attention of masses for some time, but soon faded away from their memories because the follow-up action was not correctly thought of.

If terrorism is to yield results, the activities of terrorists will have to be very well coordinated and controlled. Individual terrorists should not be allowed to act on their own. Formation of splinter groups to carry out terrorism is not advocated if some results are to be achieved. The Sikh militants have a number of splinter groups. As a result most of the time there is -no control over the terrorists. The use of terror is a very delicate and intricate affair and everybody is not supposed to apply it to any target that crosses the path of terrorists. PFLP (Popular Front for the Liberation of Palestine), a front organisation of PLA, used terrorism in an organised way. Dr. Habbad, its leader, masterminded the operations. As a result, the terrorist activities of PFLP drew considerable world attention to their cause. Though they have not yet achieved any result, the Palestinian terrorists are the most publicized group currently Using terror as a weapon not because they have killed more people and destroyed more aircraft but because they have been more selective and have exercised restraint in executing deeds of valour. Their image was, however, tarnished by the act of indiscriminate firing conducted at the Lod Airport by the professional terrorists of Japanese Red Army under the direction of Dr. Wadie who had to break away from the main group because of the above killing of innocent people.

At the current juncture terrorism has assumed a shape different from what it was primarily meant for. Instead of utilising terrorism as an instrument to bring about revolutionary changes, the present day terrorist groups have given it a mercenary touch. Terrorism has become a very profitable business in which the investment is minimal and the dividends enormous. Terrorists of Latin American ~and European countries and the Sikh extremists are resorting to terrorism without any goal in view. They commit kidnapping and hijacking either to get their comrades released from jail or as a bogey to raise funds for their activities or just to create chaos in an established order.

A handful of youths of upper middle and rich classes, frustrated and disgusted with their way of life, look for a change in the social and economic structure and ventilate their grievances by random killing and kidnapping. Their purpose is not to seize power but to create conditions for revolutionary changes adopting terror as a weapon. In their anxiety to do some action they indulge in ill-conceived operations which put a brake on their activities.

If a close study of the present-day terrorists is made it will reveal that most of the terrorists, if not all, are suffering from some sort of abnormalities. Blind fury in the national interest is acceptable but what about murdering an individual without logic or cause? An aimless murder indicates unsoundness of mind, eccentric mood and erratic actions of individuals or a group of individuals. Such individuals ate swayed by wild passion's which result in violent actions. Their actions are impulsive and irrational. In the terrorists of today is reflected waywardness, trait of eccentricity and an explosive temper, the state of mind of a sensitive and repressed class who are out of tune with the environment. Their mind is overburdened with tension and conflicts which weaken the hold of rationality and destroy the sense, though temporarily, to discriminate between good and bad. Some disgruntled and disillusioned hotheads have turned terrorism into a lucrative business proposition. Random shooting at Lod Airport, Tel Aviv, by the Japanese terrorists and at Rome and Vienna airports by Abu Nidal's men calling themselves "Martyrs of Palestine" or the killing of innocent bus passengers by Sikh terrorists in Punjab and Haryana cannot be termed as calculated moves of highly motivated terrorists. Kidnapping and ultimate murder of Mr. Moro by the Red Brigade group of Italy provided the people the drive and determination to fight political violence. Kidnapping and murder of eleven Israeli athletes by Black September terrorists emphasised the need for the study of the terrorists from the psychological point of view as the study from the ideological angle had failed to explain the complexity of their motives.

Wanton and brutal acts of terrorism reveal the whole world of frustrations, disillusionment, ambition, morbid reactions, individual misadventures and many hidden complexes, abnormalities and shortcomings. The terrorists of today are not a group of highly indoctrinated nationalists but a bunch of repressed individuals who are violent and indifferent to the feelings of others and who show little remorse for taking the life of a person. Terrorists in their mood of depression and gloom kill people only to get relief from tension and monotony of their dull life. It is thus doubtful if the violent behaviour of such fanatics would help in achieving the required results.

Terrorism by itself would bring about revolutionary changes would be too simplified a statement. Even where terrorism has been used as a weapon of guerrilla war, it has not achieved any decisive results. Terrorism in certain cases did help in forcing the general masses into submission but it is difficult to conclude that terrorism alone has won battles. Terrorism can force a government either to adopt repressive or reformative measures. It has stimulated more repression than reformative steps by the rulers. It is hard to believe that indiscriminate murder and kidnapping of a few prominent citizens of a state by a few hotheads can change the destiny of a nation.

International terrorism has further shown that present-day terrorists are not interested in the affairs of their own country. According to a CIA report published in 1977, the terrorists of Turkey were using a Palestinian camp for training in Syria. The same report also revealed the growing involvement of Cuban terrorists in operations in Africa and Middle East. Cuban instructors were training the Palestinians in Syria, Lebanon and Cuba. Shelter given to terrorists by various countries helps in spreading international terrorism.

There are distinct signs showing that the various terrorist groups which ostensibly operate independently in sundry parts of the world have been coordinating their activities. It was the Baader-Meinhof gang which helped the Black September group in the attack on the Israeli sportsmen at Munich. The bloodbath at Lod was performed by the Japanese Red Army. The hijacking of the French airliner from Athens in June 1976 was undertaken by the members of Baader-Meinhof gang. The passengers, who were mostly Jews, were rescued by Israeli commandos at Entebbe, Uganda. PFLP members hijacked a German aeroplane and demanded the release of imprisoned Baader-Meinhof gang members from the German jails. The plane was retrieved at Mogadishu, Somalia by the German anti-terrorist force.

According to newspaper reports, one terrorist of Baader-Meinhof gang who had broken away from the gang, revealed that the West German gang had even planned to kidnap the late Pope Paul VI in June 1976. The purpose of abduction would have been to obtain the release of jailed terrorists all over the world. Again, according to a report, an international hit squad was reportedly approached by the Khalistan militants offering a multimillion dollar contract for elimination of certain highly placed individuals in India. There is a common belief that the increase in international terrorist activities in recent years is the outcome of some understanding arrived at by the terrorist groups in different countries. Each organisation is committing acts of sabotage, terror and murder on behalf of the other organisation in order -to cover the tracks. All these associations enjoy many sophisticated international connections and means for action, both in finances and firearms. The free world with its libertarian regimes of limited power, serves as a convenient wound for the sprouting of international-terror.

Terrorist organisations not only exploit the democratic countries but also the countries ruled by regimes of tyranny. and terror, all under the cloak of revolutionaries. International affiliations have revealed that various terrorist groups do not have particular attachment to the happenings in their own countries. Adventure at the international level cannot, in any way, go to solve the problem in one's own country. On the other hand, international terrorism has forced the governments of various countries to establish and train anti-terrorist squads to deal with the menace of terrorism. Israel, West Germany, England and many other countries have raised special task forces to combat terrorism.

Earlier guerrilla operations were carried out to highlight the grievances of the aggrieved people and they aimed at seeking redress from government. Guerrillas consisted of the persons who were either being harassed or were the direct victims of government policies. They had a cause and a goal for which they were fighting.

Terrorists of today do not have set principles before them. They are mostly from rich strata of society and have not been drawn from the working classes whose cause they are supposed to be fighting for as per their assertions. They are also not downtrodden or the repressed sections of the society. On the contrary, they are from the privileged sections of the society. They are, in most of the cases, living in economically advanced countries where unemployment has very little or no effect whatsoever. These men and women are all educated and come from good families. They have had no experience of poor man's life or agony. Are such people capable of establishing a new society by using terror as their weapons? Their actions cannot even possibly cast an impression on the mind of the ruling power not to talk of creating a climate for revolutionary changes. They can, at the most, make the government hunt them out or negotiate with them. It was estimated that the Indian Army had to deploy ten divisions to contain a handful of militants in Punjab during operation Bluestar in 1984. More than 70,000 men of the Indian Army were deployed in Sri Lanka to deal with a few Tamil militants. Governments have to spend huge amounts in raising and maintaining anti-terrorist forces. They are forced to take certain special measures, pleasant or unpleasant, to contain the activities of terrorists. Security measures are tightened, searches intensified and some degree of censorship imposed.

Terrorists get a lot of publicity with the improvement in mass communication system, the activities of terrorists get wide coverage. News hungry newspapers, television, radio, *etc.*, always look for sensational news items and terrorists provide them with these. Terrorist activities are given front page coverage.

Coloured photographs are taken and published. The publicity given by the press encourages the terrorists to do many more acts of terrorism. It also gives an incentive to other fanatics to join the terrorist gangs.

The proliferation and incredible sophistication of modern weapons have enabled small numbers to do great harm. In 1973, for example, the Italian police burst into an apartment where five Arab terrorists were setting up SA-7 missiles four miles from Rome's Airport. These missiles were intended for use against an Israeli civilian airliner. The SA-7 is a Soviet missile that can be carried comfortably on one's back and can destroy a plane up to an altitude of 6500 feet. The, Russian built RPG-7 rockets weigh under ten pound's and can be carried on person and can destroy a tank, a speaker's platform or a car. The IRA terrorists are known to have used RPG-7 rockets against army vehicles and police stations. The IRA attacked a police station in March 1985 with a RPG-7 rocket hidden in the body of a truck. Telescopic rifles with night vision equipment have further increased the destructive power of the terrorists.

Even though terrorism has come under constant criticism, it is developing into a major industry of the world, In the materialistic world when stresses and strains on the human mind have increased manifold, persons who get sadistic pleasure by merely killing persons or destroying planes will be found in plenty among men out of work, depressed and inspired with fantasies of misguided patriotism, Such maniacs will always be there and there will always be men to exploit them. Added advantage is that in executing acts of terrorism and in forming an outfit of terrorists very few people are needed. Large liberated areas and formidable base camps are also not required. Planning can be done in small rooms of crowded localities of towns and big cities. In addition, terrorist operations are not very difficult or complicated to execute. Funds are easily available as ransom or by plundering banks. International connections between various terrorist gangs have made things much easier by way of finance, training, arms and ammunition. Foreign territories also provide terrorists and their masters necessary sanctuary to escape detection.

Terrorism is about a slow erosion of the might of a country; the threatening of its core ideals, and above all a psychological war that is aimed at wearing away even the most battle hardened troops in a war where the enemy is often invisible and where the victims are always their own people. The target of terrorism is the state itself, and the objectives it espouses today appear increasingly close to that usually sought to be achieved by conventional war. In India, and in many parts of the world where terrorism has emerged in familiar ones and guises, the present bout of violence that has been rising since the late 1980's is nothing short of a new kind of war, and this war can only be fought by completely new thinking on coünter-terrorism, state policy, and armed forces structures and training, and foreign policy.

To understand terrorism is to be at least half way towards evolving a way to deal with it. For this it is necessary to understand the processes that have made terror into a mutant of war itself. War was once an extremely exclusionary activity. It was fought by the state, with its armed forces, often in a particular battle zone, against a like enemy-uniformed, with a clear command and control structure, and for clear political objectives. War was considered an honourable activity, and so the soldier was viewed with some respect, while the population was taxed so that the soldier might fight. But for all other purposes the three-the state, the army and the population remained separate, though sometimes the first two merged when various strong men (martial regimes) ruled with an iron hand. While populations thus suffered the exigencies of errant kings or demanding dictators, war itself remained an activity that was outside the society at large. This suffered a complete reverse during two world wars which made the targeting of whole populations in Germany a "strategic" activity, and whose whole scale killing was supposed to yield certain benefits. This it did not do, but that did not stop the use of nuclear weapons against Japan, not did it stop the march of doctrine which continued to see the prosecution of terror (with nuclear weapons) as a part of intelligent strategy This component of strategy that soon found its way into the next phase of war. This global blackmail by each superpower led to the pushing of war downwards, emerging in the 1960's as terrorism in Europe and as interstate and intrastate wan in the developing world.

Along with the depredations of the Baader Meinhof gang and the German Red Brigade, came the shock of Vietnam and the realisation that intervention, in others conflicts was an expensive and horrifying business. What followed as a further degeneration downwards into proxy war-where a patron state supplied the favoured regime with the weapons that he most required to deal with the opposition forces which were provided with guns, assault rifles, and landmines that were the most appropriate to fight an "irregular" war. This was often not a war at all but a series of conflagrations and bush fires that swept across Africa, South Asia, or East Asia, or where over the great powers found their interests clashing. Thus billions of dollars of weapons flowed into the hands of various non state actors who variously espoused a dubious and poorly understood left or right wing ideology.

War thus came not only into society but was soon indistinguishable from it. The soldier was the farmer and vice versa. But these wars, dangerous as they were, set in motion another cycle of incidents. Tong of these weapons—often of a genre that was far superior to that wielded by the armies of most developing countries—soon began to spread outwards (into neighbouring countries) or inwards (into society itself) especially where a state was involved as a conduit for the supply of weapons. This led to a culture of violence within these societies, as well as the arming of states in the region with tons of weapons ideal for the fighting of low level war and terrorism with neighbours stronger than themselves.

The option of "proxy war" thus became the favoured option for those countries who had already tried and faded at their objectives through conventional war. Thus proxy war was launched as an extension of war by other means. Though clearly a part of state activity, it did mean that the state had to adopt a certain stand off position, without seeming to be too involved in what was essentially an illegal act. Ideally also this transborder operation required the crafting of a new ideology, that would provide some legitimacy to what was outright interference and sabotage. This was soon provided by a series of reactive occurrences in the Middle East and in its periphery.

The 1980's saw a considerable change, as the lure of Marxist revolution waned, and new actors appeared on the stage, espousing new ideologies of "Freedom". The Iranian revolution and its subsequent isolation led to Teheran pursuing a surreptitious support of religious extremist groups for its own foreign policy objectives. The Arab states followed likewise, with Saudi Arabia leading the way. Alongside came the most outrageously expensive and largest operation of all—the launching of the "jehad" in Afghanistan against the "evil forces" of the Soviets—a jehad, armed, funded and prosecuted by a Christian democratic state, and subcontracted to a country that was under the jackboots of a military regime, and none of the freedom that was supposedly the sole rationale of the jehad.

Around $6-8 billion worth of weapons flowed into Afghanistan from all sides, and more than 80,000 "jehadis" were trained. The "war ebbed and flowed, sometimes emerging as terrorist strikes, and sometimes like old fashioned "sieges" (as in Jalalabad) reminiscent of the Middle Ages rather than modern war. Once the Soviets pulled out, all pretences at a jehad vanished, and with it whatever little restraint that had existed. Afghanistan became a free for all, with regional actors heavily involved, and the state itself coming under the hold of a group that, was so radical that it held even the former "radicals" of the Iranian revolution in thrall.

The Afghans are still fighting for freedom, and the subcontractor state is back under military rule in all but name. The wheel has turned full circle, with all the paraphernalia of a "jehad"—the weapons, the men and the ideology—spewing out of Afghanistan and Pakistan into the rest of the region. Today terrorism has spread to parts of Russia, Tajikistan, Uzbekistan, China, Saudi Arabia, Egypt, Algeria, parts of Africa, and South East Asia. Together with the United States, there is hardly any part of the globe which has remained untouched.

Significantly, nearly all of the terrorist "spectaculars" that have taken place recently (with the exception of the Oklahama bombing) have been linked to the Afghanistar-Pakistan region. From here "terrorist"—well armed, trained, under some command and control—appears to move with surprising ease across national boundaries. Firstly, terrorism is therefore unequivocally a transnational enterprise, and secondly, much what is today called "international terrorism" emanates from our immediate neighbourhood.

Thirdly, it is increasingly motivated by an ideology that can loosely be called religious. Statisties provide some interesting points. A Rand data base of terrorist incidents notes that while there were no groups who could be classified as religious from 1968 to 1980, the first "modern" religious groups, appears in 1980—but only two of 64 counted. By 1992 this had risen six fold representing a quarter of terrorist organisations who carried out attacks in 1992 (11, out of 48). By 1994 a third (16) of 49 identifiable terrorist groups could be classified as religious in character and/or motivation, and in 1995 they accounted for nearly half (26) our of the 56 known terrorist groups active that year. By 1999, at least 64 out of a total of 96 active terrorist groups are clearly identifiable as being religiously motivated. This list is heavily tilted towards Islamic groups, but there are clearly many fractured Christian Catholic or Orthodox Church groups in the former Yugoslavia (where religious insignia was used by many parties) which are difficult to count and these do not figure in the list at all (since Europe does not classify them as terrorist). Given that the Church was accused of being heavily involved in supporting such movements like Solidarity in Poland with US encouragement, such a reticence was hardly surprising.

Fourth, it is apparent that killing of innocents is once again a part and parcel of strategy. The earlier trend of terrorism did not seem to demand high casualties. Brian Jenkins had argued in the mid 1980's that "simply killing a lot of people has seldom been one terrorist objective terrorists operate on the principle of the minimum force necessary.... as long as killing a few suffices for their purpose". Today's terrorist apparently revels in violence. This is proved again by statistics which show that while terrorist incidents world wide have dropped, the number of casualties per incident has risen exponentially. The St. Andrews-Rand data base also notes that though 1996 recorded the lowest annual tally in 23 years in terrorist incidents, it was one of the bloodiest years on record-in fact the fourth highest recorded in the chronology since 1968. Much of this data naturally is factored around just who is labelled as a terrorist group. Clearly if the terror let loose in Afghanistan is any guide, the "jehad" has killed more than a 100,000 in Kabul alone,—a figure far higher than anything that this data highlights. In Kashmir, more than 10,000 have died as a result of the jehad launched by Pakistan. Hoffman for instance in 1996 only notes 30 deaths in Kashmir for 1996, while the real figure comes close to 1159 according to government data.

While analysts arrive at the conclusion that religious terrorism is therefore more deadly than its "secular" cousin, the possibility that these terrorists are less concerned about civilian casualties may lie less in their beliefs and more due to their patronage. Today's transnational terrorist may not need the popular support that was essential in earlier times, when terror ism was basically an internal phenomenon. It is again evident that the objectives of terrorists across Asia are remarkably similar to the objectives once sought to be attained by conventional war. In India, Central Asia, parts of China and in the periphery of Russia the objective is clearly the control/acquisition of territory. In Kashmir, this is apparent enough with the movement for "liberation" centered since the early 1990's towards merging with Pakistan-an objective that clashes completely with the original objectives that had sparked off violence.

In Kyrgyzstan, religious extremists tried to wrest control of a part of that country (the Batken province) with the objective of creating a separate state. In Chechnya similar objectives prevail, while the movement of men, money and material into the Indian North East is sought to bolster separatism. The continuing conflict in Sri Lanka—which is aimed at the establishment of a Tamil homeland—is also beginning to acquire religious overtones, with the Buddhist and Muslims each supporting different groups and thus adding to the violence. Apart from objectives is the fact that the fighters in these wars, who had started as small ill organised groups have graduated rapidly into structures that are comparable in size, outfitting, and training to a small army. However their methodology of fighting is still "unconventional"—that is, they still rely on sniping, random firing, arson, intimidation, and indeed all the tactics that were once associated with "terrorism". The Harkat ul Ansar and the Lashkar e-Taiba (to quote only the most well known groupings) are known to have an enviable communication systems, a publicity cell, a well thought out recruitment strategy, and huge recruitment reservoir that springs from the madrassas. Their only rivals to such organisation are the Egyptian and Palestinian groups who are however far less well organised, nor do they enjoy this measure of state support.

Once the realisation dawns that terrorism today is a mutant of war, then the methodology of state reaction becomes that much simpler. All the panoply of options and policies that would normally come into play during a regular war needs to be considered here—keeping in mind always that terrorism has to be fought much more through the mind than by mere physical threat or persuasion. Thus a strong media policy is as important (if not more) than equipping the armed forces with weapons and technology that is suitable for anti-terrorist operations.

In a war where the objective is in part to wear down the armed forces of a country, the standard customs of bringing in huge numbers of armed forces into a conflict area must be resisted with the clear idea that this is playing into the hands of the enemy Such troops infusions leads to farther "alienation" of the people—whom they are supposed to protect—and thus further confusion among troops.

However the dangers of the present phase of terrorism are many and is only flagged here as points of concern, though each of these aspects require focused study.

— Terrorism being a transnational enterprise is much more prone to spreading the baccillus of conflict and violence into other countries. Thus areas with otherwise no relation to the conflict get drawn in. Relative to conventional war therefore, this type of terrorism has far greater "reach" in terms of damage done.

— Terrorist incidents may lead to open conventional war with very little warning time. Particular terrorist incidents may.be used by a state to launch what is in fact a premeditated decision to go to war.

— The blurring of lines between what is terrorism and what is war may also lead to rapid escalation into war.

— The close co-operation apparent between terrorism and organised crime also point to a further erosion of the authority of the state, with the one using force to achieve its objectives and the other corrupting the state from within.

— The "just war" panoply that underwrites terrorism (in the form of religion) ensures that this kind, of action is set to continue and spread into areas of low development and education,

All these factors have extremely serious implications for

international security. Though the term "security" is now open to varied interpretation, the bottom line still remains that states as actors need to have a minimum developmental progress, some safety for their peoples, and an ambience which allows the state to achieve these objectives. As brought out in large parts of the world, this is no longer possible, The future obviously lies in once again reinforcing the lines between armed forces and society.

The weapon of violence has to remain with the state-which may be the perfect model but is still a "controllable" actor, which is expected also to control those under arms and carries its insignia, and wears its uniform. This is easier said than done. States (especially the so called "international community") need to build up norms that once protected civil society. It also means a definite commitment not to instigate wars in their neighbourhood or in the region with the clear understanding that such wars do little for their own security. The spread of the weapons of war needs to be curbed urgently. The trend of controls has been to deny weapons to a state in conflict. (Since no one has yet any ideas on how to control the non state actor). However, while this has some benefits, it must be remembered that it is the state which is the victim. This denial should include sanctions of those states seen to be supporting the continuation of conflict or directly contributing to it.

There are many other "points of intervention to "cap, roll back and eliminate" these wars that are the children of a strategy that was so gladly followed in years past. Proxy war has produced its own mutants—which are resistant to the weapons that once addressed conventional war, and equally resistant to the tools of diplomacy that once sought to limit conflict. Defence industry has already embarked on the next phase of war by bringing in the weapons required in these "war-like situations" and offering technological "fixes" for problems that beset these nations. But it is states that wage war, and this is one continuity that is apparent through almost all the cycles of war and conflict. It is therefore the responsibility of the states that form the "international community" to coax war again into its former boundaries. The realisation that even a super power or a regional power really has no defence against terrorism must finally push states into acting in their own interest. States supporting terrorism thrive on inter-state differences and competitive strategies, and have become adept at playing the one against the other to achieve their own covert objectives. While it is accepted that states will continue to adopt competitive modes of conduct in their relations with each other, the bottom line is that a cooperative strategy in tackling terrorism has to be made a "stand alone" objective by those democracies who still wish to retain a measure of stability in international relations.

As every handbook on terrorists makes clear, the aims of the terrorists differ from those of ordinary criminals. Most criminals commit crimes for personal profit. But most terrorists commit crimes in support of political causes: to focus international attention on a neglected problem; or to strike fear amongst the people; or to strike at the perceived oppressors, their installations or installations identified with them.

Some of the revolutionaries who seized power in France adopted a policy of violence against their enemies. The period of their rule became known as the Reign of Terror. However perverse those causes may seem to observers, terrorists are deeply motivated individuals committed to their goals. Terrorist tactics have been used for hundreds of years.

A new dimension has, however, been added to the

genre of terrorism: *the Islamic jihadi.* Unlike other terrorists whose goals are definable in distinct political terms, the goals of the *jihadi* are no less than to establish "Islam" all over the globe, and especially to liberate regions which were once ruled by Muslims. It is this religio-civilisational dimension, and the desire to establish a *Nizam-I-Mustafa,* that the *jihadi* brings to the vocabulary of contemporary terrorism. And it is these *jihadis* that are at the foreftont of the militancy in Kashmir But not only in Kashmir. From Sudan through Egypt through Kosovo and Chechnya and much of Central Asia, through Afghanistan and Pakistan to Indonesia, there are numerous local battles being fought as part of a global civilisational war, as the Harvard political scientist Samuel Huntington would put it, between these so-called warriors of Islam and the ruling establishment.

Kashmir, as everyone knows, was for centuries a symbol of cultural and religious harmony. Not only did Kashmiri Hindus, Kashmiri Muslims and Buddhists live in complete harmony but out of Shaivism, Sufisim and Mahayana Buddhism they had created a composite cultural identity: *Kashmiriyat.* Although it faced an onslaught through much of the 1990s, it survived albeit in a latent form. Today, however, Kashmiriyat is fighting a battle of survival because of the war waged against it by these *jihadis.* But what is *jihad* and who are the *jihadis*? The concept of Jihad has been debated, over the centuries, by a number of Islamic theologians. Some of the Sufi thinkers have emphasised the importance of a "higher" jihad against one's lusts, but in the perception of the militant groups it is incumbent on every Muslim to fight a war against the infidels and the unbelievers. Islamic thought divides the world into two: the land of Islam or Peace (Dar-ul-Islam) and the land of strife of war *(Dar-ul-Harb). To* wage war against *Dar-ul-Harb* is

Jihad. The infidels have the option to either embrace Islam, pay *jaziya* (special tax), remain as a minority or face the sword. As one of the ideologues puts it:

"To fight on is incumbent on the believers till the way of life (i.e. Deen) prescribed by Allah dominates and overwhelms the whole of the world. Now the question arises whether at present Allah's Deen alone is ruling the world and whether the world order has Islam at its roots or it is based on disbelief. We need to know if economy is being run according to the commands given by Allah, free from interest and usury or whether we are forced and pressed by the disbelievers, to follow the economic system based on interest and usury and if the limits imposed by Allah are being observed in the world or not. There car, be no two answers to these questions. Islam is certainly nowhere dominant in the world. If it is so, the fact is established that Jihad is obligatory for the believers."

The ideologue adds:

Fighting is obligatory till the disbelieving powers and states are subdued and they pay Jaziya (captivation tax) with willing submission. Have the disbeliever's any where in the world agreed to come under the protection of the Muslims by paying the Jaziya? Do they feel themselves subdued by the Muslims in any part of the world'? No. Rather, at present, it is the Muslims who feel themselves subdued and humiliated before the disbelievers, 'and it is again the Muslims who have been forced to pay tribute to disbelievers. The disbelievers are plundering and exploiting all the wealth and resources belonging to the Muslims through the World Bank and IMF Should we not make any struggle to free ourselves from this state of utter disgrace? Why should we still not regard Jihad as obligatory?

He also further stated:

> When the weak are being oppressed and persecuted in any part of the world, it is obligatory to fight on (against the oppressors) till they (i.e. the weak) are delivered from this oppression and brutality. Can you name a single point in the world where the Muslims are not being harassed and oppressed? How should you not listen to the oppressed who arc crying and calling for help and deliverance in India, Kashmir, Philippine, Chechnya and Bosnia? How should we ask for some further proof to regard Jihad as obligatory in the presence of impeccable verses of the Qur'an, and viewing how our brothers have been undergoing sheer brutalities at the hands of the disbelievers?

The whole of India, including Kashmir, Hyderabad, Assam, Nepal, Burma, Bihar, and Junagadh was a Muslim territory. We lost this vast territory and it fell into the hands of the disbelievers just because we abandoned Jihad. Such is the rationale of the *jihadi*. Ostensibly rational reasons are provided for waging an irrational war against innocents. As far as the Kashmiris are concerned the *Jihadis* are primarily located in two organisations.

Earlier known as the Harakat ul-Ansar Harakat ul-Mujahidin (HUM) was designated a foreign terrorist, organisation by the United States government in October 1997. It is HUM which was responsible for the hijacking of Indian Airlines Flight 814. HUM is an Islamic militant group based in Pakistan that operates primarily in Kashmir. Its leader Fazlur Rehman Khalil has been linked to bin Laden and signed his fatwa in February 1998 calling for attacks on US and Western interests. HUM operates terrorist training camps in eastern Afghanistan and suffered casualties in the US missile strikes on bin Laden-associated training camps in Khowst in August

1998. Fazlur Rehman Khalil subsequently said that HUM would take revenge on the United States. It conducted a number of operations against Indian troops and civilian targets in Kashmir and is linked to the Kashmiri militant group al-Faran that kidnapped five Western tourists in Kashmir in July 1995; one was killed in August 1995, and the other four reportedly were killed in December of the same year.

Maulana Masood Azhar, a HUM ideologue freed in January by India in return for hostages on a hijacked Indian Airlines plane has vowed to recruit half a million men to fight Indian rule in Kashmir.

"We are going to organise a 500,000 Mujahidin force to fight against the Indians," Masood Azhar told thousands of his supporters. Azhar said the force would be recruited from all over Pakistan.

The parent organisation of Lashkar-I-Taiba (LIT) is Markaz Ad-da'wah Wal Irshad which claims to be committed to Islamic education and Jihad. It also claims that thousands of its militants are fighting the Indian security forces and 600 have been killed during encounters with the security forces. The head of the Lashkar, the so-called Ameer Markaz is Hafiz Muhammad Saeed. At a congregation in Muridke near Lahore, Lashkar leaders spewed venom against India and the United States.

For instance "addressing the annual congregation one of the leaders said that "the next target is New Delhi". LIT is probably the strongest jihadi organisation today. As with all such organisations, it is supported by various agencies within Pakistan. This new phase of terrorism is probably the most dangerous and to combat it will require a huge cooperative effort across continents. The first step is to introduce a Global Convention on

Terrorism, which makes it incumbent on states, that provide a hospitable area for terrorist operations, to clean up their act or face international enforcement action. Until then states like India and the United States must also evolve joint strategies to crush this international menace.

After the arrival of UN, the genesis of conflict and violence goes back to the history of civilisation. But use of terror tactics to resolve international conflict is relatively a new phenomenon, Its application in international relations could be traced back to political developments in the Middle East after the partition of Palestine and creation of Israel in 1948. The Palestinian leader refused the UN proposal for two separate states in the disputed territory. This was, the beginning of growth of terrorism in the Middle East. Similarly, politico-ideological divide between the US led capitalist forces and the Soviet led Communist forces created bi-polarisation of the global polity. These political developments had profound impact on the polity of the developing countries in the East Europe and Central America. These countries were used by the US and the hen Soviet Union to increase their respective areas of influence. Both the super powers and their allies used violence and terror tactics in some form or other to achieve their respective foreign policy goals. During this period i.e. 1960s and 1970s there was alarming growth of terrorism.

The super power rivalry coincided with the struggle for freedom movement in Afro-Asian countries. The movements for freedom in these countries received political and financial support from the Soviets, because the colonial powers—the Great Britain and France joined hands with the US. As a matter of fact, involvement of e super powers not merely delayed the process of freedom; it also created political mess in the international relations.

While the Soviet Union endeavoured to influence these countries towards the left, the US did the same frustrate the Soviet design, The result was the beginning of cold war and global insecurity. There was no possibility of common agenda for global security between exploiters and the exploited, and between those Who want freeze the international status quo in their own inters and those who are disadvantaged by it. The international politics was clearly divided into two blocks and international security was at stake. A huge sum of money was spent on weapons of mass destruction and defence technology.

.However, since the memory of the World War II was still fresh, both the super powers avoided an open confrontation. Therefore, the only available option for them was covert warfare or use of terror tactics to achieve their objectives. Thus innumerable state-sponsored terrorist groups mushroomed in different parts of the world. In 1972, the UN for the first time realised the hidden threat from international terrorism and decided to adopt a resolution. The year 1972 thus was the beginning of the UN contribution towards prevention of international terrorism.

The first ever text of the UN on international terrorism was adopted on 18th December 1972 in 2114th plenary meeting of the General Assembly The subject of the text was described as the 'Measures to prevent international terrorism' which endangers or takes innocent human lives or jeopardises fundamental freedoms, and study of the underlying causes of those forms of terrorism and acts of violence which lie in misery, frustration, grievance and despair., and which cause some people to sacrifice human lives, including their own, in an attempt to effect radical changes.

Recalling the Declaration on Principles of International Law concerning Friendly Relations and

Co-operation among States in accordance with the Charter, the United Nations expressed its concern over increasing acts of violence and terrorism. The purpose of adopting this resolution was mainly to draw attention and co-operation of member states. The important aspect of this resolution was concern to violent struggle for independence of people under colonial and racist regimes and other forms of alien domination, It condemned the continuation of repressive and terrorist acts by colonial and racist regime, and invited states to submit their observations and proposals to the Secretary General by 10th April 1973.

The inclusion of right to self-determination in the third paragraph of the text was important in the light of the' fact that many Afro-Asian countries were reeling under the colonial empires which inter alia was one of the causes of growth of terrorism in international politics. Unless the political grievances of these countries were addressed, prevention of terrorism was not possible. This resolution, however, did not mention about modalities for the prevention of transnational terrorism or to resolve problems in freedom movement. It just marked the beginning of the UN intervention to curb terrorism. After deliberations and debates the General Assembly decided to establish an ad hoc committee to examine the matter. The resolution was finally adopted by the Assembly with roll call vote, 80 members voted in favour, 37 against, 17 abstained and 5 were absent. The US led Western allies either voted against or abstained while the Communist Russia voted in favour. The trend was very obvious.

The ideological divide between the Eastern and the Western allies was pre-dominant. The UN adopted the resolution for the prevention of terrorism. But nothing was likely to emerge from this exercise except that the ad hoc committee was appointed to evolve an acceptable definition of terrorism, examine its causes and suggest measures for prevention. Reaffirming its commitment, the President of the UN General Assembly appointed a 35 members ad hoc committee in 1973 to examine the details towards prevention of international terrorism. The idea was to create consciousness. The member states were concerned to the growing acts of terrorism. But there was no agreement on defining terrorism. One man's terrorist emerged as another's freedom fighter. The committee submitted the report without adopting any acceptable definition of terrorism, though it suggested number of measures for prevention of terrorism and sought co-operation among nations. The UN General Assembly Report of the ad hoc committee on International Terrorism (28tb session/A/9028 1973) was an important document in the history of terrorism. For the first time member nations worked on different aspects of international terrorism. Three separate sub committees were established to examine definition, causes and prevention of terrorism. Seven draft proposals were submitted by different nations. While Non-Aligned Group (consisting of Algeria, Congo, Democratic Yemen, Guinea, India, Mauritania, Nigeria, Syria, Tunisia, Tanzania, Yemen, Yugoslavia, Zaire, and Zambia) submitted a collective proposal, France, Greece, Haiti, Iran, Venezuela made separate representations on definition of terrorism.

The Non-Aligned Group defined international terrorism as acts of violence committed by group of individuals which endanger human lives or jeopardise fundamental freedoms the effects of which are not confined to one state. This should not, however, affect the inalienable right to self-determination under colonial and racist regimes. The French proposal defined international terrorism as heinous act of barbarism committed in foreign territory. The proposal by Greece was an attempt to distinguish between freedom fighting and terrorism. It defined international terrorism as criminal acts of violence against innocent persons committed in the territory of a third state with the aim to put pressure on any dispute or for personal satisfaction. Haiti added political purpose in the agenda of terrorism, Iran included violence against freedom movement also as acts of international terrorism. Nigeria and Venezuela also submitted similar observations.

Apparently, none of the proposed definition received general support. The house was divided and no conclusion could be drawn from the draft proposals. Finally member nations decided to drop the subject of definition and decided to focus on prevention of international terrorism. Thus no definition of terrorism could evolve until 1987 when the Secretary General convened an international conference to define terrorism and differentiate it from freedom fighting. Taking note of the Secretary General's report, the UN General Assembly condemned all acts of terrorism except those fighting for right to self-determination against foreign and racist regime as 'criminal' wherever and by whomever committed, including those which jeopardise friendly relations among states and their security. Overwhelming majority adopted this resolution. The US and Israel, however, voted against this resolution while Honduras abstained.

Having analysed the menace of international terror ism, the UN members were all set to adopt resolutions that could restrict growth of terrorism in international politics. Recalling the original Charter the General Assembly adopted international conventions for the prevention of terrorism. It took long for the UN to define international terrorism. From 1973 to 1987 the international community struggled to distinguish between freedom fighters and terrorism. The UN could arrive at some definition in 1987 precisely because by this time most of 'the colonies in Afro-Asian countries were either set free or were at the verge of freedom. But international terrorism was on its peak during this period and the UN could not remain a silent spectator.

In 1976 the UN General Assembly decided to establish an ad hoc committee to draft an International Convention Against the Taking of Hostages which came into effect on 29th November 1978. The following year a detail report of the committee was submitted for ratification by the member nation states. The Articles 1, 5 and 10 of the convention were vital to curb international terrorism. Article 1 described any person who seizes or detains and threatens to kill, to injure or to continue to detain another person (hereafter referred to as the (hostage) in order to compel a third party, namely, a state, an international intergovernmental organisation, a natural or juridical person, to do or abstain from doing any act as an explicit or implicit condition for the release of the hostage commits the offence of taking of hostages (hostage-taking). The Article 5 sought for nations cooperation and judicial action against the offence. But the most important of all was the Article 10. This Article made it clear that hostage taking shall be deemed as extraditable offence in any extradition treaty existing between two states. It further reiterated that if a state receives a request for extradition from another state with which it has no extradition treaty, the requested state might at its option consider this convention as the legal basis for extradition in respect of the offence.

Another important aspect of this convention was Article 13 that emphasised that this convention is not applicable when the offence is committed within the country and the offender is national of the same nation. By doing so, the UN made it clear that it doesn't intend to interfere in the domestic affairs of member nations, and this is why this convention was adopted by consensus. However, by 1981 international community had realised that terrorism is sponsored by nation states and its prevention is not possible unless such activities are restricted.

In the 85th meeting of the General Assembly, 1981 it was decided that the ad hoc committee would draft an International Convention against the Recruitment, Use, Financing, and Training of Mercenaries, This convention was finally adopted in 1989. It took eight years for the members to submit their observations on the basis of which the convention was drafted and finally adopted without a vote on 4th December 1989. This convention consisted of 21 Articles of which first two were dedicated to definition of a, mercenary and Article 4 to the acts of violence committed by the mercenaries. The most important, however, was Article 5. It emphasised that member states 'shall not recruit, use, finance or train mercenaries and shall prohibit such activities in accordance with the convention.'

The convention also reiterated that such instruments should not be employed by states to oppose legitimate struggle for right to self-determination of people. Rest of the Articles dealt with different approaches towards prevention of terror ism by member nation states. Taking note of previous reports of the Secretary General and recalling all the resolutions the UN General Assembly decided to include yet another resolution. This was solely dedicated to elimination of international terrorism. Calling attention to the growing connection between drug-traffickers and absence of extradition treaty among member nations, the Assembly decided to draft a

Declaration on Measures to Eliminate Terrorism. On 9th December 1994, this Declaration was adopted. The Declaration expressed concern over linkage of drug traffickers and money launders with paramilitary gangs which resort to all types of violence and endanger constitutional order of states by violating human rights. The importance of this declaration could be analysed from the fact that coordination and cooperation among states to combat terrorism was given utmost priority.

The need for extradition treaty among nations and efforts at regional and bi-lateral level was reiterated. International terrorism had come to such a sorry pass that by now every year the General Assembly adopted one after another resolutions calling upon member states to co-operate, co-ordinate and investigate matters related to suppression of international terrorism. Based on the documents of Group of Seven Major Industrialised countries, Ministerial Conference on Terrorism of Russian Federation, held in Paris and Plan of Action adopted by the Inter-American Specialised Conference on Terrorism, held at Lima in 1996, the General Assembly established another ad hoc committee.

The purpose of this committee was to elaborate on International Convention for the Suppression of Terrorist Bombings, and thereafter an International Convention for the Suppression of Nuclear Terrorism. In 1997 the draft for this convention was prepared. The following year it was implemented. The important subjects for discussion in this committee were extradition, sharing of information about mechanism, investigation and prosecution of terrorists. Recalling the 1997 resolution, the General Assembly urged the member states on 8th December 1998 to bring about domestic legislation on priority basis to implement the provisions of the convention. In accordance 'with the commitment Foreign

Ministers and Heads of States of Non-Aligned Movement (NAM) met on 23rd September 1999 in New York. Reiterating decisions of its previous meetings held at Durban in South Africa, the NAM members called for an international conference under the auspices of the UN to form a Joint Action Group against terrorism. On the similar line a separate Terrorism Prevention Branch was set up in the Centre for International Crime Prevention of Vienna to enhance UN capabilities through research and technical capabilities. Meanwhile, taking note of all the efforts at the General Assembly, Security Council also adopted a resolution (1269) on 19th October 1999 and called for co-operation among member nations. These developments were well acknowledged by the General Assembly, On 19th November, 1999, a Working Group came into being to draft a Comprehensive Convention on International Terrorism within the framework of the existing convention.

It was decided that the ad hoc committee meeting would be convened in 2001 for this purpose. France was the first to submit a draft proposal for the International convention for the Suppression of Financing of Terrorism. This proposal received overwhelming support from the members. Thus an Anti-Terrorism Working Group was formed under the chairmanship of Phillippe Kirsche of Canada. The proposed convention mentioned a number of new provisions. It excluded political purpose in defence of terrorist acts, restricted extradition if the purpose is to discriminate and also dealt with illegal practices in financial institutions and bank secrecy.

Responding to press conference the chairman highlighted problems in implementation of these conventions which require 22 ratifications for enforcement. Normally the conventions do not receive the requisite number, e.g. the 1997 Convention for

Suppression of Terrorist Bombings received only eight ratifications though there were 52 signatories. Thus the UN has set the basic agenda and has provided innumerable prescriptions for elimination of terrorism. The problem is not with lack of agenda or programme of action. The problem lies with the implementation. These prescriptions can not be imposed on nation states by force. They could be persuaded to adopt these prescriptions and implement them at bi-lateral and regional level. But the complex nature of international politics often interrupts the process of implementation. Terrorists take advantage of this situation, and thus continue to threaten mankind.

The term 'international terrorism' is often used so loosely that it implies only that terrorism is a world-wide problem or that most terrorism has some influence, however marginal and indirect, on international opinion and behaviour. More rigorous standards of definition are required for such tasks as scholarly investigation or legal codification. Even academic publications, however, sometimes betray extreme carelessness in the use of the term. A 'Chronology of Recent Incidents in International Terrorism' presented to a major conference committed the *faux pas* of including provisional I.R.A. attacks in London while omitting cross-border terrorist raids in the Middle East. Moreover, progress towards more rigorous definition is a precondition for effective analysis and policy prescription, particularly at the levels of inter-governmental negotiation and political and judicial action. When does an act of extreme violence and coercive intimidation for political ends become international? The most obvious case is that of the state which uses coercive or repressive terror in the process of conducting foreign war, conquest, annexation or colonisation. Second, there is the direct terroristic attack by a faction or movement against the citizens and property of a foreign state: such attacks range from the cross-border raids of the type Israel has experienced almost ceaselessly since 1948 to long-range forays such as the Munich massacre in 1972 or the OPEC Conference hijack of 1975 in Vienna. Next there is the terrorism commited by government, faction or movement operating in their own country of origin or in third countries against foreign citizens, property or means of transport. Terrorist acts can also be accurately designated 'international' if they are committed as the result of connivance, collaboration or alliance between terrorists and the governments, terrorist movements or factions of foreign states. In short, political terrorism becomes international in the strict sense when it is; (i) directed at foreigners or foreign targets; (ii) concerted by the governments or factions of more than one state; or (iii) aimed at influencing the policies of a foreign government.

The definitional debate has become somewhat confused in recent years by the introduction of the term 'transnational terrorism'. And one writer has gone so far as to suggest that terrorism 'becomes transnational when it involves individuals of different nationalities'. This seems unnecessary, because the term 'international' has never been restricted exclusively to inter-governmental relations as such and is generally used to apply to cultural, economic and other activities and transactions involving citizens of different countries. Other writers have suggested a more specialised use of 'transnational', applying the designation to those terrorists who operate internationally with the express long-term aim of global revolution or of establishing a revolutionary supranational world order. According to this stricter definition transnational terrorist groups clearly constitute a small, though exotic, minority of international terrorists.

The vast majority of acts of international terrorism

have clearly far more limited objectives, such as national liberation, secession or seizure of power over a specific political regime. Examples of international terrorist movements in the transnational category would be the Bakuninist Anarchist International active in Europe in the 1870s, or the Japanese United Red Army with its professed aim of 'world revolution'. But the Popular Front for the Liberation of Palestine would not be included because its primary declared aim is the liberation of the Palestinian people and the establishment of a secular Marxist Palestinian state: it is to a high degree international in its targets and *modus operandi,* but this does not make it a transnational organisation in the same league with the Bakuninists or the modern anarchists and nihilists.

Force and Violence in International Relations

In the context of the liberal polity, the distinction between force and violence is of the greatest importance. Responsible and limited constitutional government provides a formula by means of which citizens may enjoy the highest degree of individual liberty compatible with security against the violence of tyrannical government, foreign enemies, private persons or groups. But we also noted the agonising dilemmas that may arise in liberal political practice when force and violence become so blurred as to be almost indistinguishable. For example, if the laws of the state require a man to act contrary to his private morality, under what conditions should he place obedience to conscience above obligation to the state? Are there circumstances when, even in a liberal polity, one may be morally justified in resorting to political violence? It was not suggested that there are any easy general answers to such questions.

However if we consider the problem of force and violence in the context of international relations as a whole the moral problems involved are infinitely more complex. For there is no world sovereign authority with the power to make universal law, order, peace, and justice.

The noble hopes of the liberal internationalists have been sorely disappointed by United Nations experiment. For while idealists looked eagerly for signs of an embryonic world authority emerging from Lake Success, the sickening realities of deepening division into armed camps, the strategic arms race, and continuing ideological and military struggles have dragged the organisation into the Slough of Despond. In the absence of any effective world body with the necessary authority and power to impose peace and order it is, as always, the strongest states or alliances that have determined for themselves when war is necessary and, hence, justified.

In this desert of ruined hopes there remain some miraculous blades of hope. There is the historic but painfully slow progress towards a more comprehensive and effective international law. Yet this remains tenuous and vulnerable because, unlike the positive laws of states, international laws must depend solely on a combination of international consensus, appeals to reciprocal self-interest, and retaliatory sanctions. According to some legal theorists this makes international law more closely analogous to customary law and convention than to law proper. History abounds with examples of states that have defied such rules with impunity.

The development of a more elaborate body of international law may in itself be encouraging evidence of greater international co-operation and interdependence. And since the Second World War this development has been vastly reinforced by the movements towards greater international organisation in the economic, technical and scientific spheres. But no realistic statesman pins too many hopes on the grandiose rhetoric of brotherly love or treaties, protocols and agreements, for it is all too easy for statesmen to sign resolutions and treaties to which they have no intention of adhering. And inter-state relations can still shift from toleration to envenomed conflict with astonishing rapidity as a result of revolution, coup or other dramatic internal changes.

Internationally liberal theory has to come to terms with these realities. Liberal states inhabit a hostile environment, and the greatest immediate dangers they face stem not only from the Soviet Union with its explicit world revolutionary aims and rapidly growing offensive military capability, but also from 'crazy' states led by fanatics such as Colonel Gaddafi and Ayatollah Khomeini. Moreover, liberal democratic states are becoming an increasingly beleaguered minority, as evidenced by their growing isolation and frustration in the U.N. General Assembly.

According to a survey only 19.6 per cent of the world's population live in free countries. The vast majority live under military regimes or one-party states of one kind or another. It is absolute utopian nonsense to speak as if an international community of shared liberal values already existed. In an unfriendly and dangerous world what alternative have liberal states but to arm themselves for their own protection and to form defensive alliances to try to insure against Soviet aggression? Only an absolute pacifist would want to deny them the right of self-defence.

International Terrorism and International Relations

Any honest survey of violence in contemporary international relations would have to admit that, even in the very shadow of nuclear weapons, internal and international conflict is endemic. Liberal statesmen are already, in this sense, struggling to build peace within a framework of failure. Since the Second World War there have been over 200 internationally significant outbreaks of violence. And although less than 10 per cent of these have been direct military conflicts between two states, a large proportion of the major internal conflicts and revolutionary civil wars has involved considerable covert or indirect foreign intervention.

Hence there has been no diminution of what has been earlier designated as epiphenomenal terror, that is the large-scale terror which is an inevitable cocomitant to wars and mass insurrections. And it would clearly be dangerously naive to assume that the preservation of a merely formal peace between the major powers is enough to secure a significant reduction in the degree of epiphenomenal terror.

For the Soviet Communist leadership has clearly demonstrated that it believes the pursuit of detente and the so-called, peace-offensive' on the diplomatic front to be entirely compatible with the waging of ideological and armed struggle in furtherance of the world-wide aims of Soviet Marxism-Leninism. Not only have the Soviet leaders never renounced Lenin's injunction that any means are justified to further their world revolutionary aims, they have actually refined and added to their repertoire new and more insidious modes of unconventional war.

In an age of nuclear stalemate the Russian leaders are astute enough to realise that there is no need for them to put at risk all their hard-won economic development by provoking all-out nuclear war. By the selective adoption and covert promotion of a host of 'armed liberation struggles', by subversion and sabotage, and by terrorism, they have been able to nibble away piece after piece of the non-communist world. The new generation of their satellite and client regimes—in Cuba, in Vietnam, in Ethiopia and now in Afghanistan—is ample testimony to their growing success in techniques of internal subversion and takeover in Third World countries. And unless the Western powers can find an effective counter-strategy all their nuclear strength and military technology will not be able to prevent the fall of the non-communist world by a thousand cuts.

As Liddell-Hart observed: 'The implied threat of using nuclear weapons to curb guerrillas was as absurd as to talk of using a sledgehammer to ward off a swarm of mosquitoes. The policy did not make sense, and the natural effect was to stimulate and encourage the forms of aggression, by erosion, to which nuclear weapons were an inapplicable counter.'

There are a number of very widespread misconceptions about the nature of unconventional and irregular war in general, and about revolutionary and subrevolutionary terrorism in particular, which need correction. The case of international terrorism is especially appropriate to illustrate the falsity of a number of these assumptions. First, it is a widely held belief that guerrilla struggle is essentially a defensive response to superior military power, that it is always the weapon of the weak. But this is to overlook a significant shift in the strategic environment in favour of indirect means: 'In the past, guerrilla war has been a weapon of the weaker side, and thus primarily defensive, but in the atomic age it may be increasingly developed as a form of aggression suited to exploit a situation of nuclear stalemate. Thus the concept of "cold war" is now out of date, and should be superseded by that of "camouflaged war". The peculiar aptness of Liddell-Hart's term 'camouflaged war to terrorism hardly needs emphasis.

Of course it is undeniable that in many cases the guerrilla struggle is an asymmetrical conflict with cumulative advantages accruing to the incumbent regime. This has been true of most, though not all, national liberation wars waged in Third World countries. But it is really a question of who is calling the shots. We now have a situation in which the Soviet Union and other communist states and Islamic fundamentalist states have actually initiated, armed and directed struggles in foreign states.

We have seen the second most powerful military power in the world waging a kind of proxy war by means of guerrilla movements, terrorism and subversion in many countries.

It is clear that where powerful states exploit such methods, and provide the very latest weapons and training for the guerrilla or terrorist operatives, one is confronting a new and dangerous variety of offensive war, 'camouflaged' but deadly enough to its targets.

There is considerable evidence that the Soviet Union has not been content merely to give diplomatic support to national liberation movements for its own purposes. Since 1967 the Russians have reconsidered the potential of the plethora of new Left revolutionist and anarchist movements in Western industrialised states. They have shifted from regarding them solely as ideological heretics to using them in certain circumstances to weaken and disrupt liberal democracies through terrorism and student strife.

Soviet encouragement and indirect assistance to the Provisional I.R.A. has taken the form of allowing Soviet arms to be supplied to the terrorists. A large shipment of arms from Czecholsovakia, which must have been cleared by the Russians, was intercepted *en route* to the I.R.A. at Schipol Airport in Holland in October 1971.

There are the numerous supplies of Soviet-made

equipment to terrorist movements of almost every ideological hue channelled through Libya, in addition to the massive aid they provided for the P.L.O. Evidence has even come to light of communist willingness to assist the anarchist-nihilist group, the Baader-Meinhof terrorists.

There are only two real surprises about the fierce and confused debate that has raged since the Reagan Administration, in its first week in office, bluntly accused the Soviets of complicity in terrorism around the world, and the State Department released a dossier to prove Soviet and Cuban involvement in terrorism in Central America. The first is that some usually well-informed people expressed genuine surprise at these 'revelations'. The second is that a C.I.A. analysis, either through incompetence and naivete or for more devious political reasons, sought to deny the link. One had become aware that, since Vietnam and Watergate, the C.I.A. had become dangerously run-down and inadequate as the intelligence arm of the elading Western power; but most people did not expect it to start operating as an agency of disinformation. The C.I.A. seems also to be suffering from a bad bout of amnesia, for one of its own research studies on international terrorism, published in April 1976, stated:

After a period of hesitancy, the Soviets began channeling funds, weapons, and other assistance to fedayeen groups through a number of intermediaries in 1969. All indications are that they continue to do so today. Similarly, they have continued their long- standing programme (the more innocuous aspects of which are publicly associated with Moscow's Patrice Lumumba University) of bringing young revolutionaries from ali parts of the Third World to the Soviet Union for training and indoctrination. And ... some of these individuals have subsequently cropped up on the transnational terrorist scene... There is also a considerable body of circumstantial evidence linking Moscow to various terrorist formations in Western Europe.

The same 1976 C.I.A. report goes on to emphasise that much of the work of channeling aid to terrorist movements is done by intermediaries and proxies such as the Warsaw Pact countries. Cuba, Libya and the P.L.O., 'who, if exposed, can be plausibly represented as having acted on their own initiative'. The study concluded that although 'the true dimensions of Soviet involvement remain extremely difficult to ascertain... their efforts to gain some handle on extremist activity have, together with their pursuit of less congruent objectives, done more to aggravate than to contain the current rash of transnational terrorist activity'.

This cautious assessment did no more than endorse the conclusions of the small, but fast- growing, Western community of academics, security analysts, and investigative journalists specialising in the study of terrorist phenomena in the mid-1970s. But over the last few years we have had more and more material brought to light which confirms that Soviet leaders, operating through the machinery of the International Department of the Secretariat of the Soviet Communist party, and the K.G.B. have been up to their necks in direct support for terrorist activities, pumping vital training, cash and weapons, and valuable propaganda and diplomatic support to selected 'national liberation movements' (such as the P.L.O., the Omani Liberation Front, the Polisario, the Armenian Secret Army, and SWAPO) on an opportunistic basis, with a view to using them as instrument of proxy war to further Soviet interests abroad.

One valuable source of evidence about the precise

nature of Soviet help has come from interviews with captured terrorists. For example, David Shipler of *The New York Times* has published a very full account of his conversation with Adnan Jaber, commander of a P.L.O. terrorist squad that killed six Jewish worshippers in a Sabbath ambush at Hebron in May 1978.

The two-hour interview was arranged at the request of *The Times* and conducted in the presence of an Israeli Army public relations officer and with no guards or interrogators present. The Soviets must, of course, be aware that it is impossible to keep their terrorist training activities secret, even if they particularly wanted to.

For the organisations they assist, such as the P.L.O., openly admit its extent: indeed they boast about it, no doubt in the belief that it adds to their movement's status and credibility and the impression of power and invincibility they wish to create. Jaber claimed that he was selected for special training in the Soviet Union, following preliminary courses in Syria and Lebanon. He was sent to a camp at Skhodnya, about twenty miles from Moscow, where he received training in the use of weapons, how to command a group of about thirty guerrillas, military tactics, political ideology and propaganda techniques. Jaber said he and his fellow trainees were not allowed to have any contact with Soviet citizens other than their instructors.

Further details of the terrorist training camps within the Russia were revealed by Herbert Krosney in a September 1979 article in New *Yorker* magazine and in his T.V. documentary on the P.L.O. shown by the P.B.S. and C.B.C. the following week. Drawing on intelligence reports and interviews with P.L.O. officials, Krosney was able to provide a very interesting description of the six-month specialist training course made available to selected members of major P.L.O. factions at the Soviet foreign-military academy at Sanprobal near Simferapol on the Black Sea. Under the innocent title 'engineering', selected 'national liberation' movement personnel are taught the following: regular and electric detonators; production of incendiary devices; preparation of an electrical charge using a detonator; fuse types; blowing up vehicles and ammunition dumps; and many other technical skills of terrorism. Krosney's sources estimate that, up until 1979, roughly 1,000 P.L.O. operatives had been sent to training camps either in the Soviet Union or in other Soviet bloc countries. This programme was stepped up after 1977-8, when the Soviets decided to make greater use of the P.L.O. to counteract the Sadat peace initiative with Israel and the Camp David process.

The P.L.O. Representative to Moscow, Muhammed ash-Shader, confirmed the continuing importance attached by the Soviet regime and the P.L.O. to this programme when he said, in February 1981: 'Hundreds of Palestinian officers holding the rank of brigade commander have already been accredited by Soviet military academies, and members of the P.L.O. use arms of Soviet and East European manufacture.' It is important to stress that such support given by the Soviets to the P.L.O. has a far wider significance in the furtherance of international terrorism, because the P.L.O. was the most important conduit for weapons, funds and expertise to other terrorist movements, including some of the main groups active in Western Europe.

Following its major military defeat in Lebanon in 1982 the P.L.O. is no longer the major conduit for aid to other terrorist movements. Cuba, Libya, Iran, Vietnam, and North Korea all play a significant role in training and in provision of weapons. Shipler's informant, Jaber, claimed that Vietnamese training was particularly highly valued by the terrorist groups, because it was so up-to-date. Libya has also been an important centre for training and weapons supply. For example, Thomas McMahon, the I.R.A. man found guilty of the murder of Lord Mountbatten and members of his family, acquired his expertise in constructing remote-control bombs in a camp in Libya, under the direction of Soviet specialists. There is a network of Libyan training camps catering to a wide variety of West European and other terrorist groups. Apart from the Libyan role in helping train and arm the P.F.L.P., and other groups such as the I.R.A., Gaddafi has recently concentrated efforts on training terrorists to subvert his adversaries in the Arab world, such as Egypt and the Sudan.

Cuba's participation in funnelling practical assistance and armed 'advisers' to foreign movements is fully documented. Its activities as a Soviet proxy in Africa are well known, and it is clear that the K.G.B. has taken a particularly close interest in the establishment and supervision of a Soviet-style terrorist training in Cuba. The State Department's dossier on the tragic situation in El Salvador underlines the importance of Cuba as a Soviet proxy for the subversion of the vulnerable and unstable regimes in Central America. What is less well known is that Cuban 'advisers' and support are increasingly being channeled to areas and insurgent groups further afield, such as within the United States' own borders, and in the Middle East.

The great advantage for the Soviets of this use of proxies for subversion and terrorism is, of course, that they can disclaim any responsibility while in practice reaping the strategic benefits of undermining non-communist states, increasing the dependency of their client states and movements, and thereby hoping to gain still greater control over them. By helping 'national liberation movements' in strategic areas of the Third

World, such as the Gulf, the Horn, the Caribbean and Southern Africa, they clearly hope to gain control over key strategic 'choke points' where they could sever vital sea-lanes which supply the West, and gain control over key suppliers of strategic natural resources such as oil, 'yellow-cake' uranium and bauxite.

Prospects of rather different tactical gains may attract them to aiding the often tiny but potentially disruptive terrorist groups active within the NATO democracies' own borders. Except in certain cases—for example, Turkey in 1979-80—the Soviets must know that terrorism in Western countries has little chance of destabilising the whole political system. On the other hand, it has great prospects of weakening them by disruption and attrition. The Soviets are not unaware that protracted terrorist campaigns in democracies tend to force Western governments to spend more on internal security and to divert their already inadequate conventional forces away from the tasks of external defence, thus weakening NATO in its major task of countering the Soviet and Warsaw Pact build-up. Soviet Leaders would not find it easy to refrain from aiding, at least covertly, groups that are such a thorn in the throbbing flesh of their adversary capitalist states. And, the export of political violence constitutes a low-cost, low-risk weapon in the service of Soviet interests. Because it is undeclared, and, to a large extent, clandestine, it can be used without bringing the danger of a major conventional war escalating to nuclear conflict between the superpowers.

Needless to say, the Soviet Union is not prepared to explain its true motives and interests in promoting terrorism and political violence on an opportunistic basis around the world. The U.S.S.R. does not want its true role revealed because it would destroy tactical advantages, such as surprise—or the opportunity of helping both sides simultaneously (as happened in the Horn of Africa) so that they are bound to be ultimately on the winning side. Where their cover is blown or they officially admit involvement, of course, the last thing the Soviets will do is to attempt to justify it purely in terms of national interest.

We must remember that the Soviet leadership and the media they control need a convenient ideological framework that both explains and justifies direct and indirect use of violence beyond the borders of the U.S.S.R. under certain circumstances. Where a particular national liberation movement or revolutionary faction is judged to be on the side of the 'progressive forces' of Marxist-Leninism, as led and interpreted by the Soviet vanguard, and hence against the 'capitalist-imperialist reactionaries', it can be ideologically legitimated as part of Moscow's mission to further the world revolution's inevitable march to final victory. This is precisely how the Kremlin justified its (ultimately decisive) role in supporting the Vietcong. They use the same terms when they 'adopt' movements such as the P.L.O. today. History tells us that in every recent struggle by national liberation movements, terrorism has invariably been adopted by some, if not all, of the movement's factions, as one of their weapons of struggle. Yet the Soviets, of course, angrily disavow the terrorism label for any of the campaigns or actions they support. They claim that, as the leading revolutionary power in the world, they have the duty to aid national liberation movements to the fullest possible extent, and they can even quote U.N. resolutions on struggles for self-determination to support their claim that these activities are perfectly within the rules of international law. Moreover, the Soviets constantly reiterate their belief that this kind of aid is totally compatible with East-West detente, for they have never regarded the process of negotiating agreements on such matters as arms control, trade and scientific exchanges as precluding their right to continue to wage ideological warfare in support of world communism whenever and wherever they wish.

Hence, we should observe that the great dispute between the West and the Soviets over 'international terrorism' is not really about the basic facts. The Soviet Ambassador in London admitted in a B.B.C. radio interview, in March 1981, that his government is involved in the activities described. What is really in dispute is the interpretation of these facts. The Soviets claim that they are engaged only in aiding legitimate national liberation struggles. Many Americans and other Western observers, including this writer, question the credentials of some of the national liberation movements the Soviets are sponsoring, and point out that these movements, now and in the past, have carried out barbarous acts of terrorism, deliberately and systematically attacking the innocent.

As many historians of Russia have pointed out, the official attitude of the Soviet regime toward terrorism has always been highly equivocal. On the one hand, Lenin condemned individual terrorism as a waste of valuable revolutionary lives, as a possible provoker of repression that would only inhibit the development of the revolutionary movement among the masses, and as a possible means of turning the people against the revolution. On the other, Lenin and the Bolshevik party eagerly embraced mass terror as a method of extirpating 'counter-revolutionary' elements and consolidating their control over the new revolutionary state. And a dictatorship that has used and experienced mass terror on the scale of a Stalin is hardly likely to hesitate at the thought of using terror as a weapon beyond its borders when it sees it as expedient. Nor should we neglect Richard Pipes's insight, in 'The Roots of Involvement' in *International Terrorism: Challenge and Response,* that the Bolsheviks were the beneficiaries of the process of terrorism in Russia that had helped undermine the country's traditional values and institutions, in the pre-revolutionary period. Thus, Pipes argues, despite their rhetoric rejecting terrorism, this experience left 'an indelible imprint on the minds of the Soviet leadership', and thus they adopted terrorism as part of their repretoire of global strategy because this was 'a natural adaptation to foreign policy of methods which had been learned by the Bolsheviks and their allies when they were in the underground fighting the Imperial regime'.

Although the Soviet Communist party's *apparatchiki* have an almost instinctive feeling for the use of terror as a weapon of internal control, may be there are at least three powerful reasons why they continue to show considerable caution in employing terrorism as a tool of Soviet foreign policy. First, they must be afraid of the weapon's rebounding on their internal system of control. The Soviet Empire is full of disaffected groups and persecuted ethnic and religious minorities who might all too readily emulate terrorism as a means of fighting the Soviet regime, especially if they saw the method working against other East European Communist regimes with a less secure grip on their populations. Richard Pipes may be correct in his claim that the Soviet Union has in reality a lower tolerance for terrorism than the pluralist states of the West.

If the omniscience and power of the Soviet state were to be seriously challenged by internal violence, then the whole system of Communist party control could readily crumble. This may help to explain the Soviet leaders' paranoid reaction to dissent of any kind, and their massive repression against its smallest manifestations. Perhaps it was this kind of consideration that helped persuade them to stop aiding the Red Army Faction terrorists in Germany and to initiate a limited co-operation between their Warsaw Pact allies and West Germany in tracking down German terrorists who had escaped to Eastern Europe.

Second, the Soviets must be well aware of the dangers inherent in their own lack of control over their protege foreign terrorist movements. It is true that the Russians can always conceal or disown their connection, but suppose the protege using the firepower and expertise acquired from the Soviets, causes a major international conflict that threatens to escalate out of control? If it is difficult for the Soviets to completely subjugate individual Warsaw Pact states to their will, if they become vexed with the idiosyncratic policies of a more distant ally like Gaddafi, just imagine the problems of trying to control a national liberation or terrorist movement sustaining itself on the basic belief that it is a self-determining actor, the sole true representative of its 'own people'. Whatever the realities of dependency in terms of cash and arms, the Soviets must be aware that they are dealing with highly autonomous volatile entities that, with the aid of modem weapons of mass destruction, could cause conflicts endangering the Soviets' interests and national security.

Third, the Soviets are clearly aware that for them to be associated with sponsorship of international terrorism is a definite disadvantage in their attempts to woo sectors of opinion in Western and Third World countries. Terrorism is defninitely what T. D. Weldon, in *The Vocabulary of Politics,* once called 'a boo word'. The touchy, indeed angry, reaction of the Soviets to the Reagan Administration's charge of Soviet complicity in international terrorism is evidence that the Kremlin realises that any visible sign of their backing for terrorism may be counterproductive in the longer term by alienating international opinion.

The truth is that, for all their aggressive and exaggerated rhetoric, the Russians have been forced on to the defensive about their role in exporting and sustaining violence and terrorism. Soviet radio supported the 1981 I.R.A. hunger-strikers, and portrayed Britain as 'oppressors' and the Maze prison as a 'concentration camp', but tried to emphasise that the Soviets did not endorse the I.R.A. and its 'extreme forms of struggle' which, they claim, do not help solve the Irish problem.

It has been repeatedly suggested" that, in this offensive role, international terrorism is a form of 'surrogate war' between movements or states, but this term is dangerously misleading. International terrorist attack is simply a different mode of war, not an alternative to war as such. Indeed it may actually parallel conventional conflict, as in the case of many Palestinian attacks, or the conflicts in Lebanon, or it may be designed to act as a catalyst for a wider conflict. A more accurate description of the involvement of states in mounting long-range terrorist attacks in 'enemy' states would be 'proxy war'. International terrorism evinces similar characteristics to those of terroristic acts in the domestic context; arbitrariness, indiscriminateness in effects, non-recognition of any rules or conventions of war, inhumanity and barbaric cruelty. As has been argued earlier, terrorism represents the militarisation of politics. Instead of seeking negotiation, diplomacy and compromise, terrorists see their struggle in zero-sum terms. They will not rest until they have secured final 'victory'. Anything that aids their struggle is good and justified.

It is because revolutionary terrorists perceive themselves as being engaged in a zero-sum conflict rather than a 'mixed game of conflict cooperation"' that it is so dangerous to assume that governments can bargain meaningfully with them. The most frequent mistake is to confuse their short-term tactical demands with their strategic objectives. The latter are strictly non-negotiable. Hence the suggestion that terrorists and governments have 'a common interest and consequently the possibility of a mutually advantageous outcome' is illusory. The terrorists always have their eyes not merely *on a specific confrontation, but on* winning their campaign. In dealing with terrorists with determined political objectives totally opposed to its own, governments have far more to gain from holding fast and attempting to defeat the terrorists. Deterrence and bargaining will not suffice. Any government weakness encourages further assaults, and any release of terrorists as part of a bargain simply strengthens the terrorist groups staging such assaults.

A second major misconception is that guerrilla and terrorist movements invariably wage war in a noble and just cause. It is so often tacitly assumed that anyone who takes guns and plastic explosives aboard an aircraft to stage a hijack must be a *bona fide* victim of oppression or injustice. This is by no means always the case. A more balanced view has been expressed by General Frank Kitson:

> Many regard subversion as being principally a form of redress used by the down-trodden peoples of the world against their oppressors, and feel, therefore, that there is something immoral about preparing to suppress it. Undoubtedly subversion is sometimes used in this way, and on those occasions those supporting the government find themselves fighting for a bad cause. On the other hand, subversion can also be used by evil men

to advance their own interests in which case those fighting it have right on their side. More often, as in other forms of conflict, there is some right and some wrong on both sides ...

A third common error is to assume that international terrorism is a new invention. There were numerous incidents of international terrorism in the nineteenth century. One of the most famous was the attempt by the Italian patriot, Felice Orsini, to assassinate the Emperor Napoleon III and the Empress Eugenie on 14 January 1858. The Bakuninist International believed it was engaged in a campaign of European dimensions. After the First World War inter-national terrorist attacks were endemic in the new Balkan states and the internicine feuds of the Internal Macedonian Revolutionary Organisation (I.M.R.O.) spilt over into Vienna and Milan. Hence it is nonsense to suppose that international terrorism was invented by Latin American guerrillas in the mid-1960s. However, there *has* been a remarkable increase in the incidence of international terrorism during the past decade.

A recent study of acts of international terrorism—i.e. attacks against foreign targets in the state of the terrorists' origin or attacks across international frontiers—recorded a total of 6,714 incidents between 1968 and 1980. The annual incidents climbed from below 200 in 1968 to 400 in 1970, over 600 in 1972 and over 800 in 1978.

Explosive bombing remains far and away the most popular international terrorist tactic, but since 1975 there has also been a very steep rise in assassinations and attempted assassinations. Only a quarter of all attacks in this period caused death or personal injury, through a worrying trend since 1980 has been the increase in indiscriminate and lethal attacks such as massive bombings in public places and truck bombings: 1,435 incidents between 1968 and 1980 caused at least one casualty. And the number of attacks causing death and/or injury has increased each year since 1968. Over 30 per cent of incidents occurred in Western Europe, 20 per cent in Latin America and 20 per cent in the Middle East. Between 1968 and 1980 the most victimised were United States nationals, with West Europeans coming second, U.S. diplomats, businessmen and military—seen as symbols of Western power and affluence— remain the major targets. It is significant that over 38 per cent of all incidents in this period involved U.S. citizens or premises.

Statistics on international terrorist bombings and attacks on diplomats from 1977 to May 1983 provide useful data on targets, victims and venues of attacks, but they do not provide any clearcut evidence of the success of particular states' anti-terrorist policies. For example, although France, which suffered 126 international terrorist bombings in this period, may be thought to be especially vulnerable because of its weakness in dealing with terrorism, this is contradicted by the fact that West Germany, a country of similar size and political vulnerability comes third in the league with 118 attacks. It is also significant that among the thirteen countries which accounted for 68 per cent of all explosive incidents are included some of the hard-line anti-terrorist countries such as the United Kingdom (64), Spain (61) and Israel (49). Moreover, the greatest number of incidents involving diplomats occurred in the U.S.A. in this period (377). This shows that there must be much more complex causal factors at work, capable of producing higher levels of international terrorist activity even against a country with a well-known hard-line policy against terrorism, and with stringent immigration and entry procedures.

Any serious and prolonged terrorist campaign has implications for the international system. If it succeeds, alone or in combination with other methods of struggle, in overthrowing a regime, then foreign policy, alignment and the international balance of power will all be affected. Even when the challenge to the regime is unsuccessful the terrorist movement and its target regime inevitably seek moral and diplomatic support, resources or even military aid from potential allies abroad. Today, as a result of modem revolutions in communications and technology, serious domestic terrorist conflicts almost invariably spill across international borders or catch foreign citizens in the cross-fire.

For the purposes of the present discussion, however, terrorism is defined as international when it is directed across international frontiers or when the targets are foreign citizens or property located in the terrorists' country of origin. Using these crude criteria, the figures show a 30 per cent rate of increase in international terrorist incidents between 1980 and 1982 and an even higher rate of increase in 1983. More worrying still is the fact that since 1980, taking domestic and international terrorist incidents together, there has been an annual increase of 13 per cent in the number of deaths caused by terrorism.

Roughly 25 per cent of these incidents are either state-sponsored or state-directed. The sponsorship involvement of these rogue states in international terrorism ranges from moral and diplomatic encouragement to material assistance by such means as weapons, training, funds and sanctuary.

A smaller number of these terrorist states resort to using directly controlled hit-squads to undertake bombings, assassinations and other missions abroad. But the more usual method is to employ proxies, such as a client terrorist movement already based in the country, or expatriate volunteers.

States resorting to international terrorism are in most cases simply exporting the violence which they routinely use as a weapon of internal repression and social control. The present chapter will not be addressing the huge and important subject of domestic state terror.

There is an extensive historical and social science literature on this field. However, as Richard Falk and Michael Walzer, among others, have pointed out, it is much harder for the international community to evolve any effective humanitarian intervention or constraints against this internal regime terror. The very framework of international law and organisation is designed to preclude international interference in the domestic affairs of states, even in cases of the most blatant and massive violation of human rights.

It is also important to note that state-sponsored international terrorism is not a novel phenomenon. Stalin sent his agents abroad to murder those he judged to be enemies of the Soviet Union. Trotsky was perhaps the most famous victim of Stalin's international terrorism. There were scores of others. The fascist states also used international terrorism between the wars.

The present international situation is clearly conducive to the increasing use of state-sponsored international terrorism. The Soviet Union has always been prepared to use this weapon on a very selective and opportunistic basis, wherever it thinks that this will serve Soviet strategic interests. It has encouraged its Communist allies to take a major share of the burden of assistance to client movements. Ideologically, the Soviet Union justifies this as fraternal help to national liberation struggles and giving history a push towards the inevitable victory of world communism. At another level, the Soviet Union and other Communist countries have also used the weapon of international terrorism as a means of silencing and intimidating exiled dissidents and hunting down those alleged to have betrayed the Party.

State-sponsored terrorism, along with all the other modes of unconventional warfare, is particularly attractive in an age of nuclear strategy. It does not carry the degree of risk of escalation to superpower involvement and the nuclear threshold which accompanies full-scale conventional war. It is cheap. It can also bring high yields. The Khomeini regime in Iran was able to inflict a crippling psychological blow on the American Administration by the most daring act of state-sponsored terrorism in recent history, the seizure of the entire American diplomatic mission in Tehran in 1979. It was a blow from which the Administration never really recovered, and undoubtedly ensured that President Carter would not be re-elected. The massacre of 241 American marines in Beirut by a truck bombing was another instance of the impact of terrorism on the policy or the world's strongest military power. In the wake of this horrifying event, President Reagan had no real choice but to succumb to the chorus of domestic demands for American military withdrawal from Lebanon.

There is still some debate as to whether this attack was instigated or abetted by the Syrians or the Iranians. What we can be sure about is that other hostile states will be tempted to emulate this method of intimidating and coercing rival regimes and their citizens. Not least of its attractions is that the true identity of the state behind the attack can be disguised. If the terrorist action proves abortive, the state sponsor avoids the humiliation of a conventional and public military defeat. The major characteristics of this method of unconventional warfare can be briefly summarised as follows:

(1) State-sponsored international terrorism is always conducted clandestinely. Even though terrorist states such as Libya and Iran have frequently uttered general threats of exporting violence against alleged enemies, they naturally avoid any precise reference to the timing, targets and nature of the attacks, for this would rob them of the advantage of surprise, and could enable the victim state to take necessary measures to prevent the atrocity.

(2) Terrorist states always deny responsibility for specific international terrorist acts. This places the onus of proof on the victim state. It also thwarts any concerted international legal sanctions against the rogue state. Terrorist states, unlike terrorist movements, do not need to leave their signature on the crime. They do not resort to international terrorism to become known to the world. Their generalised public threats are enough. The real purposes of state-sponsored international terrorism are somewhat different: the hunting-down of exiled opponents and dissidents, the waging of surrogate war against an adversary state, and the export of revolution by means of supporting client terrorist groups abroad.

(3) State-sponsored international terrorism invariably involves the use of specialist intelligence and security agencies. These recruit and fund the assassination teams or client groups used to carry out missions. On occasions they carry out the attacks themselves. Almost invariably, they operate with the full knowledge and co-operation of their diplomatic missions in the target country: this provides them with an invaluable cover, the guarantee of diplomatic immunity, and the use of diplomatic premises and the diplomatic bag for obtaining and storing weapons, ammunition and explosives.

(4) State-sponsored terrorists almost invariably have access to more advanced weaponry and greater firepower than autonomous 'freelance' groups. For example, states have made available rocket launchers, SAM-7s and a whole range of modern automatic weapons. In addition, many of the terrorist states, such as Libya, North Korea, South Yemen and Iran, offer intensive training in weapons, explosives and tactics, in camps within their own borders. They can provide much more substantial funds to support terrorism than the ordinary freelance terrorist group could ever command. And, last but not least among their advantages, rogue states can also provide the necessary sanctuary and protection for the members of the terrorist cell after the mission has been completed.

(5) To an even greater extent than with domestic terrorist groups, the state waging international terrorism has the tactical advantage of surprise. It can use its superior resources and communications to hit the target state at any point of its choice, not only within the boundaries of the victim state, but also against its diplomatic personnel, embassies, business premises, aircraft, ships and expatriate personnel, and families anywhere in the world. In messages sent to American, British and French embassies in Cairo and Jakarta recently, the Iranian-backed Islamic Jihad threatened attacks of this very nature against what it called 'imperialist' countries which had participated in the multinational force (MNF) in Beirut. And in 1980 Colonel Gaddafi sent his hit squads into seven different countries. They carried out fourteen separate attacks abroad against Libyan exiles in 1980 alone, murdering eleven. British and international outrage and condemnation following the shooting of the policewoman, Yvonne Fletcher, by an armed member

of the Libyan People's Bureau in St. James's Square has not brought any apparent shift in the behaviour of Colonel Gaddafi. In a speech at Miaitiqah air base in June, Gaddafi stated:

> We are capable of exporting terrorism to the heart of America... We are also capable of physical liquidation and destruction and arson inside America. If we have to export, then we shall export terrorism to America.

(6) A common feature of all state-sponsored international terrorist incidents is the strong psychological reaction among the people of the victimised state. Almost invariably, and with the encouragement of government and media, the blame is attached to the state which sponsored or directed the attack. The people will direct their outrage and desire for retribution against the rogue state, its representatives and its regime. Thus, however much the perpetrator tries publicly to deny any responsibility for a specific crime, the public in the victim state will demand some immediate and forceful punitive action. This immediately worsens formal relations between the countries, heightens tensions, and places the victim government under enormous pressure to act to avenge the attack in some dramatic way. This psychological effect was vividly demonstrated after the shooting in St. James's Square on 17 April 1984.

State-sponsored international attacks are undoubtedly presenting the Western democratic states with the most difficult problems of response. On the one hand, public and media outrage is creating pressure for urgent forceful action. On the other, governments which take seriously their responsibilities under international and domestic law are severely constrained by the limitations of the law and legal processes. It is by no means always a straightforward matter for the police and the authorities to obtain the necessary evidence to establish the precise identity of the perpetrator of the crime. It is still more difficult to obtain the necessary legal proof of the role of a foreign power as instigator and abettor. The terrorist state will, for reasons that have already been mentioned, do its utmost to hide its fingerprints.

Even if these severe handicaps to judicial response against state-sponsored terrorism are disregarded, there are other major obstacles to forceful punitive action. First and foremost is the fact that the victim state is likely to have diplomats, businessmen and perhaps a whole expatriate community living in the territory of the rogue state. From day one of the Libyan Embassy siege, the British government was acutely aware of this dilemma. It knew that British people could be taken hostage in a Teheran-type action, with all the agonising consequences suffered by the Americans in 1979-80. Gaddafi's reputation for unpredictability and fanaticism is certainly comparable to that of Ayatollah Khomeini. One could not gamble with the lives of the British people at the mercy of such a regime..

A second major constraint is that even where circumstances may permit a forceful unilateral response against the terrorist state, strong international action against the offender, even by friendly Western countries, is almost impossible to obtain. Other states will instinctively place other considerations above any general concern about terrorist threats against the innocent and the rule of law. All the Western democracies generally make a ritual condemnation of international terrorist outrages, but they are apparently unwilling to put at risk potentially lucrative trade links or to close the door to what are possibly valuable commodities and markets. They fear that if they take any strong stand to boycott or sanction the offending state, commercial competitors will simply move in to take over their share of the market.

A sad but vivid illustration of the Western states' failure to take effective combined action against state-sponsored international terrorism occurred in 1980. America, Western Europe's major ally and protector, was looking to the European Community states to join in firm economic sanctions to bring pressure on the Iranian regime to release the American hostages. After much hesitation and evasion, the E.E.C. foreign ministers did, rather to their own surprise, hammer out an agreed package of European trade sanctions. But when the British Foreign Secretary brought the proposed measures to the British Parliament for approval, they were sabotaged as a result of a well-timed back-bench revolt led by the Labour M.P. for West Lothian, Mr T. Dalyell. Because the British would not implement the package, the whole effort at a European Community stand on the issue was undermined. Should anyone be very surprised that there has been a similar absence of concerted Western response following the St. James's Square outrage?

It is more realistic and sensible to concentrate on trying to learn some appropriate lessons from the Libyan People's Bureau affair and similar events, and try to minimise the chances of any similar abuse of diplomatic privileges in future.

It is to be hoped that the government's understandable insistence on keeping their inquiry into the affair confidential will not mean that it is any less rigorous and searching in its investigations. Why, in view of the Libyan Embassy's known activities in 1980, was the so-called People's Bureau allowed to continue in London? Why was there not more stringent control over the accreditation of diplomats and the granting of diplomatic immunity? What is the truth about the transfer of American intelligence about Gaddafi's instructions to London? Was it passed on to London? When? And why was no counter-action taken?

It was largely because of the insistence of the British Prime Minister and the Foreign Secretary that the subject of international terrorism appeared at all in the discussions of the London Economic Summit, 9-10 June 1984.

It might have been expected that the inclusion of international terrorism would be supported by all the major participant states. Almost half of all international terrorist attacks in recent years have been directed at American personnel and facilities abroad. No less than 17.6 per cent of all bomb attacks against diplomatic targets in the period 1977 to May 1983 were directed at the United States. It may also not be generally realised that the United States was the second most popular venue for terrorist explosive bombings in this same period, with 122 attacks.

The most favoured venue was France with 126 international terrorist bombings compared to Britain's mere 64 in the same period. Yet France was reportedly totally against including a discussion of terrorism at the Summit, and the French were apparently the major obstacle to any more binding and effective commitment to international action on the subject. The French Foreign Minister, Mr Claude Cheysson, argued that the Summit was designed exclusively for economic matters, and had no remit to deal with 'political' subjects. On the specific matter of sanctions against terrorist states, the French candidly stated their opposition to taking any steps that would damage French economic interests in these countries.

The final Summit declaration on international terrorism was, therefore, patched together with considerable difficulty. There are general complaints that it is not sufficiently precise and that it fails to issue any binding resolution on collective sanctions against states engaging in international terrorism. Nevertheless, the declaration does combine some eminently sensible general statements which together amount to a viable overall policy for Western response.

The Summit viewed with serious concern the increasing involvement of states and governments in acts of terrorism, including the abuse of diplomatic immunity. Apparently it was unable to secure unanimous approval for a set of anti-terrorist measures, but it reported that the following proposals 'found support in the discussion':

— Closer co-operation and co-ordination between police and security organisations and other relevant authorities, especially in the exchange of information, intelligence and technical knowledge;

— Scrutiny by each country of gaps in its national legislation which might be exploited by terrorists;

— Use of powers of the receiving state under the Vienna Convention in such matters as the size of diplomatic missions, and the number of buildings enjoying diplomatic immunity;

— Action by each country to review the sale of weapons to states supporting terrorism;

— Consultation and as far as possible co-operation over the expulsion or exclusion from their countries of known terrorists, including persons of diplomatic status involved in terrorism.

What has been entirely overlooked by many commentators is what the declaration does not say. It does not make any reckless commitments to a policy of totally militarised response against terrorist states. Yet there were some strident voices in Washington demanding what was misleadingly called 'proactive' measures against such states, by which was apparently meant the bombing of terrorist training centres and bases, or even the removal of the regime by force. If such dangerous policies were ever implemented they would not eradicate international terrorism. They would only succeed in substituting the greater evil of full-scale war, with all its attendant death and devastation and dangers of escalation, for the lesser evil of terrorism.

To the great credit of the Summit leaders such false panaceas were discarded. The policy of response contained in their declaration is, as it must be, entirely compatible with the preservation of the democratic values and the rule of law which they had so strongly proclaimed earlier in their proceedings.

6

Brownback-Harkin Amendment

The latest legislative move in the US Congress is likely to boost Indian hopes for long term relief from many of the American nuclear sanctions. But they might also suck India into the quagmire of American domestic politics over the ratification of the Comprehensive Test Ban Treaty (CTBT). A Bill introduced by a bipartisan group of Senators, called the Brownback-Harkin amendment, proposes to suspend for a period of five years a number of American sanctions currently in force against both India and Pakistan.

The proposed legislation seeks to delink the suspension of sanctions from Indian and Pakistani signatures on the CTBT and deny the US President, Mr Bill Clinton, the discretionary power to selectively lift the sanctions against India and Pakistan.

Senior officials of the Clinton Administration, however, are cautioning against expectations that India and Pakistan can walk out of the sanctions regime without an adherence to the CTBT. "It will be a misreading of the Bill to believe that sanctions against India and Pakistan will be removed without concrete progress in the nuclear talks," a senior official of the Clinton Administration said. There is a long way to go, however, before the Brownback-Harkin amendment becomes US law. The legislation will have to be approved in the Senate and a similar move will have to be approved by the House of Representatives.

Once the Senate and the House reconcile their differences, the President will have to approve the Bill. Even if the President signs the Bill and the sanctions go, the official said, the President has he authority "to reimpose the sanctions against India and Pakistan and lift them at the discretion of the Administration". Senior Senate staffers involved with the Brownback-Harkin amendment concede that Mr Clinton has the power to reimpose sanctions but want to make it "politically difficult" for him to do so.

The Brownback-Harkin amendment comes at a time when the US nuclear negotiations with India and Pakistan are poised delicately, and the Clinton Administration is getting ready for the hard political battle in the Senate to get the CTBT approved.

The Brownback-Harkin Bill is the first step in the current legislative year to extend and expand the Brownback amendment passed last, year to give some immediate sanctions relief to India and Pakistan.

After the Pokhran and Chagai tests of last May, Mr Clinton imposed sweeping economic and military sanctions against India and Pakistan that were mandated by the US non-proliferation law called the Glenn amendment.

Last year a group of Senators led by Mr Sam Brownback led the legislative initiative that gave the President authority to waive some of the Glenn sanctions. Citing the progress in the nuclear dialogue with India and Pakistan, in particular their readiness to adhere to the CTBT by September 1999, Mr Clinton eased some of the sanctions last November. Senate staffers say the

Brownback-Harkin amendment takes a "long-term view of US relations with India and Pakistan" and hopes to move them forward".

With this in mind, the new legislation expands the Brownback amendment through a five-year suspension of many sanctions, and broadens it by opening the door for limited military assistance. But it retains the restrictions on the transfer of daul-use technologies to the subcontinent and the sale of arms that will significantly improve the combat capabilities of India and Pakistan.

Administration officials welcome the Brownback-Harkin amendment as reflecting the new political willingness in the US Congress to construct "a post-Glenn regime for South Asia", but will not accept efforts by the Congress to undercut the Administration's negotiating strategy with India and Pakistan. They insist that the President, who has the responsibility to conduct American foreign policy, needs "greater flexibility" and the discretionary power to pursue US non-proliferation objectives as well as a "sanctions-free" relationship with the subcontinent.

Senate sources are confident of gaining substantive political support for the Brownback-Harkin Amendment cutting across political and ideological differences in the US Congress. It enjoys the backing of Mr Jesse Helms, the powerful chairman of the Senate Foreign Relations Committee. But they concede the Administration could put up a tough fight by mobilising the strong non-proliferation sentiments in the Congress.

A senior Administration official said in Washington that India and Pakistan should not "concern themselves with the US ratification debate on the CTBT and delay their own decisions on adhering to the treaty". He hoped that the decisions in New Delhi and Islamabad to join the treaty would be based on the "calculation of their own national interests".

The economic sanctions imposed against India in the wake of the nuclear tests at Pokhran last year have begun to hurt. During 1998-99, external assistance is likely to show a shortfall of over Rs 1,227 crores, resulting in the net external assistance falling sharply to Rs 910 crores against the Budget estimates of Rs 2,337 crores.

The biggest shortfall has been in the case of the World Bank (International Bank for Reconstruction and Development). In this case, a major portion of the expected assistance failed to materialise during the current financial year, with the result that against an expectation of Rs 1,527 crores, what India received was only Rs 626 crores. The shortfall was in the region of Rs 901 crores. On the bilateral front too, India's two major donors, Japan and Germany, provided less than what was expected. The shortfall in case of Japan was as high as Rs 378 crores while Rs 117 crores did not come from Germany.

However, some other donors contributed slightly more than what had been committed earlier, which helped in making up the shortfall somewhat. Consequently, the year-end estimates show that multilateral assistance would be short by Rs 693.63 crores while bilateral assistance would be short by Rs 533.43 crores.

The shortfall in assistance has occurred in case of grants and commodity assistance also. Against the Budget estimates of receiving Rs 1,053 crores during 1998-99, actual inflow is expected to be Rs 812 crores only. This figure is likely to go down further to Rs 715 crores during 1999-2000. At the same time, India's repayment obligations are rising. Against an estimated total repayment of Rs 7,657 crores during 1998-99, the actual repayment is likely to end up slightly higher at Rs 7,856 crores, In the coming year, the repayments are expected to go up even higher to Rs, 8,155 crores.

Though India has a comfortable foreign exchange reserves at present, the inflow of external assistance helps in meeting the repayment obligations on past loans. This process has been on for a long time, with the multilateral and bilateral assistance for every year being decided a the India Development Forum held sometime in May-June.

In 1998, this meeting was scheduled for June 30 at Tokyo, but was one of the first meetings to be put off indefinitely immediately after the Pokhran tests. No dates have been fixed for the current year's meeting either and as things stand today, the meeting is unlikely unless there is some concrete positive movement in the on-going Indo-US dialogue being conducted between the External Affairs Minister, Mr Jaswant Singh, and the US Deputy Secretary of State, Mr Strobe Talbott. In case the current impasse continues for the second year running, India will start feeling the pinch in terms of an outflow of foreign exchange to meet its repayment obligations.

US nuclear and other sensitive high-tech will continue to be out of bounds for India as long as it does not sip the non-proliferation treaty (NPT) even if current problems between the two sides over India's nuclear tests are sorted out, a high-ranking US official has said. "Even if current problems following the Indian nuclear tests are resolved, India will not get access to nuclear aid and other high-tech on the same basis as China as long as she does not sign the NPT," Mr Matthew R Daley, a member of Deputy Secretary Strobe Talbott's negotiating team, said in Washington on Jan. 13. However, an exception could perhaps be made regarding civilian nuclear power, he told a seminar on "Recent and prospective developments in Southern Asia", days before the two sides were scheduled to meet to iron out differences over disarmament and proliferation issues following the May tests.

The forthcoming round of talks between key interlocutors—Mr Talbott and External Affairs Minister Jaswant Singh—in New Delhi later in January will promote better understanding of mutual concerns but no breakthroughs are expected, he said at the Henry Stimson Center, a Washington-based think-tank. Significantly, India has called for lifting of sanctions on sale of high technology besides recognition of New Delhi's right to a credible minimum deterrent, a deterrent that is survivable and provides adequate response to an attack, before its signs the NPT.

Outlining the progress on key issues after several rounds of talks between the two sides, Mr Daley said that both sides had developed a better appreciation of each other's concerns and positions than they had in June but much remains to be done. The US, he said, "is trying of reconcile its interests in the viability of the global non-proliferation regime with the security interests of India and Pakistan ... both sides recognise that there is progress is to be made." "There is no deadlock and there is ample scope for further discussion, for understanding and refinement in positions, and I am hopeful there will be further progress," he said. "But we don't expect dramatic breakthroughs certainly at this stage." "I don't just see in this narrow discussion rubric right now the makings of a deadlock. We may end up there but we are not there in the middle of January," Mr Daley said. "Obviously; the shape of our ties is going to be influenced by what kind of common ground we reach on the non-proliferation agenda." At the core of talks with Pakistan, Mr Daley said, are "various points of contention between Islamabad and New Delhi, including in particular

Kashmir, that the two countries would have to resolve bilaterally." India, he said, has been adamant in rejecting global initiatives. That does not help resolve these issues. "While the US understands India's position, that will not exclude offering our views and specific suggestions as to how India and Pakistan might address their disputes."

On Prime Minister Vajpayee's statement that India must have a credible minimum deterrent, Mr Daley said, "We will discuss what that means in concrete terms." He expected this to be helped by India's strategic defence review now under way.

On the CTBT, he said, "the Indian Prime Minister has said India is committed to converting its voluntary moratorium to a de jure obligation." "India is engaged in discussions with the US and other countries which it is prepared to conclude successfully, for the purpose of ensuring that the entry into force of the treaty is not delayed beyond September this year.

US officials on Jan. 23 expressed surprise over reports in a section of the Indian media suggesting that the Clinton administration was willing to lift economic sanctions without India signing the Comprehensive Test Ban Treaty (CTBT) or abandoning its proposed missile test. They dismissed the reports as "erroneous"; making it clear that there was no change in US policy. These were mandatory sanctions and would be withdrawn only after India had met the non-proliferation concerns outlined by the international community, including the UN Security Council.

The reports, appearing days before the 8th round of the US-India non-proliferation dialogue in New Delhi, created a virtual stir in the State Department's South Asia bureau. Originally it thought of issuing a "clarification" but a meeting of its senior officials decided against such a formal response, fearing that it might only add to the confusion on the eve of Deputy Secretary of State Strobe Talbott's visit to New Delhi.

In fact, it is claimed that the reports were based on a January 16 speech of Mr Talbott at Stanford University and US officials maintained that the Deputy Secretary had not said what had been attributed to him. He had not given any indication of unconditional lifting of sanctions as had been made out in the news reports. According to the text of the speech, he referred to his trip to India next week for the parallel dialogues the US has been conducting with India and Pakistan in the aftermath of their nuclear tests. "Because of those tests, we are confronted with a lamentable but for the foreseeable future, irreversible fact: India and Pakistan have formally and overtly demonstrated that they have nuclear weapons. In so doing, they made themselves in 1998 even more part of the problem of regional and global proliferation than they were before," Mr Talbott said. He, however, said, "They can, in 1999, if they so choose, move back in the direction of being part of the solution—and they can do that while enhancing their own security at the same time." "One way they can move back in the right direction in the political sphere is by intensifying contacts and confidence-building measures, including the issue of Kashmir," Mr Talbott remarked.

He said they could also do so by taking four "important steps." These are: adhering to the CTBT, agreeing to a moratorium on the further production of fissile material, demonstrating prudence and restraint in the development, flight testing and storage of ballistic missiles and nuclear-capable aircraft and strengthening export controls. "The essence of the argument that were making to the Indians and Pakistanis is that in presuming what we believe in their ill-advised reliance on nuclear deterrence, we hope very much they will not jeopardise the other, political and economic dimensions of their own safety," he added.

India had not agreed to sign the Comprehensive Test Ban Treaty (CTBT) and there was no change in the Government's stand on the issue, the External Affairs Minister, Mr Jaswant Singh, told the Lok Sabha on Feb. 24. "The answer is a clear, explicit and unambiguous no," Mr Singh said to a spate of supplementaries during Question Hour on whether the Government had agreed to sign the CTBT during the several rounds of Indo-US strategic talks. "The Government has not agreed to sign it.

The Government's stand remains what it has been, what it has stated in the House, what the Prime Minister had stated in the UN General Assembly," Mr Singh said to a question by Prof P.J. Kurien of Congress(I). The Prime Minister, Mr Atal Behari Vajpayee, had stated that India was prepared to bring to a successful conclusion discussions with key interlocutors on a range of issues, including the CTBT, so that the entry into force of the treaty was not delayed beyond September this year.

On the issue of minimum nuclear deterrence, Mr Singh asserted that India "will not accept any aspect that attempts to explain what its minimum nuclear deterrent ought to be" either through "suggestion or intrusive measures or in any other aspect." He said, "India shall define its own requirements and parameters of nuclear deterrent on the basis of our assessment of what our security requirements and considerations are. This is a sovereign function." "It is, of course, subject to review and alterations in accordance with the alternate security requirements," he stressed. Asked about progress in talks with the US on nonproliferation issues, he said the discussions had narrowed and were now focused on four issues—CTBT, FMCT, defence posture and export control—from the earlier 13 items. "That in itself is an arithmetical measurement of the movement that has taken place," he said while apparently referring to the eight rounds of talks he has held with the US Deputy Secretary of State, Mr Strobe Talbott.

It is perhaps not known by many people that India has been one of the earliest advocates of the Fissile Material Cut-Off Treaty (hereafter referred to as the FMCT). This was strictly in consonance with the stand taken by India from the days of Jawaharlal Nehru in favour of general and complete disarmament, specially nuclear disarmament.

Way back in 1966, India joined a group of the non-aligned nations to urge the cessation of fissile materials production for weapons purposes. This proposal was designed as a collateral measure to the NPT.

Years later in 1988, it also formed part of the famous Rajiv Gandhi plan for nuclear disarmament to be pursued within a time-bound framework. In 1993, India co-sponsored a resolution, alongwith the United States, in the UN General Assembly on the FMCT.

In 1995, the then Prime Minister P.V. Narasimha Rao said that India shared the US views on the imperative for a universal ban on fissile material production for nuclear weapons.

In other words, India was agreeable to negotiate the FMCT. Recently on August 11, 1998, the Conference on Disarmament (CD) in Geneva finally agreed—after years of impasse—to convene an Ad-hoc Committee to negotiate a ban on the production of *new* fissile material, mainly plutonium and highly enriched uranium (HEU) generally used in the production of nuclear weapons. Paradoxically, post-Pokhran-II India has overcome its initial hesitancy and agreed to participate in good faith in the negotiations for the early conclusion of a universal, non-discriminatory and internationally and effectively verifiable treaty banning the future production of fissile materials for nuclear weapons and other nuclear explosive devices. This has been described by the Geneva-based diplomats as a significant move in India's contemporary nuclear diplomacy.

International pressure and sanctions might have been additional factors in India's decision to participate in the Geneva negotiations on the FMCT. Post-Chagai Pakistan too has joined the negotiations and so also Israel (reluctantly though and reportedly after US assurance in regard to its security sensitivities). Indian Ambassador at the Geneva negotiations, Savitri Kunadi, said that India had always taken a pro-active position on the FMCT (the introductory remarks justify that) and added that India was ready to participate in appropriate activities to move the negotiations forward.

In view of the above, the debate should now be focused on how India should carry out its diplomacy in Geneva when the Ad-hoc Committee reconvenes for negotiations in early 1999 and not on whether India should participate in the FMCT negotiations or not.

The Prime Minister's statements in recent weeks and his Ambassador's statement at Geneva referred to earlier have shown beyond all proof that India is very much in the FMCT negotiations. The various options available to India are: sign the FMCT as it is, sign it with conditions, sign the CTBT, declare moratorium on the FMCT, and reject the FMCT.

The conditions could broadly be:

(1) That we must be allowed to retain our existing stocks of plutonium and HEU, side by side India must

ensure that it has the minimum nuclear deterrent available to it.

(2) An agreement commitment by the NWS to destroy the excess plutonium stock available with them and reportedly stored in their warheads; a point on which they have not agreed so far. They cannot obviously continue with this stand once serious negotiations on the FMCT begin in Geneva.

(3) Insist on tritium and deuterium fuels available with the NWS—these are used in the production of thermonuclear devices—be brought under the FMCT ban. As of now, the ban is confined to only plutonium and HEU. Alternatively if India has acquired the capacity to extract tritium from the heavy water used in power plants, we would lose in no way by agreeing to the FMCT provisions in this regard.

(4) Oppose IAEA inspection of our sites and plants and favour some kind of a new agency set-up for this purpose. It is reported that China and Russia are favourable to this idea. India should coordinate its strategies with them as well as Pakistan and Israel in this regard. Questions of violations of sovereignty are very sensitive issues and they have the potential to block the conclusion of the FMCT. Hence they should be handled carefully. This issue has to be looked at from the perspective of the need for enhancing the confidence levels of countries like India, Pakistan and Israel, against the background of their threat perceptions.

(5) India should retain the right of deployment of its missiles and warheads in sectors and at the time it perceives it necessary. Security considerations do not permit a moratorium on fissile material production. Alternatively, this condition can be relaxed if Pakistan

is prepared for a ban on deployment and China agrees to withdraw its deployments on its India sector. This issue, which has a direct bearing on India's national security, needs to be handled with finesse by the government and its negotiators at the Geneva talks. The key issue with reference to the FMCT is not just as to whether the Treaty is discriminatory or global, but whether India has a minimum nuclear deterrent to ensure its national security which can be adequately safeguarded. This condition must be kept in mind before acceding to the treaty.

(6) India must also press for early negotiations on the need for signing a convention on banning tactical nuclear weapons.

(7) Now that India is a declared nuclear weapon state (reportedly when the Indian Ambassador at the Geneva meeting referred to India being a nuclear weapon state in her statement, no delegate protested, something which has been seen as a positive sign for India by the Western diplomats) it is only fair that India demands equal benefit to her and other NWS from the FMCT.

In addition to the above conditions, our ruling elite must also ensure that the major Opposition parties are taken into confidence and brought round to their point of view.

On their part, the Opposition parties should refrain from taking partisan views and cooperate with the government. We could also perhaps wait for the ratification of the CTBT by the US Senate and our own accession to it. An unratified CTBT would render the FMCT largely meaningless. Our decision-makers would do well to keep this factor in mind.

As regards the possible benefits to India from

adopting the strategy of signing the FMCT with conditions, the following benefits can be identified:

(a) India would succeed in forestalling Pakistan's planned reprocessing programme;

(b) maintain the balance in its favour vis-a-vis Pakistan insofar as fissile material stocks are concerned;

(c) succeed in freezing China's fissile material stock;

(d) if we succeed in committing the US and other NWS to destroy the excess stock of fissile material they reportedly have, we, would be contributing to security;

(e) if tritium and deuterium stocks are also brought under FMCT ban, that would be an additional input for international security and eventually nuclear disarmament.

As for the risks involved, signing the FMCT with the conditions outlined above, would entail no great risks to our national security and sovereignty. The NWS might, however, argue that a weak FMCT may not be very effective and the signatories will find loopholes in it and might as well cheat it on its provisions, which of course no signatory should try to do.

The reactions of the United States and the other NWS to India's accession to the FMCT would hopefully be positive. They would be happy that we are part of the FMCT and their non-proliferation regime/agenda.

May be they will do greater business with us, remove sanctions (hopefully, sanctions of all types will go much earlier contingent on the bargain that India is seeking to sign the CTBT), consider India for technology transfer and may be even willing at some later stage to consider India's claim for a permanent seat in the UN Security Council. China might be happy to have India on board and so would Russia be in all likelihood. As for Pakistan, their leaders would predictably follow, the Indian model/strategy vis-a-vis the FMCT. Signing the Treaty with the conditions like a ban on tritium, convention on tactical nuclear weapons, insistence on destruction of excess stock of plutonium available with the P-5 nations would result in the FMCT becoming genuinely effective and a catalyst for a time-bound elimination of nuclear weapons.

The FMCT should in the longer run lead to greater confidence building and consequently reduce the damages/risks from nuclear weapons to regional and international security. Finally, it is only appropriate that we should remind ourselves that signing the FMCT would result in a strengthening of India's national security and strategic position, as it would prevent possible arms race and an escalation of Pakistani and Chinese threat.

It would also lead to an overall improvement of the strategic environment and pave the way for improvements in non-political fields and in turn lead to nuclear restraing by India, Pakistan and hopefully China.

The challenge lies in negotiating an FMCT which would confer benefits on all, the old-time NWS and the new entrants to the nuclear club, and India's role in the dawn of such a treaty can neither be minimised nor given up.

7

Roller-Coaster Talk

In an amazing and outright denial of what had been widely reported in the American press after the latest round in New Delhi of the Jaswant Singh-Strobe Talbott talks, the Indian Parliament was categorically assured by the Minister for External Affairs that there had been no agreement of any kind reached between the two sides about India's signing the CTBT as things stand at present.

This is all the more surprising since the statements originating from Washington were not only attributed to Talbott himself reporting to the US Secretary of State Madeleine Albright immediately after his return to Washington, but had emanated variously and in quick succession from Assistant Secretary of State Charles Inderfurth, National Security Adviser Sandy Berger, and State Department spokesman Arthur Rubin.

The distinct impression sought to be given in these statements was that, in return for the Indian side agreeing to subscribe to the CTBT, even ahead of the deadline of September this year, the US would no longer stand in the way of World Bank and IMF loans from being extended to New Delhi. Many serious questions arise from the piquant situation that has arisen from all this. First and foremost, why should Talbott have conveyed to his immediate superiors something so different from what had actually happened at the Delhi talks, if the statement now made in the Indian Parliament is to be believed? On the other hand, why was there no immediate clarification given by the Indian Government when the Talbott statement came out in the press? Why did seasoned American officials make public their version of what is said to have transpired at the confidential negotiations on such a sensitive matter? In plain words, who is telling the truth or is the truth to be found somewhere in between these conflicting statements?

Perhaps, as Professor Brahma Chellaney has written in a thoughtful article in the winter 1998-99 issue of Survival, published by the International Institute of Strategic Studies, the situation has arisen because India is "at odds with itself and increasingly marginalised through its vacillations and 'revolving-door' politics", which makes it vulnerable to external coercion. He goes on, "It has not built the military power needed to command respect, the economic strength to gain leverage or the distinct political philosophy to lead others." If that is indeed the case, it is highly regrettable and no time should be lost in setting matters right.

Let us examine the statement made on February 26 by the External Affairs Minister in Parliament, bearing in mind that it was in response to an uproar created by all the opposition parties in regard to the testimony by Secretary of State Madeleine Albright before the US Senate that India had agreed to adhere to the Comprehensive Test Ban Treaty by the end of the year.

The Minister had categorically denied that there was any change in the official stand as outlined by him on February 24. "I can hardly be held to account for what someone says in Washington. Our stand is clear". It was rather curious for him to say this, since it was not just 'someone', but the US Secretary of State giving her testimony before the Senate, and has to be taken very seriously.

Moreover, the question arises as to why no clarification was issued by the Indian Government, when so many statements by senior officials were being floated in the US media and also carried in the Indian press, about Talbott's version of the New Delhi talks.

In his statement in Parliament on February 24, the Minister had maintained that at the eighth round of Indo US talks, no secret understanding had been reached on the US lifting some of the economic sanctions imposed on India in return for subscribing to the CTBT. He categorically declared that India will not let any other country decide what should be our minimum nuclear deter rent.

If that was so, why was there the need for India to have embarked on so many rounds of talks with the US in which, by all accounts, pressure had been mounted to get us to spell out not merely the level of nuclear deterrence that we intended to have, but also the disposition and deployment of these weapons, besides tying to place stringent limits on our missile development? As it is, an essential aspect of our nuclear deterrence is the development and testing of our missiles which has been now put on hold.

There is no indication todate as to when this will be resumed. One would be fully justified, in these circumstances, to view the ongoing talks with a high degree of scepticism. The desire to be all things to all men has been Indians' bane throughout history. The anxiety to be applauded by others was evident in the Indian Government's unilateral statement, immediately following the nuclear tests in May 1998, that India would not conduct any more tests and would be prepared to missile production and deployment. An expert level meeting of officials was held in New Delhi in November 1998 and India assured the US side that as a responsible nuclear weapon state it would not only behave responsibly but also take steps to make stringent laws regarding export controls.

Both the sides described the talks as helpful and saw great prospects for continuing cooperation between the two countries in that area. Prime Minister Vajpayee's address to the UN General Assembly earlier in New York, where he had talked of India doing its best to bring to a successful conclusion its negotiations with the key interlocutors and not delaying the entry into force clause of the CTBT beyond September 1999 were seen as positive and helpful signals emerging from India. It is against this background that the eighth round of India-US strategic dialogue took place in New Delhi for three days in January this year.

The eighth round of talks was significant because a conscious decision was taken by both the sides to broaden the scope of Indo-US strategic dialogue-to a level where something should be done to improve the bilateral relations between the world's two richest and largest democracies.

It is also useful to remember that the talks between Mr Talbott and Mr Jaswant Singh were preceded by a telephonic conversation between the American President and the Indian Prime Minister. This only goes to show how much importance the two sides attached to the strategic dialogue. Prime Minister Vajpayee showed yet another gesture by agreeing to a meeting with Strobe Talbott after the two negotiators had concluded their parleys. That India and United States were serious about resolving the strategic content of their bilateral relations were demonstrated by the meeting that the

Vice-Chairman of the US Joint Chief of Staff, General Joseph Ralston had with top Indian defence officials. These talks were seen as an effort to remove the constraints and Irritants that had crept in following the conflicting perceptions on the nuclear issue and open up the possibilities of cooperation in other areas including the military sphere. The New Delhi talks were preceded by a remark by, Mr Strobe Talbott which gives a cue to the importance attached by him to his parleys with Mr Jaswant Singh. He told the Presspersons before his talks with Mr Singh: "I think it is high time this relationship is put on a much stronger footing." And after the first day's talks Mr Singh said: "We have had positive and very encouraging talks... on that positive note we have decided to continue our talks tomorrow," Echoing Mr Singh's sentiments, Mr Talbott said: "The discussions were most worthwhile." Together the two of them addressed the Press after the conclusion of the dialogue.

As regards the substantive issues in the Indo-US strategic dialogue and the manner in which they were addressed by Mr Singh and Mr Talbott, spread over the eight rounds of talks, the following assessment can be made. On the most important issue of signing the Comprehensive Test Ban Treaty, the Indian side has communicated clearly: (a) that our moratorium on further nuclear testing coupled with the pledge of no first use of nuclear weapons is a significant step in adhering to the spirit of CTBT; (b) that India is willing to adhere to the Treaty once coercive measures like economic sanctions are removed; (c) that we do not any more insist on *de jure* recognition of our nuclear weapon status; (d) that we are perhaps getting reconciled to the ban on transfer of dual use technologies not being removed in the short run; (e) that we also expect the other countries as indicated in Article XIV of CTBT, to adhere to the Treaty, without any conditions. All this means that the Vajpayee Government subscribe to the CTBT. In the case of the Kashmir issue, too, similar premature actions intended in good faith had only served to complicate matters.

By going to the United Nations at a time that Indian forces were pushing out the tribal invaders from the territory of Kashmir, one-third of the state has continued to remain with Pakistan. Thereafter, because India gave the unsolicited assurance that she would not use force to take back the occupied area, Pakistan was emboldened to lay claim to the remaining two-thirds of the state, and the stalemate continues.

Again, after the Indo-Pak War of 1965, India returned strategic areas of PoK which had been captured, indirectly legitimising Pakistan's position there. In 1971, after the liberation of Bangladesh, 90,000 prisoners of war were returned to Pakistan, on the assurances of Bhutto, without seeking to ensure a final solution of the Kashmir question. The problem with such impulsive gestures is that they increase the appetite of the other side to demand more. For example, the permanent extension of the Nuclear Non-proliferation Treaty, instead of leading the nuclear weapon powers in the direction of genuine nuclear disarmament, resulted in their losing all interest in striving towards that goal enshrined in Article VI of the treaty.

Similarly, the CTBT has not removed the appetite of nuclear weapon countries for developing new generations of these weapons, through conducting sub-critical tests in their test sites. The tests are conducted without any international monitoring or verification and there is no way of ensuring that the tests are as harmless as they are made out to be.

Above all, the danger of adopting a casual attitude towards signing the CTBT lies in the provision that it contains no national and international technical means of monitoring and verification.

However, under the so-called permissible activities accord, negotiated among the P-5 countries, they remain free to carry on improvements of their own nuclear stockpiles.

On the other hand, the same accord gives them enormous leeway to act as CTBT policemen and to charge any country which is a signatory of the CTBT with violating its obligations, and to carry out intrusive inspections and overflights as and when they deem fit! The object lesson of what happened to Iraq, in the name of UN inspections to determine whether there were any weapons of mass destruction hidden in that country, should serve to alert us to the very real danger of rushing in to sign the CTBT without ensuring sufficient safeguards for ourselves from possible abuse of this provision.

8

Politics and Economics of Sanctions

Imperceptibly—perhaps irrationally—Indo-US relations are headed towards a new elevated interaction, gradually shedding the style and agendas of the past. It is ironical that this new phase has been triggered by the Indian nuclear tests of May 11 and 13 last year which initially elicited a ferocious reaction from Washington.

The eight rounds of Talbott-Jaswant Singh talks are a piece of this new style Indo-US engagement. Closed-door confidentially locked negotiations and bargainings are laced by public postures which continue to stress the declared fundamentals of US and Indian foreign policy. This new style diplomacy is obviously necessary because the usual channels have been found too rigid and unsuitable for a volatile agenda.

Continuity of foreign policy is a sound precept, an accepted norm of diplomacy. But there are exceptions to this rule: exceptions where continuation of policies takes the country backwards, or keeps it stuck in a rut. Such is the case with Indo-US relations in today's fast changing world—when muscle power and technology, diplomacy and economics interact to create a new foreign policy brand. It has been no smooth climb to the present phase of Indo-US interaction littered as it still is with plenty of potholes. The Indian nuclear blasts in themselves created a wild response from the United States: Washington's global strategic scheme had been rudely shaken. It became clear that the American administration would not easily accept India's gate crashing into the nuclear club with the claim of a nuclear weapon status. Thus, in the first round of response, a series of American actions followed which showed imbalance in search of a stick to punish India without itself getting hurt in the process.

One such was the black-listing of 200 odd Indian institutions and corporate bodies in two phases, which ranged from the Tata Memorial Centre, India's preeminent cancer treatment hospital to Gas Turbine Research Establishment, Bangalore; Directorate of Estate Management, Mumbai; Institute for Systems Studies and Analysis, Delhi; Agricultural Research Unit, Almora; and of course all major R.&D institutions. Alongwith came denial of visas to eminent scientists like AEC Chairman, Dr R. Chidambaram, IGCAR Director, Dr Placid, Rodriguez, and Special Materials scientist, Dr Baldev Raj, in a farcical bid to isolate them from the community of world scientists. And to cap it all, came imposition of all-embracing economic sanctions against Indian government and all Indian corporate bodies and institutions, seeking to carry the battle against India's economic growth to the World Bank, IMF and other international financial institutions.

The attempt to keep Indian scientists out of international scientific, councils proved to be a farce since it was found unworkable, and was repudiated by America's own scientists. Minus India, organisations like the International Atomic Energy Agency would loose all credibility.

Similarly, the move to quarantine Indian organisations such as cancer treatment institutions, agricultural and modern systems management bodies—in fact all Indian institutions which have a scientific approach—makes the USA a laughing stock in the Third World, more at home with Talibanism in so far as developing countries are concerned.

But it was a different story with economic sanctions and export blockade of all variety of equipment and components in the name of sensitive industrial uses.

Contrary to the Indian government's claim, the cascading effect of the projects that have been hit by American sanctions as well as the slow down of new economic projects, particularly those in the power sector, infrastructure and a wide range of industries can hardly be minimised.

The damage could run into many thousand crore, while the extent of economic slow down of economic recovery may be difficult to quantify in monetary terms. The power sector, the largest segment in external assistance (31 per cent, of total) from both bilateral and multilateral sources, has been badly affected by the economic sanctions imposed by USA and major creditors Several ongoing projects in Central and State sectors, including the 1000 mw Simhadri in Andhra Pradesh, with funds totalling 5,661 million dollars, mostly committed and in the pipeline, have been hit for the duration of the sanctions.

Another example of the magnitude and nature of problems created by sanctions on the power sector alone is the Bakeshwar power project with a cost of Rs 2,500 crore, funded by OECF, Japan. The blocking of condenser tubes exports by the United States, valued at just Rs 6 crore, has held up the project for six months in terms of delayed project completion and denial of power for these six months, costlier credit by Rs 250 crore, while the cascading effect of denial of power for user industries could run into a damage of a few thousand crore rupees.

Some hydro projects also face uncertainties. If sanctions last more than a year, the borrowing cost is likely to increase by three to four per cent and if new loans fail to materialise within reasonable time, the power sector would face pressures in the domestic market in raising funds, all of which would no doubt further delay commissioning of projects.

Loan approvals are also pending in the World Bank and with bilateral sources for new projects including transmission, lines. All said and done, the parameters set for the end of Ninth Plan (2001-02) would be hard to realise hitting industrial and all round economic growth sizably.

An addendum is that restructuring of SEBs which is so very necessary for streamlining of electricity, management, would be delayed in the absence of financial support since the Power Ministry says that continuing sanctions would effect the flow of funds from the Power Finance Corporation to SEBs. At the other end, the United States has also begun to realise that its non-multiple losses from imposing sanctions on India are considerable—direct export losses as well as loss of clientele to its other business rivals. Alongwith, hitting economic growth of India is causing immense damage to global economy and holding up international economic recovery.

The political damage that the USA suffers by alienating a vast population under a democratic regime is perhaps even more vast. But putting its super power strategic interests above all else; the United States can afford to hold on in the hope that it has the power and immense economic-political clout to bring India round to its terms on the contentious nuclear issues. In this backdrop, the question one should ask is what brings a change in stance of the United States, from a ferocious look to sweet reasonable posture. Is it to cajole India with minor concessions for the same strategic aims in the nuclear realm which it could not obtain through economic sanctions and political threats?

A supplementary to the same question is: what is the clout that India can muster to face the world's sole super power? Has India enough leverage to engage the United States in confidentiality locked talks for a fair deal on the nuclear issues, obtaining a status of equality with other nuclear weapon states? The answer to these last two questions is an emphatic 'yes'. Which also provides the raison d'etre for the change in the American stance to one of sweet reasonableness. In the first place is American realisation that the Indian tests demonstrate the triumph of India's science and technology, and that its sustained efforts over the last three decades to stiffle India's nuclear capability growth have entirely failed.

One notices that change in American stance towards India's nuclear concerns has progressed as feedback poured in from American think tanks and nuclear technologists. The first shift in American postures came with the feedback from its nuclear monitoring organisations which for full six months were engaged seriously in assessing the work of Indian nuclear technology, and the extent to which Indian scientists claims on the two-day tests—the thermo-nuclear test in particular—were justified. American monitoring organisations as well as the reliable CIA scientific assessors (some of them hold key positions in IAEA which has complete know-how of Indian nuclear capability) have given full marks to the Indian nuclear scientists and hold the May 11 and 13 tests to have been totally successful in all the objectives laid out.

This poses several serious questions for the American State Department The most critical is India's place in the American non-proliferation objectives woven round the CTBT and FMCT. It now becomes clear that without India's active participation and backing, the FMCT will be unrealisable, and minus the fissile material cut-off, the CTBT will be a lame-duck in the American non-proliferation bid.

There is perhaps inadequate realisation of the Indian clout on this score. The fact is that India's accession to the CTBT does not hamper Indian clout or negotiating strength to win a place of honour as a nuclear weapon capability state, and in the first place, immediate end to the sanctions regime.

The American effort on the other hand is to avoid these awkward aspects and prevent them from surfacing. The best way to do so is to keep the Indian side engrossed in the game of passed lifting of sanctions, with Indian accession to the CTBT being followed by a preemptive termination of its fissile materials capability.

So far, the quid pro quo offered is a limited de facto, not de jure, recognition of Indian weapon capability. The assessment that the Indian nuclear scientists and R&D institutions were ahead of all others in the developing world, even China, has raised American apprehensions about India catching up with futuristic trends for laser ignited fusion weapons bypassing the CTBT and FMCT.

From this arises the demand, articulated by the American Ambassador, and subsequently by Talbott himself, about the limits of Indian deterrence and transparency of Indian nuclear weapons. It would be worth examining whether the United States is prepared to strike a matching deal with India if the latter offers its earnest cooperation in genuine non-proliferation moves—to begin with the CTBT and FMCT.

While on the question of India's clout vis-a-vis the

United States, in the ongoing talks, the Indian economic leverage is often minimised. India does not, of course, have a trade surplus with the US as China has. Nor is the Indian foreign exchange reserve anything like that of China.

India does not have a steady and consistent economic reform and growth policies. What then is Indian economic clout? The answer comes from Dean R.O'Hare, Chairman of the US-India Business Council, who said during a recent tour of South.

India was emerging as a global economic player in the "leading growth, sectors of the 21st century." In a technology driven world, this statement counts for a lot. Dean O'Hare obviously referred to Indian strides in info-tech, besides the front runner laser and nuclear technologies. The Indian strides in software are a case in point, and soft ware exports promise to soar to some 8 billion dollars in the next few years.

An American columnist put the matter in the right perspective when he noted that without India, their information technology industry—now the largest sector of the US economy—could be in a soup. One-fourth of the world's programmers are Indian. And according to a recent publication from the University of California, one-third of wages paid in the entire IT industry goes to Indian info-tech technicians working in the United States, India's own infotech industry and the government knows that US demand for Indian programming has become massive. That explains the paradox that just when American ire over the Indian tests was being voiced, Clinton decided to support an increase in the quota for Indians who wanted to immigrate in response to pressure from high-technology companies and to a Department of Commerce report which estimated a shortage of over one million programmers, particularly in the light of the danger from Y2K menace that could be a disaster. That also explains why within two months of the imposition of sanctions against India, the US Congress passed a bill increasing the quota of H-1 work visas from 65,000 to 90,000 this year, and to 115,000 by the year 2002, a large part of which would benefit Indian infotech experts in the United States.

This is a clout which Indian negotiators have hardly taken into account, just as there has been inadequacy in pressing home India's indispensable status in taking the fissile material cut-off to fruition, and in seeking a quid pro quo.

Obviously, nuclear diplomacy in the new world setting cannot be divorced from America's, technological and strategic pursuits and of the major powers. Political and muscle power has got tied in a close knot with technology and economic pursuits in the world of today.

The new moorings of diplomacy are all about this. To engage the United States successfully, without getting side-tracked, these are the facets that have to be kept in view on a global scale—especially in relation to India's periphery, China and Pakistan.

9

Quest for New Partnership

Since the beginning of the eighties, India has made concerted efforts to improve relations with the United States. It had concluded that it relations with the Soviet Union had reached a plateau and it needed high technology and investment from the West to raise the level of its economy.

The Reagan administration positively responded to the Indian overtures. As a result it was able to improve relations with both India and Pakistan simultaneously. There were, however, two impediments.

Many American policy makers believed India to be closer to the Soviet Union and considered its support of the government in Kabul to be against the United States. These impediments disappeared with the end of the cold war.

A Soviet Union which was dependent on the West for economic assistance and leaned heavily towards it was no longer a threat to the security of the United States. India discovered to its dismay that in the post-cold war era it could no longer depend on the Soviet help. It lent greater urgency to the task of mending fences with the United States.

The Gulf War against Iraq was the first war of the post-cold war era. which revealed how much the balance of power had shifted in favour of the United States. India tried to steer clear of the conflict. It did not join the coalition led by the United States.

Its priority was to evacuate thousands of its nationals from the war zone. During the war it extended the facility of refuelling to American planes going to the war zone in West Asia. When the secret arrangement came out in the open there was an uproar in and outside the Parliament.

The government was forced to withdraw the facility. The Bush administration was grateful for the cooperation it received. India's decision to liberalise its economy and integrate it with the global economy was enthusiastically welcomed by the United States as it opened another window of opportunity for trade and investment for the United States.

India embraced the market economy and gave up its policy of export substitution in favour of export-led growth. Keen on attracting foreign investment it offered counter guarantee in power sector. It may be noted here that the bilateral trade with the United States grew by nineteen per cent in 1995 alone, going up from $7.6 billion in 1994 to $9 billion in 1995. US exports to India increased by 44 per cent while imports from India rose by 8 per cent.

US was also the largest source of investment and technology for India. In four years since 1991, US investment aggregated to $3 billion which was more than the total US investment in India since 1947. Trade and investment continued to grow. These were affected in 1997 because of the economic crisis in the countries of southeast and east Asia. According to the Indo-US Chamber of Commerce the total approval for FDI from the US stood at $9.6 billion at the end of July 97. But the actual inflow was far less. The estimate of the US embassy in India was that the market value of the US investment would be between $6 to 7 billion.

According to the estimate of the Security and Exchange Board of India the portfolio investment in India between January 1991 and to September 1997 was $8.7 billion.

Out of which the US share was $4 billion. The US investment in India peaked in 1993 at 44.1 per cent of the total investment flow. It came down to 28.4 per cent in 1997. It touched the lowest point at 12 per cent In 1998. The total inflow also considerably declined as the result of the combined effect of the widespread recession as well as the sanctions imposed by the United States after the Pokhran tests.

The spurt in trade and investment was not without its share of controversies. The United States demanded from its trading partners free and equal access for its exports and investment. Where it could not obtain its objective through multilateral agreement it was not averse to twisting arms in bilateral negotiations.

During four years of the Bush administration, efforts were made to resolve controversies amicably or at least nothing was done to exacerbate the differences. The insurgency in Kashmir began in late eighties. Pakistan supported insurgency from across the border. It trained the militants, provided them with arms and finances. It raised the Kashmir issue in every international forum and tried to draw the attention of the US to the violations of human rights in Kashmir by the Indian security forces. It succeeded to some extent with the help of some India basher Congressmen.

India's demand that Pakistan be declared a terrorist state was not accepted. The Bush administration gave, however, some satisfaction to India by insisting that the

Kashmir issue be resolved through bilateral negotiations under the Shimla agreement and by arguing that plebiscite was not a practical solution. It also put pressure on Pakistan to close its training camps for the militants.

Things began to change with the coming in of the Clinton administration. It declared that the entire state of Jammu and Kashmir was a disputed territory. Its accession to India did not finally settle its status. This contradicted the Indian stand that Kashmir was an integral part of India as much as Texas was part of the United States.

The United States stated that it considered militancy to be an indigenous movement which went against the Indian contention that but for the support it received from across the border the movement would have collapsed. The US officials regularly visited Kashmir and met with the leaders of secessionist movement. It stated that it regard the people of Kashmir to be the third party in the dispute.

India believed that such statements encouraged the militants of keeping their hopes of success alive. The United States conceded that the militants carrying on terrorist activities in Kashmir were receiving support from Pakistan but at times it exonerated the government and shifted the blame to private fundamentalist organisations. It thus accepted the claims of the government of Pakistan that it was only extending political and moral support to the people of Kashmir in their struggle to decide their own future. The government of India could not agree with the assessment. The United States repeatedly raised the issue of human rights violation in Kashmir. It demanded that human rights organisations like Amnesty International and International Red Cross be permitted to come to Kashmir and investigate the charges. It demanded punishment of the guilty. India contended that, some violation was inevitable when a government was dealing with insurgency. However, it was punishing these who were found guilty. The United States later conceded that there was an improvement in the situation.

With the establishment of National Human Rights Commission, India took several measures to introduce transparency which blunted criticism. Pakistan repeatedly pleaded for its intervention in the Kashmir dispute. The United States contended that it would mediate in the dispute only when invited by both the parties.

As India opposed third-party mediation in Kashmir the US intervention remained a non-starter. India acceded neither to the NPT nor to the Missiles Technology Control Regime. It favours global elimination of all nuclear weapons.

A position which is unacceptable to the United States as well to all other nuclear powers. In 1995 in a review of the NPT the United States succeeded in getting the NPT extended unconditionally and indefinitely. But it did not result in a major row between the two countries because India expected this outcome. Major dispute erupted during the consideration of the draft of the CTBT in Geneva.

Just before opening of the conference both China and France conducted nuclear tests indicating clearly that they not only wanted to hold on to their stockpile but wanted to upgrade their capability. India strongly opposed the draft. It wanted the nuclear powers to give a time frame for eliminating their nuclear weapons stockpile. It argued that the draft was not comprehensive as it permitted nuclear simulations and sub-critical tests. These objections were ruled out and India was asked not to stand in the way of the approval of the draft of the

CTBT. The nuclear powers were opposed to giving a time frame. The United States argued that the prohibition of computer simulations was not feasible as it would be impossible to monitor thousands of computers in thousands of labs.

China objected to the provisions for inspection and verification which it said were too intrusive. Its point of view was accommodated. India objected to the enforcement clause which stated that the treaty would come into force only when 40 countries, including India, having nuclear reactors, have signed it. This meant that the CTBT was being imposed on India.

Three years after the treaty is opened for signature a conference of countries signing the treaty would be convened which would decide the future course of action. Ambassador Wisner had predicted that India would follow the policy of three nos; not sign the treaty, not stop it, and not veto it. But angered by insensitivity shown to its point of view India vetoed the draft. But the treaty was introduced through the backdoor in the United Nation General Assembly and was adopted and opened for signature. The Indian Parliament endorsed the stand of the government. The CTBT became a major source of friction between the two countries.

After India carried on nuclear tests in Pokhran, Rajasthan on 11 and 13 May 1998, the nuclear issue became the most dominant issue in India's relations with the United States. Due to the failure of the American intelligence to forewarn the authorities of the impending nuclear tests, the tests came as a complete surprise to the United States and contributed in no small measure to its feeling of outrage. It strongly condemned the Indian nuclear tests and rejected India's claim to be treated as a *de jure* nuclear power. After its efforts to persuade Pakistan not to retaliate by carrying on its own nuclear tests failed, it warned both the countries that they would never be treated as nuclear powers under the NPT. It demanded that both the countries should immediately and unconditionally sign the CTBT and NPT.

It said that the nuclear tests have created an explosive situation which threatened the peace and stability not only of the region but of the entire world. Both countries should take steps to root out all the basic causes of tension in the region including Kashmir.

The United States promptly suspended India's participation in its International Military Education and Training Programme and stopped issuing licenses under munition list. It declared that it had no other option than to impose economic sanctions under the Glenn Amendment.

The United States took the lead in enlisting the support of the P-5 countries. Though France and Russia agreed with the United States that both India and Pakistan should sign the CTBT and the NPT immediately and conduct no more test, they did not favour the imposition of sanctions. China, Britain and the United States favoured taking hard stance. Differences within the P-5 prevented mandatory sanctions being imposed on India.

The Group-8 and the UN Security Council passed similar resolutions condemning the nuclear tests in South Asia. The task was easily accomplished because of the overlapping membership of these groups. The United States remained the only country which imposed economic sanctions on India under its own laws.

India took a conciliatory rather than a confrontationist approach. Prime Minister Vajpayee wrote to a number of heads of the governments explaining the reasons for India's decision. India announced a voluntary moratorium on further tests and proposed "no first use" and "no use" against non-nuclear states. It declared that its nuclear tests were not directed against any country but were considered necessary in the interest of national security. It was willing to discuss its security concern with the United States but would not accept any unfair conditions. Speaking before a gathering of intellectuals in New York in September 1998 Vajpayee declared that "We were forced to exercise the nuclear option both for reasons of national security and as a powerful challenge to the practitioners of nuclear apartheid." Had the nuclear powers accepted India's previous attempts to set up global nuclear disarmament, India need not have gone in for its current testing programme.

India began secret talks with the United States on nuclear issue in June. The talks have completed eight rounds and there is still no end in sight. As time passed both the sides reported progress in the talks. Jaswant Singh, Prime Minister's special representative for the talks, and the Prime Minister himself expressed satisfaction at the progress made in the talks.

Strobe Talbott, Deputy Secretary of States, leading the American side, also expressed his satisfaction. In a speech on the World net before coming to India for the eighth round Talbott indicated what was being discussed. There were five issues: adherence to the CTBT, moratorium on further production of-fissile material till a treaty was concluded at the talks in Geneva; unilateral strategic restraint by forgoing development and deployment of missiles capable of carrying nuclear weapons, strict control over nuclear and missile technology in keeping with international norms and direct dialogue between India and Pakistan on all disputes which are at the root of tension in the region, including Kashmir.

Secretary of State Madeleine Albright pleaded before the Senate for flexibility in the implementation of sanctions.

In October, the US Congress passed the Brownback Amendment which gave authority to the President to waive such economic sanctions for one year which are not related to nuclear, missile, and military applications in national interest. In September, a special waiver had already been approved under pressure from the US agriculture lobby to enable sale of wheat to Pakistan. In November, the United States decided to partially lift the economic sanctions.

The decision was primarily motivated by the desire to help Pakistan which was on the brink of defaulting on its repayment obligations. Only Pakistan was to get American support from World Bank for loans and debt restructuring. Both India and Pakistan could now get loan guarantees from American financial institutions like Exim Bank, Overseas Private Investment Corporation, and Trade Development Authority.

Pakistan was favoured because its collapse would have adversely affected others. On the other hand economic sanctions had only marginal effect on the Indian economy. India had no objection against economic assistance to Pakistan but it resented discrimination against itself. *The Wall Street Journal* believed that this waiver was given to India and Pakistan to save the American corporations from being hurt. American corporations like Boeing, General Electric, Enron and others ran the risk of losing business to competitors from Europe and Asia.

The partial removal of sanctions restored competitive financing. The United States policy was not moving in a straight line. In December, it issued a list of forty entities and their 200 subsidiaries in India which were debarred from having any trade and commercial relations with American concerns.

Indian scientists working in American institutions of higher learning and research in the areas of nuclear and missiles technology were asked to leave. American scientists were denied permission to attend seminars in India in related fields.

Yet neither India nor the United States believed that the nuclear issue could not be resolved eventually, Albright stated: "We have to draw a very fine line here between making it clear that what the Indian and the Pakistanis did was unacceptable and that they are not now members of the group; but at the same time they are not isolated or treated as pariah. They need to be part of the solution." The statement clearly indicates American intention to remain engaged. India and the United States decided to keep the talks secret and no information is available as to what exactly is being talked about.

The limited available information reveals a wide gap between the perspective and expectations of the two countries. India insists on having a minimum nuclear deterrent. The United States wants India to quantify what it considers to be minimum deterrent. India contends that minimum cannot be defined as the concept is dynamic and changes with the threat perception. India and Pakistan's accession to the CTBT is of great concern to the United States.

The Senate Foreign Relations Committee has not yet recommended its ratification. The Clinton administration believes that if the countries of South Asia which have flagrantly violated the NPT agree to sign the CTBT it would be able to pressure the Senate to ratify the treaty. India and the United States are giving contradictory statement regarding India's willingness to sign the treaty.

Since Prime Minister Vajpayee stated in his UN General Assembly address in September last year that India would not stand in the way of the CTBT coming into force in September 1999, American officials have been saying that India would sign the CTBT.

Latest in the series of such statements is the one by Albright who recently stated before the Senate Foreign Relations Committee that India and Pakistan have agreed to join the treaty. But Prime Minister Vajpayee has stated on numerous occasions that India has not agreed to sign it. Jaswant Singh, now Minister of External Affairs, a few days ago stated before the Parliament that India has agreed to bring the CTBT to a successful conclusion so that it is not delayed beyond September 1999.

He asserted that national interest determined government's position. When two days later he was confronted with Albright's statement in the Parliament, he reiterated that India has not agreed to sign it.

After Jaswant Singh's statement, Karl Inderfurth, Assistant Secretary of State for South Asia, again stated before the Senate Committee that India has agreed to sign it. These contradictory statements have created confusion and uncertainty as to what has been agreed to and who is telling the truth. The Indian government has repeatedly stressed that it would sign the CTBT only after developing a national consensus on it.

The Indian opinion on the issue is divided. Even those who appear to be in favour of signing it as the treaty is not discriminatory and it was India that had first mooted the proposal, stipulate that it should be signed only after the United States has signed it. There is a large body of opinion which is opposed to India signing the CTBT

There are some indications of change in US posture.

It is coming face to face with the reality of the two countries of South Asia being nuclear powers.

Before coming to India for the eighth round of talks, Karl Inderfurth, Assistant Secretary of State for South Asia, said that "the major challenge before the United States in South Asia are not so much about prevention but management of threshold that have been already crossed."

The United States is working towards "transforming the India-US relationship in a true partnership". It wants to remain engaged and hopes to reach an understanding on non-proliferation issue. The United States has many interests in the region and these would not be served if the relationship is "defined by a single issue agenda". He realistically acknowledged that though the United States has been "warmly disposed towards India's democratic tradition yet somehow that never seemed quite enough to get us beyond correct but rather chilly exchanges with various governments" Inderfurth argued that neither democracy would be the principal basis of India-American relations nor could the US take the Indian democracy for granted and "try to force India into positions for which there is no national consensus or that violate its concept of sovereignty or self interest."

One can infer from the above that there is some awareness now in the United States that punitive measures alone can not deliver the goods.

No Indian government can afford to give an impression that it is giving up a policy option which is overwhelmingly popular under external pressure and hope to survive. The United States would, therefore, like to try persuasion by pointing out how a new approach could be beneficial for India.

After the nuclear tests, American media strongly

condemned India for its wrong priorities for spending large amounts on its nuclear programme while ignoring the basic needs of its people.

The argument resonated in India. American officials also pointed out how costly it was for the United States to maintain nuclear deterrent.

India, they said should not fall in to the same trap. It will be relevant in this context to recall Indira Gandhi's remarks made in an interview with a Bangladesh magazine. She said: "Americans have to appreciate not only India's problems but the need for us to take our decision independently, to make our judgment independently."

India finds it very difficult to accept a world order which gives the right to possess and further upgrade nuclear weapons in their national interest to some countries, while denying the same right to others. India considers that there is an organic link between the global nuclear disarmament and its own nuclear deterrence. Inderfurth said that India and the United States should get ready for a partnership for the twenty-first century. Prime Minister Vajpayee also spoke of the need to restructure Indo-American relations which should be based on equality and mutuality of interest.

Prime Minister's complaint was that since independence, the United States has pursued a policy of technology denial despite the fact that there has been no leakage of technology from the country due to strict control exercised by the government.

Even though the unipolar moment may have passed, the United States will continue to be an important global player in the twenty-first century. It can facilitate India's economic and technological development. The United States also looks at the potential Indian market with expectation, The interest of both the countries converge here. How much important economic relations can be in the post-cold war era has been shown by Sino-American relations. Both of them have common interest in continuing it despite sharp difference on many issues including human rights, nuclear proliferation, relations with Taiwan and violation of MTCR. More than anything, India wants to be treated with respect, as much as the United States gives to China. The partnership in the twenty-first century between the two countries has to be based not only on mutuality of interests alone but also on mutuality of respect. India would not want only to be a junior partner of the United States.

Ten months after Pokhran II poured sand over the palimpsest of Indian foreign relations, we can attempt to read what new words have been inscribed on it, and how much of the old writing remains visible, especially with respect to India-United States relations. These relations also strongly influence and are affected by India's other important binary relationships, especially with China, Japan, Pakistan, Russia, and Western allies of the US.

All international relations are being conducted in a world which is no longer bipolar because the Berlin Wall was torn down almost ten years ago and then the Soviet Union disintegrated; but nor is the world truly multipolar because the United States so far exceeds every other state in every single attribute of power, hard or soft, and regards itself as the 'one indispensable nation'; yet the 'new world order' of President Bush's imagining turned out to be no more than a momentary unipolar illusion.

Moreover, the international capitalist system has been strained by financial-economic crises in East Asia and elsewhere, and the United Nations system has been badly attenuated. In short, the international landscape in which India (and Pakistan) dramatically asserted its claim to be recognised as a nuclear-weapons state safeguarding its own security interests is a quickly changing one in which established powers, notably the US, naturally cling to the edifices of order and hierarchy they had earlier created.

First among these structures are the various treaties, conventions, domestic laws, and multilateral suppliers groups that make up the 'nuclear non-proliferation regime'. This was explicitly designed to prevent the further spread of the technology and materials needed for the manufacture and deployment of nuclear weapons and ballistic missiles, and to limit the number of nuclear weapons states to the five recognised as such in the Non-Proliferation Treaty (NPT) of 1968. Upholding this regime is central to American foreign policy of the Clinton administration, and identified with American national interest in uncompromising terms, as the immediate imposition of sanctions on India (and Pakistan) last summer, and continued refusal to explicitly or implicitly concede their new nuclear status, reflect.

Not surprisingly, therefore, the nuclear issue dominates India-US relations in 1998-99. (It is discussed in detail elsewhere in this journal.) Of equal importance, and perhaps surprisingly in the context of India's public commitment to building a 'minimum credible nuclear deterrent', the most recent (January 1999) round of a high-level dialogue sustained by Jaswant Singh and Strobe Talbott since June 1998 left the impression in New Delhi that the two sides were also discussing larger issues of Indo American engagement and cooperation, transcending sanctions, many of which have been eased. And Talbott has said more than once that the US still looks forward to partnership with India and its emergence as a global power. This article is addressed to the desirability of, and the obstacles to, constructing a broad-based, non dependent, cooperative India-American relationship in the near future. Earlier writings on the palimpsest reappear.

There have been moments during the past 50-odd years—in 1961 and 1985 for example—when it seemed as if India and the US might use the enormous commonalities between them to direct their relationship towards cooperation and mutual benefit. These moments passed, leaving behind little beyond hope to tide over experience.

There have been moments of animosity as well—1971 and 1980 for example—when it seemed as if strategic divergences between India and the US might drive them toward open and sustained antagonism. These moments too passed, leaving behind frustrating experiences to dilute hope.

With the end of the cold war more or less coinciding in time with the Narasimha Rao government in India initiating a well articulated policy of economic reforms and multi-directional international engagement, some people endeavoured to build a positive and enduring Indo-US equation, for good reasons in both countries. Their Steady efforts had progressed to the point of making complete arrangements for President Clinton's State visit to India in early 1998.

The last American President to visit India was Jimmy Carter in the winter of 1978-1979. Clinton's visit was postponed, first because of unexpected general elections in India, and then by the abnormal situation created by Pokhran II and US sanctions.

However, having surmounted impeachment proceedings against him, Clinton's expressed desire to visit India soon, knowing that it can only take place in a positive atmosphere, is one indication that the reasons for building a broad-based partnership remain valid, on both sides. Part of the American reasoning was spelled out during the first Clinton administration which also made it clear in a range of international fora that the driving forces of US foreign policy were ideological commitment to nuclear non-proliferation, the enlargement of democracy, protection of human rights, resolution of regional conflicts, and open markets for American products, services, and investment.

The instruments of policy were a mixture of engagement and pressure, multilateral involvement as well as US good offices and/or unilateral military action when necessary India and nine other countries (including China) were identified as 'big emerging markets' offering opportunities for the US. As actual or potential regional powers with influence, they also posed challenges to American global leadership.

With strong cultures of their own, and having values and customs that did not necessarily coincide and could be antithetical with those of the US, they presented ethical and strategic dilemmas. Moreover, their potential political and/or economic instability could create havoc spilling far beyond their borders.

A multifaceted strategy for dealing with these ten countries through both government and business was devised. The essence of this strategy was constructive engagement. An additional reason for US attention to India was the hope of winning Indian agreement, or softening India's antagonism, to indefinite extension of the NPT in 1995 and passage of the, Comprehensive Test Ban Treaty in 1996.

Clinton received Narasimha Rao in 1994 and spoke of partnership. A spate of high-level official visits were made to India in 1995, including one by the President's wife, Hilary Rodhman Clinton. Though visiting Defence

Secretary William Perry then concluded (rightly) that both India and Pakistan would stay outside the non-proliferation regime, US officials and non-officials continued care to diminish the chances of a 'flashpoint in Kashmir' erupting into open conflict on the subcontinent.

There was growing if puzzled American appreciation of the strength of Indian democracy and the contributions made within the US by some 22,000 Indian students and close to a million Asian Indian-Americans.

American scientists protested exclusion of Indian scientists from international conferences held in the US because of stringent application of sanctions against 261 specific 'entities' in Indian scientific and industrial establishments in October 1998.

Earlier, important bodies, including the Council of Foreign Relations, urged more assiduous cultivation of India. The Golden Jubilee of India's independence was enthusiastically celebrated in the US. Furthermore, in 1996 the US and China had a controlled but serious military face-off over Taiwan, and notwithstanding strenuous efforts on both sides and spectacular summit meetings, relations remain anything but easy.

Some influential Americans look to India and are troubled by the irony of the US signing a joint communique with 'Communist China' in July 1998 to which democratic India inevitably took grave offence.

In New Delhi Strobe Talbott had to explicitly deny any intended "Sino-American condominium" over South Asia. Other Americans, including Samuel Huntington writing in *Foreign Affairs,* March-April 1999, have criticised Clinton's foreign policy variously as being evangelical, arrogant, or ineffective, alienating 'civilisational' friends (such as Europe and possibly India), and ignoring the manifest preferences of the

American people not to be involved in foreign adventures. Faced with the problems posed by so-called 'rogue' states such as North Korea or Iraq, Americans saw partnership with a mature and reasonable India as natural.

Younger Americans, not yet influential perhaps but not unimportant either, said last summer than Americans were bound to become increasingly interested in India, once the hype over nuclear tests had died down. The accuracy of their predictions may be judged by the continuing trickle of US businessmen and other visitors to India, the initiatives taken by the US Congress to lighten sanctions and give the executive discretionary powers of application to September 2000, and renewed feelers by the US Defence Department for establishing cooperative relations with India's defence forces, probably because of convergent interests in such important international issues as controlling terrorism and maintaining freedom of navigation on the seas. India's reasons for seeking vastly better, broader, and deeper relations with the US are both simpler and more profound.

India's aspiration remains constant since independence: to act as an independent power and be recognised as one, and to ensure its all-round national security, which means economic prosperity and social harmony at home as well as territorial integrity and a peaceful environment abroad.

Pursuing this goal in today's world-post-cold war and post-Pokhran II—means that there is no alternative to dealing with the US. (The obvious alternative of completely sealing off India to subsist or sink into itself alone is too horrendous to consider here.) First, the US is India's largest single trading partner, (the European Union is composite) the largest single source of approved private investment, a store house of knowledge, science and technology in every field, including the military, the preferred destination for students in the professions and skilled Indian emigrants.

The success of India's economic reforms, to which even the United Front and BJP-led coalition governments committed themselves, are predicated on India joining the rest of the world and enjoying friendly but not subordinate or dependent relations on the world's leading player, the US. India's skilful participation in the World Trade Organisation is of a piece with this expectation.

In the many criticisms of the US voiced by Indians over the years, it is remarkable how few have contemplated cutting off all ties with it! Secondly, foreign relationships are now synergetic rather than exclusive; they tend to work together.

While it is highly commendable and desirable that India has resumed non-official and even official dialogues with important partners such as Australia, Britain, Germany and Japan, as it has succeeded in doing in recent months, it may be suggested that these moves are not entirely separate from progress made in the US-India dialogue. For example, looking East, to ASEAN and the Asian Regional Forum, to Australia, to Japan, we come face to face with prolonged American presence and influence there and sometimes more visceral reactions to Pokhran II.

US dominance in raw materials distribution and production of energy is as unchallenged as India's imperative for more supplies; energy is one of the specified areas of possibly immediate Indo-US cooperation. Not so nuclear power and safety.

Looking West, to Britain, to Europe, even to Russia,

we meet the American non-proliferation agenda again. France and Russia might want to soften or supplement this for the sake of their own commercial interests, but cannot replace it.

It is extremely unlikely that any member of the Group of Eight rich and developed nations, which uphold the international status quo would 'break caste', so to speak, for India's sake. The same can be said about the five permanent members of the UN Security Council, of whom China is one. Looking to neighbouring China and Pakistan then, we encounter their complex webs of relationship with the US and with each other, and various implicit or explicit obligations. Thus, just when Indian columnists were happily pointing out that the list of items discussed by Talbott and Singh had shrunk from 13 US demands to four suggestions, China publicly reminded the US that it must enforce the UN Security Council Resolution, they had jointly sponsored, setting 13 harsh 'benchmarks' for India to meet. And while we can all cheer Prime Minister Vajpayee's pathbreaking bus-ride to Lahore and welcome the declaration he and Pakistan Prime Minister Nawaz Sharif signed there on February 21, 1999 as a most important step towards, a less conflict-prone subcontinent, we also knot, that President Clinton had been talking on the telephone to both of them at length, presumably urging each to recognise ground realities.

The above is not intended to imply that the US controls or even directs the foreign policies of the, aforementioned states, but rather to indicate the synergy and interdependence of diplomatic relationships in the world today.

To the extent India has normal relations with its neighbours and other powers, it becomes a desirable partner rather than a problem for the US and also is protected from intrusive or divisive, American policies. Similarly, to the extent India has good relations with the US, it enjoys access to many more capitals and international resources than if it did not, and also has safeguards against jealous neighbours, or adversaries turning the most powerful force in the world against India.

Thirdly, while rejecting the notion that what is good for America is good for the world, we do maintain that what is best for India is what is most appealing to America. Those aspects of India that attract US ideas of partnership—democracy, open society, rule of law, constitutional respect for human rights, potential for prosperity, rationality, an incredibly rich and diverse culture, expertise but moderation in the use of force, power to affect the natural and strategic environment of a substantially large part of the world, a vital voluntary sector and a large middle class—are precisely those qualities that make for achievement, progressiveness, vibrancy and realisable prosperity in India. Those aspects that repel Americans from making a stake in India—deep and enduring poverty, hideous social abuses, corruption, violence, lawlessness, institutional breakdown, infrastructure inadequacies, opaque and non-accountable administration, the absence of a work culture, dilatory and changeable decisions, in short, misgovernance and thralldom to *baboodom*—are precisely those features that burden the fives of Indians with misery.

The desirability of a multi-layered broad-based enduring relationship between the US and India is recognised by many people in both countries, but is none-the-less hard to build because of inhibitions and obstacles on both sides in addition to the immediate nuclear tests/sanctions problem. Perhaps the greatest inhibition is ignorance of each other among the higher echelons of policy makers, irrespective of political party in either country. Close personal relations at that level not only prevent misperceptions and stereotypes from determining policy, they ease the way for resolving difficulties and disputes.

The easiest way of building close personal relations is through regular institutional interaction over many years, inside and outside government, inside and outside educational centres. But it was this kind of institutional interplay that was prevented by cold war considerations and measures taken by Indira Gandhi's government to keep out American academics. Obviously, a big obstacle is the legacy of the cold war. Not only did it feed on and nourish Pakistan-India disputes, it left a destructive detritus of gun-happy militants on India's borders, and shaped popular imagery.

Thus, there is, a general American perception of India as a 'troublesome thorn' in its side, neither ally nor enemy and so impossible to deal with in a straight-forward manner. And there is a widespread Indian tendency to see the US as *the* adversary, responsible for most of the trials and tribulations India faces in the world.

Sometimes, honest but limited difficulties such as farmers may experience with, seeds distributed by Monsanto Company are blown up into a full-scale take-over 'conspiracy' which is patently absurd. Present-day US recognition of India's genuine security concerns beyond the subcontinent, and India's recent willingness to explain itself to larger American audiences and elicit their understanding may help to overcome US prejudices.

Americans too need to be more persuasive of their self-proclaimed benevolence in India and cease pretending that history has come to an end, but they have become victims of budget cuts and their own lack of access to many Indian circles.

The most serious obstacles to improved Indo-US relations are harder to overcome. One is India's continuing light weight in the worlds of commerce, finance, industry; and investment and its seeming lack of drive for economic excellence. India's potential is internationally recognised and continues to attract some interest, from the US as elsewhere.

What is incomprehensible and intolerable to Americans (and others) is the unpredictability, unreliability, red-tape tied and endlessly procrastinated decision making process in India on all matters having to do with money.

Though Enron Company displayed fortitude and entered. Phase II of its Dabhrol Project, many other American companies small and large have waited several years for things to improve and are giving up for greener pastures elsewhere—of which there are not a few.

Yet, were American business to have a substantial stake in India's success, problems of US difference to India's concerns would quickly disappear because commercial ties would stimulate enough political and educational interest in India to dissipate ignorance. The other seemingly insuperable obstacle to quick improvement in Indo-US relations comes from the particularities of both governments.

The American political system divides decision-making power between fiercely competitive and partisan institutions, the Presidency and the Congress. Irrespective of what understanding Strobe Talbott and his State Department colleagues reach with Jaswant Singh, they still have to face their own ideologues as well as the formidable Jesse Helms, Republican Senator from North Carolina, who heads the Senate Foreign Relations Committee and is sometimes referred to as a Neanderthal; keeping him happy most inevitably take priority over making India feel good! Other obstructing examples could be cited from the US, but they pale in comparison now with the vagaries of coalition politics in India.

It took time for Washington to understand that India's nuclear tests were something more than an impulsive action by a nationalist political party new to power. Now it as accepted (reluctantly), India's determination of define for itself and build a 'minimum credible deterrence', partly be cause it has accepted Prime Minister Vajpayee's declarations in the United Nations and other places that India will not stand in the way of the CTBT coming into force in September 1999, that India will negotiate in good faith on limitations of fissile materials, that India will exercise stringent export controls on nuclear materials and technology, and that India is committed to the universal elimination of nuclear weapons. But at times it seems to Americans as if there is no effort to create a, national consensus on these issues, and so no guarantee that Vajpayee (or some other Prime Minister) will be empowered to carry his statements through to implementation.

If that is the case, any incentive Washington may have to enlarge the high table and accommodate India on it is likely to give way to increased punitive pressures. In other words, the most essential tasks India must undertake to be taken seriously by the US and other powers as a worthy partner, are at home.

Also in its immediate neighbourhood where a good start has been made but needs to be strengthened. And finally, it must be repeated, the surest way of overcoming the present impasse in Indo US relations is to build a broad-based, multi-layered, long term oriented relationship which will sustain itself through the interactions of two democratic peoples who have so much to share with one another.

10

Indo-American Relations

A further and partial lifting of sanctions against India by President Clinton in October, 1999 has generated optimism about Indo-US ties. Certain sections of our print and audio-visual media have indulged in hopes about "a paradigm shift" in favour of India in US policies. It is relevant, therefore, to assess whether there is such a shift in US policies towards India.

The purpose and meaning of President Clinton lifting the sanctions should be examined. The purpose is two-fold, namely to create a positive atmosphere in Indo-US relations in preparation for his visit to India and Bangladesh. Secondly, it is a gesture to encourage India to fall in line with the US agenda on non-proliferation, which remains, intact despite the US Senate's vote against the ratification of the CTBT. The meaning of the removal of the sanctions can be interpreted as reflecting certain nuances in US policies towards India. First and foremost, it is a signal that the US desires to engage India constructively on important issues about which there are differences of opinion between the two countries, whether they are related to nonproliferation or the WTO, and so on. Secondly, the removal of sanctions implies an acknowledgement by the US that India is not likely to succumb to punitive attitudes or economic pressure at the cost of its basic national security interests. Thirdly, sanctions which have been removed in their specificity imply a willingness to expand bilateral economic and commercial relations and to slowly revive cooperation in the field of defence cooperation, wherever possible. Clinton has removed sanctions on development aid and on private US banks' participation in Indian commercial and economic operations. Bilateral defence training and exchange programmes can be revived under this dispensation.

The US has moved forward in conveying a desire to expand bilateral relations based on mutual trust. As far as the more substantive sanctions go, the US is likely to relate them to the non-proliferation benchmarks because non-proliferation still remains a matter of high priority in Washington's global and regional strategic agenda.

However, the US is not taking a punitive or confrontationist stand *vis-a-vis* India on this matter. Bruce Reidel, a, senior official of the US National Security Council, and Karl Inderfurth, the US Assistant Secretary of State for South Asian Affairs, have confirmed that India signing the CTBT or conveying indications regarding it is not a precondition to President Clinton's visit to India. In fact, the frequency and number of high level discussions between India and the US since mid-August indicate a mutual desire to transcend differences of opinion on some basic issues and to establish a practical and working relationship.

As far as economic policies go, indications given by Finance Minister Yashwant Sinha provide a basis for a gradual interaction between the two countries. We should also remember that meeting our mounting fiscal deficits will depend on the US endorsing the flow of funds from the IMF and IBRD to India. As far as managing relations with Pakistan are concerned, we must appreciate the fact that the US has delinked its relations with India from its relations with Pakistan. While remaining aware that the US will deal with General Pervez Musharraf, as far as he remains in effective power, there is no point in opposing this element in America's South Asian policies.

There is no paradigm shift in the United States' India policies, but there are notable undercurrents and impulses indicating Washington's desire to structure a stable and mutually beneficial relationship with India. We should be responsive to these trends, without of course, wishing away basic differences with, the US on some vital issues.

11

Strategic Dialogue

This chapter attempts to analyse the circumstances under which India and the United States decided to initiate the dialogue, the objectives of the two nations in this regard as articulated by the leaders of the two countries, and, more so the key interlocutors, the way the parameters of the dialogue have been widened after a few rounds of talks and finally what is it that the talks have achieved so far.

Since the dialogue is an on-going one—the ninth round of talks is scheduled for mid-June of this year—necessarily no attempt is made here to arrive at any definitive conclusions. The Indo-US strategic dialogue that is going on between India's present Foreign Minister Jaswant Singh and US Deputy Secretary of State Strobe Talbott is by any standards the longest bilateral dialogue between the two great democracies of the world.

The dialogue's beginning represented a desire on the part of both the countries to end the diplomatic isolation that followed the Vajpayee government's historic decision to exercise India's long pursued nuclear option through the nuclear tests of May 11 and 13 1998 and the declaration of India as a nuclear weapon state.

Since the dialogue is an on-going one—the ninth round of talks is scheduled for mid-June of this year—

necessarily no attempt is made here to arrive at any definitive conclusions.

The 'assessment' is only tentative in nature keeping in mind the fact that the final outcome of the talks will depend upon how the leadership of both the countries will feel as to how they have achieved their objectives without compromising on their national requirements and without alienating the groups opposed to the kind of conclusions they want to bring the dialogue into.

As mentioned at the outset, the necessity for indo-US strategic dialogue arose after India's May 1998 nuclear tests, conducted in utter secrecy and the manner in which it led to Pakistan also going nuclear overtly. The Indo-Pak nuclear tests, specially the Indian tests, were widely criticised by the United States and the rest of the international community.

It was a blow as it were to Clinton's non-proliferation agenda and his plans for bringing the Comprehensive Test Ban Treaty (CTBT) into force. Though Indian leaders put up a brave front, international condemnations and the slapping of sanctions by the US and the Western community led the Indian leadership to initiate measure to contain the diplomatic isolation (and condemnation).

Prime Minister Vajpayee made a statement in the Parliament—and through that he was addressing the international community—on May 27, 1998 that India was declaring a moratorium on further nuclear testing and gave a pledge for a no first use of nuclear weapons. Further, he sent feelers to the United States that India was prepared to enter into a dialogue with the key interlocutors on India's position regarding the CTBT.

While Mr Vajpayee's special adviser Mr Brijesh Mishra, went to Moscow and Europe, Mr Jaswant Singh was sent as the Prime Minister's special envoy to Washington to soothe the anger of the Clinton administration.

Mr Singh's discussions with the US officials on June 12,1998 marked for all practical purpose the beginnings of the strategic dialogue between India and the United States. The first round of talks were predictably characterised by both the Indian and the American sides, stating their official positions, India elaborating on the security rationale, for its nuclear tests and the United States insisting on India signing the NPT and the CTBT without, any conditions and with no further delay.

The US side was harsh on India for unleashing the spectre of a nuclear arms race in, South Asia with unbearable consequences to both India and Pakistan. Many newspaper columnists were in a hurry to describe the first round of talks as a 'failure'.

Actually the two sides conducted their negotiations in utter secrecy and even in their press briefings later on they only made routine statements saying that they discussed broad range of issues including nuclear proliferation and security matters. In any case, they decided to carry forward the dialogue. The second round of Indo-US dialogue took place in Frankfurt, Germany on July 9th and 10th 1998.

Prior to the second round of talks it was announced from the Indian side that the government was willing to discuss positively the CTBT accession issue and that India would not insist on CTBT being amended to include some of its concerns like committing all nuclear weapon states for a time bound reduction and eventual elimination of nuclear weapons. In other words, India, was signalling that she was prepared to remove the linkage between CTBT and nuclear disarmament as a concession which drew criticisms from some quarters as, surrendering to US pressures. Reportedly, Mr Singh and Mr Talbott discussed for two days India's security situation, India's perception of threat from two nuclear neighbours who are allies—China and Pakistan—and how they impinge on India's strategic and defence policies.

It seems Mr Talbott was personally getting convinced of the security rationale behind India going nuclear overtly, but was constrained to push forward the Clinton administration's agenda for non-proliferation and the successful completion of the CTBT process for realising the ultimate objective of nuclear disarmament. The Indian side insisted on the removal of economic sanctions by the P-5 and the G-8 countries and the lifting of ban on transfer of dual use technologies as a quid pro quo for India considering to accede to the CTBT.

Though the talks were held in highly cordial and malice-free atmosphere, apparently Mr Singh and Talbott could possibly not arrive at any specific decision regarding the requirements of both sides.

The US administration was apparently not agreeable to any linkage between India's signing of the CTBT and the relaxation of controls on dual use technology. New Delhi's compliance, it said, should be without any 'pre-conditions'.

Credit goes to the tenacity and diplomatic skills of both Talbott and Singh and the concern of the two Governments to continue their search for a solution which made the two sides issue a statement at the end of the Frankfurt meeting that the talks were very useful and that constructive consultations would continue.

Prime Minister Vajpayee made a statement in the Rajya Sabha during a debate on foreign policy coincidentally on the same day the second round of talks ended. He, said that although India was ready for talks on CTBT, it would not sign the treaty unconditionally under pressure.

The Parliamentary debate also noticed strong statements being issued by the Congress and Left parties cautioning the Vajpayee government against any compromises on national security. They virtually chided the Government for hinting at signing the CTBT without taking the opposition parties into confidence. Against this background of strong domestic condemnations, the third round of talks-between Mr Singh and Mr Talbott were held on 21st July 1998 in New Delhi.

The US appreciated that the Indian Government needed time to elicit a national consensus. The fourth and fifth rounds of Indo-US talks were held against the background of US air strikes on Sudan and Afghanistan and the Geneva negotiations on Fissile Material Cut-off Treaty (FMCT).

India's participation in Geneva deliberations, along with Pakistan and Government of India's assurances that it would participate constructively in negotiations for the successful conclusion of a multilateral verifiable FMCT— which also formed, part of Singh-Talbott dialogue brought some cheer to the US side that the strategic dialogue was progressing well, albeit slowly.

During the sixth and seventh round of parleys Mr Singh and Mr Talbott debated not only the CTBT issue, but also other important issues like India's defence posture and the need for maintaining adherence to, export control regimes. The issues being ticklish involving sensitive questions of sovereignty etc., the talks did not make any serious headway, though there were enough indications, to the effect that the US side was able to understand the practical problems faced by India in giving any definitive commitment on questions of

has *not yet* given its *final* consent to sign the Treaty. This is clearly the import of the statement made by the Prime Minister earlier in the Parliament on 15th December 1998 and the, statement issued by Foreign Minister Jaswant Singh recently in Lok Sabha on February 26, 1999 when his attention was drawn to the statement of US Secretary of State Madeleine Albright made before the US Senate Foreign Relations Committee that India (and Pakistan) have agreed to adhere to CTBT before the year end. Mr Singh further told the Parliament: "For the successful conclusion of the talks, creation of a positive environment is a necessary ingredient". Mr Singh was no doubt repeating the Prime Minister's statement in this regard. But this only goes to show that the Indian Government expects the 'positive environment' to be created before the ninth round of strategic dialogue scheduled for June this year or that these issues would need to be clinched at those talks.

So, it remains to be seen—unlike what many of the analysts have already said—whether the Indian side would relent or that its requirements are going to be met.

In the meantime, the Government should take the major opposition parties into confidence and build up a national consensus on the question of acceding to the CTBT. Needless to emphasise, the opposition parties too should refrain from politicking on this vital issue and cooperate with the Government. As regards the Fissile Material Cut-off Treaty (FMCT) the US side is happy that India is participating in the Geneva deliberations.

On the more substantive issue of accepting a ban on the production of fissile material pending successful completion of the negotiations for the conclusion of the FMCT—that would indeed take a long time—India has rightly not obliged the United States, keeping in mind its security requirements. So, the criticism that the Vajpayee

Government is compromising on FMCT is really unfounded. But being alive to the larger issues, the Government has agreed to participate in multilateral negotiations in this regard and rightly so.

On the all important issue of our defence posture, which is also one of the important issues in Indo-US strategic dialogue it bears noting that the Government of India has not really given away anything.

It has rightly emphasised that these are questions, of national sovereignty on which we would not like to be dictated to by any one. At the same time, Mr Jaswant Singh seems to have succeeded in convincing Mr Strobe Talbott about India's security concerns.

US officials like Mr Karl Inderfurth and Congressmen like Mr Gary Ackerman have admitted in recent times to the seriousness of the Chinese threat in India's security calculus.

Neither Mr Singh nor the Prime Minister have yielded to the US administration on questions concerning the size of our minimum nuclear deterrent and when and where would they be deployed. At the same time, India has done well to reaffirm its commitment to reduce the nuclear danger in South Asia.

Prime Minister Vajpayee's bus journey to Lahore and the subsequent Lahore Declaration—Mr Nawaz Sharif needs to be complemented too in this regard—pointing to the Indo-Pak decision to remove the dangers of unauthorised use of nuclear weapons and pursue vigorously other confidence building measures to promote peace and security in the sub-continent are worthy of appreciation. It is no secret that the United States played a quiet but helpful role in bringing Vajpayee and Nawaz Sharif together at Lahore. Thus the US trilateral dialogue's role in the Lahore Declaration needs perhaps an acknowledgement. Finally on the question of export controls, the fourth issue in Indo-US strategic dialogue, luckily there has not been much of divergence between the two countries. The expert level meeting which took place earlier in November 1998 and the next round of export controls talks scheduled for March 1999 at the expert level will help clarify issues further.

India's impeccable record of effective control over sensitive technologies is appreciated by the US administration. It is with this record that India is asking for better access to dual use and high technologies, which may hopefully materialise in the near future.

As noted earlier, the ninth round of talks will take place only in June this year. It is hoped that things will get straightened out in the meantime or during the talks itself. The devil may lie in the detail as Talbott noted in Delhi, but as he also noted the dialogue between the two democracies has to be a non zero sum game and result in a win-win situation for both.

One last word. This strategic dialogue should not only lead to a broader improvement of Indo-US bilateral relations but also to a strategic coming together of India and the United States as in the perception of the new millennium the strategic challenge to both of them would come from China. Recent reports about China having developed advanced varieties of nuclear warheads and missiles are indicative of the likely trend.

Sooner the decision-makers and opinion-moulders in both the countries realise this, better it is for the two great democracies whose areas of convergence otherwise are steadily expanding.

A remarkable feature of the eight rounds of Indo-US dialogue in the wake of India's nuclear tests last May has been the distinct difference in the perspectives that each side carries away from the confabulations. This has been particularly true of the last three or four rounds of talks. After each such engagement, spokesmen for each side would talk in glowing terms about "edging closer" and "narrowing the differences." They also invariably averred that progress had been achieved, which would, indeed, make the next round that much easier.

The waiting public never came to know the specific details of what had been discussed and what had actually been achieved because the two sides had joined in a compact from the beginning not to publicise the give and-take that went on behind closed doors. They did not wish premature disclosure to stymie future progress. In a sense, that is an understandable sentiment. But it had a down side: It gave rise to the wildest speculation. None of which was officially countered because of the stipulation about silence.

A few days after each round, however, officials from each side would begin briefing newsmen they considered discreet about what "really" went on. And that is where the surprise came in: going by the two versions. It was difficult to believe that, the two delegations had attended the same conference. In both cases, there is obviously a lot of wish being farther to the thought.

The most glaring instance of the two sides looking at the same, scenario and seeing different things has been with regard to India's stance on the Comprehensive Test Ban Treaty (CTBT). Ever since Prime Minister Atal Behari Vajpayee stated in his United Nations General Assembly address last September that India would not come in the way of CTBT coming into force in September 1999 as long as certain conditions put forth by India were fulfilled, US spokesmen have been going to town praising India's decision to sign the CTBT this year. A constant drumbeat of that propaganda has been kept up, with everyone from President Clinton down congratulating New Delhi for its wise and statesman-like decision.

What the US forgot was that notwithstanding the agreement not to reveal details of ongoing negotiations, the talks were not going on in a vacuum, but within the confines of each nation's political calculus. The more US propaganda succeeded about India's imminent move to sign the CTBT, the more intense was the pressure brought to bear on the Vajpayee government, with the opposition flaying it for knuckling under to the US.

The darn finally burst on February 24 when External Affairs Minister Jaswant Singh announced in Parliament that India had not agreed to sign the CTBT, nor would it permit another country to decide its minimum nuclear deterrence. Singh's most forceful rebuttal was his statement that the government would not even respond to claims reportedly made by some US officials that India was close to signing the CTBT.

Jaswant Singh's forthright statement has now put the issue in perspective. But it is also a cautionary tale for the US with regard to its relations with Pakistan, the other new nuclear state. Many US officials seem to believe that Pakistan, beset as it is with financial crises and dependent on US generosity, or at least the absence of hostility, is easier to handle than India. They appear sanguine that the threat of sanctions and the promise of continuing largesse will induce Islamabad to toe the American line.

But they fail to see a salient political reality: however big the stick and however enticing the carrot, Prime Minister Nawaz Sharif can never be persuaded to commit political harakiri, especially with his predecessor,

Benazir Bhutto, waiting in the wings, ever ready to pounce on any sign of weakness that can be politically exploited. Meanwhile, have India and the US moved closer through the series of meetings they have had? Or have they only sharpened their own stands and become more precise in their language? In other words, are they mistaking clarity for convergence? It certainly seems to be the case.

What are US and Indian perceptions after eight rounds of talks? In an article to appear in the March/April issue of *Foreign Affairs*, Deputy Secretary of State Strobe Talbott, who leads the American delegation in the talks with India (and Pakistan), made the point that the US "cannot concede, even by implication, that India and Pakistan have by their tests established them selves as nuclear weapons states." Jaswant Singh's response to that is straightforward: "Facts cannot be disinvented. India is a nuclear weapons state." The External Affairs Minister has made it clear during the dialogue with the US that matters relating to defence postures are sovereign functions and, therefore, not negotiable. Yet, according to Talbott: "A key objective of our discussions with the Indians and the Pakistanis involves restraint in the development and deployment of missiles and aircraft capable of carrying weapons of mass destruction." There is very little common ground between the two positions.

Talbott also says that the "starting point and near-term objective of the US diplomatic effort underway since last June" is to persuade India and Pakistan to "stabilise their nuclear competition at the lowest possible level". There it is again: the equating of India and Pakistan. Somehow, the US appears to have some difficulty in appreciating that India's strategic concerns include China, now America's "strategic ally." This, despite Talbott's own admission that in developing nuclear weapons, Pakistan "sought and received help from China, which further stoked India's mistrust of both nations".

It should be no secret to Talbott, given the numerous US intelligence briefs he must have read, that Beijing has for long been fishing in troubled South Asia waters, trying to build up Pakistan as a counterweight to India. China has no real need to fear India here and now, but it is certainly disquieted by India's potential to challenge its regional hegemony.

The US has been talking long and loud about the need for "tightened export controls on sensitive materials and technologies that could be used to develop weapons of mass destruction". This is an issue which the US says it has been raising with India. But as Jaswant Singh pointed out the other day in Parliament, "our record is better than that of the P-5 countries."

Will the Indo-US dialogue ever arrive at a meaningful conclusion, or will it go on endlessly like the Middle East peace talks? To a large extent, it depends on whether and how the US adjusts to 21st century realities.

Commentator Garry Wills points out in the same *Foreign Affairs* issue that was host to Talbott that since the Second World War, to get its- way as the self-styled leader of the free world, the US "has ignored the American public and used covert action, sabotage, and threats against hapless foreign countries." Wills suggests that in order to lead in the 21st century the US will have to listen to other's opinions, act in partnership with other nations and get used to persuading allies rather than browbeating them.

Harvard Political Scientist Samuel P. Huntington says the unipolar moment has passed. Even old allies stubbornly resist American demands, while many other nations view US ideals as openly hostile to their own. Huntington suggests that the US relearn the game of international politics as a major power. His conclusion: "US policymaking should reflect rational calculations of power rather than a wish list of arrogant, unilateralist demands."

The point, therefore, is not whether India will see the light of strategic restraint, but whether America will absorb the ground realities of a changing world.

12

Clinton's Visit: A Cheering Experience

It is only when you see him up close that you understand why US President Bill Clinton is not just the most powerful leader in the world but is such an extraordinarily attractive survivor. The energy he exudes, the legendary empathy he builds up instantneously, his cosummate skill in putting across his view and the easy boyish charm that Indian politicians who packed the Central Hall of Parliament on March 22 to listen to him were no exception. In his speech, Clinton described how the uniqueness of Indian classical music was its elasticity where the composer lays down a foundation, a structure of melodic and rhythmic arrangements, which the player then improvises to bring the raga to life. As his five-day trip to India progressed, Clinton charmed his way into the heart of India by being unafraid to strum different tunes and explore new ragas in a relationship that had strangely been out of step for more than five decades. The overall effect had much of the country enthralled and dramatically redrew images the two nations shared of each other.

In Parliament that morning, Clinton came across as a soulful speaker, shorn of the arrogance that characterised most Americans in power, subsuming his role as a global headmaster, willing to laugh and be laughed at, pandering to India's inflated ego and appealing to the country's rectitude.

It was diplomacy at its mellifluous best. The 1,000-odd parliamentarians, both present and past, knew that it was a decisive moment in the relationship between the two countries. As Clinton walked to the exit, suddenly, as if the dam of hostility had been breached, almost everyone wanted to shake his hand. Some of the MPs even climbed on benches to reach out to him and a Tamil Nadu MP wrapped a colourful angavastram around his neck. It was as if half a century of rancour and suspicion that had marred relations between the two countries were being washed away by the flood of goodwill that Clinton had created.

Congressman Jim McDermott, a seasoned Democrat from Seattle, who was watching the proceedings with a mixture of awe and surprise, said, "I tell ya what, when I saw them climbing one over the other to shake hands with him, I knew then that not just a new leaf, not just a new chapter, but a whole new book was unfolding in our relations with each other." Jim Greenwood, a Republican Congressman from Pennsylvania, who was sitting next to him, was as effusive: "For me it was a historic moment. As significant as President Nixon going to China." Even Prime Minister Atal Bihari Vajpayee stood bemusedly watching the rapturous reception that Clinton received. Madhavrao Scindia, deputy leader of the Congress in the Lok Sabha, acknowledged, "The US President was candid, positive, constructive and exhibited a great sensitivity to India's needs. It augurs well for us. " For someone whose trip many cynical experts had dismissed as the extended waddle of a lameduck president, the outcome came close to being epoch-making.

Much of it had to do with the dazzling facets of the

personality that Clinton exhibited. It shattered all stereotypes of him. Before he landed, the army of security that descended on Delhi and wherever else he had to visit only increased the notion that Mr Big Guy was in town and you had better not mess with him. But as soon as Clinton landed on March 19 in Delhi and checked into Room 1683, the Chandragupta Suite, at the ITC Maurya Sheraton, he went about dismantling his carefully choreographed trip with its iron rings of security. He dropped by at a reception for India Americans hosted by US Ambassador to India Richard Celeste. That was an unscheduled stop. Immediately after that, he strolled through the corridors of the hotel, shook hands with staff members at random, visited shops in the building, and even bargained over the price of a carpet. He then wanted to play the saxophone at the hotel's jazz Club. But with jet lag catching up and the yawns becoming obvious, he postponed his "Millennium performance", as he joked, for another night.

The next morning before setting off on a day's trip to Bangladesh, he continued to keep his Secret Service guards off balance. In the wee hours, wearing a grey Nike T-shirt, he exercised on a stepper in his room. He then had his favourite breakfast-coffee with bagels, assorted breads and fresh pomegranate juice. While coming down the elevator to get into his motorcade, he suddenly decided to walk through the coffee shop and, much to the delight of the chefs, began asking them questions about what they were cooking and even tasted some of the fare. While the President was away in Dhaka, Chelsea flew down to Jodhpur where the former Maharaja's black Cadillac waited to drop her off at a Holi celebration amidst regal surroundings. When they both returned to the hotel that night, Clinton opted for dinner at the Bukhara restaurant where he took a particular fancy to the burra kababs and couldn't resist having a second helping. He downed the meal with gulps of diet Coke. For dessert he finished an entire portion of kulfi and faluda.

On March 21, the day his official tour of India began, Clinton, sporting a dark blue suit and a mustard tie, drove up to Rashtrapati Bhavan in a blast-proof stretch limousine. He had already been briefed by Sandy Berger, his national security adviser, about the dastardly gunning down of 35 Sikhs in a village near Anantapur early that morning, When Clinton got off to greet President K.R. Narayanan and Vajpayee, he seemed genuinely grieved by the incident and extended his condolences.

As the ceremonial guard of honour began, Clinton was alert and curious to his surroundings. Naresh Chandra, India's ambassador to the US, recalls that the President "soaked in" the sights and sounds of India. It was as if Clinton wanted to savour every moment he was in India and feel the intensity of an ancient civilisation that his countrymen had always failed to understand. Soon after the brief welcome ceremony, Clinton and Chelsea, wearing a dark business suit, drove to Gandhi Smriti where the President again exhibited an eye for detail and was extremely polite. A senior member of the Indian delegation observed: "He wanted to be *pucca* in whatever he did and was careful not to offend anyone's feelings." Apart from just laying the customary wreath, he tried his hand at Gandhi's charkha and enquired about the words "Hey Ram" engraved on the stone. He loved the peace of the place and said as much.

Again showing that he didn't really care about convention, Clinton arrived almost half an hour early at Hyderabad House for what was to be his only political session of the trip. Vajpayee had had half a dozen telephone conversations with Clinton but this was their first face-to-face dialogue. Despite the age difference of close to 20 years, the two leaders got along well. Chandra believes that the Indian prime minister's style of speaking his mind "without prevarication and hypocrisy" was something that the US President appreciated. Brajesh Mishra, principal secretary to the prime minister, described the chemistry between the two leaders "as good". A US diplomat said Clinton "respected Vajpayee for his forthrightness". On its part, the Indian delegation, which had come prepared for some finger-wagging by the President on the Kashmir and nuclear issues, was surprised and disarmed by what the members termed as his "friendly tone that had no rancour and recrimination".

Part of the reason for the ease with which the two sides sidestepped their differences was the extensive dialogue that External Affairs Minister Jaswant Singh and US Deputy Secretary of State Strobe Talbott had in the past two years over the nuclear question and relations with Pakistan. The Indian delegation noticed two significant departures from the past on Kashmir. They found that for the first time, the US delegation did not refer to Kashmir as a "disputed territory". Also, Clinton did not say that a solution to the problem would have to involve the "wishes and aspirations of the people of Kashmir", a sentence that always came as a rider whenever any official referred to the issue. "Don't just look at what he said but also pay attention to what he did not say," said a senior US State Department official. Clinton did choose his words carefully condemning "violence" in the Valley but nowhere describing it as an act of cross-border terrorism. So Pakistan needn't feel all that awful. During lunch, soon after, India made sure that of the seven state chief ministers, it was the articulate Farooq Abdullah of Jammu and Kashmir who was seated next to the President, giving him a large dose of how Pakistan was messing up on Kashmir.

On the sensitive nuclear issue, Clinton's tone was firm but not offensive. He admitted that India had the "right to determine its own security needs" but wanted India not to enter into a debilitating arms race or conduct further tests. Vajpayee, it is learnt, reassured the US that the "Indian policy was not a threat to the US" and that India was not keen on a war with Pakistan or for that matter on an arms race. At the end of the hour-and-a-half dialogue at Hyderabad House, the Indian side felt that "the US was making a sincere attempt to lay the foundation for a longer relationship with India". After that Vajpayee and Clinton had a 10-minute discussion without their aides. No details were made available. At the end of it the two countries issued a vision statement which, says former foreign secretary Maharaja Krishna Rasgotra, "puts the past behind and looks at the future and newer ways to explore it". Importantly, they called for ways to institutionalise the dialogue between the two countries and Vajpayee accepted Clinton's invitation to come to the US for a summit meeting.

In the evening at a banquet held by Narayanan, there were some discordant notes over the tough speech made by him. Some circles in the Indian Government too seemed upset. Narayanan, a seasoned diplomat, appears to have decided that since no one else in the Government was mouthing the shibboleths of non-alignment and the multipolar world that India subscribed too, it was time to tell the US about it. While the Government fumed, the President's office pointed out that there was no real departure from the norms and previous presidents had made far sterner speeches to visiting US presidents.

The next morning, before he addressed Parliament, Clinton met a Congress delegation headed by Sonia Gandhi. There were some embarrassing moments when he sought to know from the team why the party won fewer parliamentary seats, even though it polled more votes than the ruling BJP. It was left to Madhavrao Scindia to explain the first-past-the-post system.

After Clinton's well-received address to Parliament, Vajpayee in his reply preferred to stick to Hindi. But he quoted an English verse from a Walt Whitman poem that began, "Sail forth, steer for the deep waters only." As the prime minister went on, Clinton shifted uneasily wondering whether the host had by oversight forgotten that he had presented Monica Lewinsky with a special edition of Leaves of Grass by the same poet.

After the official engagements, it was time for Clinton to shed his suits and "Tear trendy T-shirts and shorts. His first halt was the Taj Mahal where he couldn't stop exclaiming "wow". He also charmed those who were there. "What a dashing personality. I wish he came to Agra more often," sighed little Ashita Verma, a class V student at St Patrick's junior School, Agra. The doe-eyed beauty queen Priyanka Chopra even got a handshake. How did it feel? "Shaking the hands of power did things to me," gushed the dusky beauty. Appropriately, a loudspeaker was blaring the Hindi film song *"Tu mera hero No. 1"* at the Taj.

March 23 was Clinton's day out with Indian women and he seemed to enjoy every minute of it. From being garlanded to having the traditional red thread tied around his wrist—friendship band, they called it. He left the women of Nayla, a village near Jaipur where he had gone for a taste of grassroots democracy, gasping while their menfolk looked on a trifle angrily. More so when the women held his hands and took turns at twirling with him to the tune of Rajasthani folk songs. "What am I supposed to do?" Clinton asked his interpreter, Kanchan Mathur, when he saw the women swaying to the sound of music. "Why don't you dance?" she replied and before anyone knew, Big Bill was out there in the middle tapping his feet. Later expressing astonishment and appreciation for the work under the Panchayati Raj, he said computers in every village would soon revolutionise the locals' struggle and even create jobs for their children.

Clinton seemed quite pleased when he was presented a smart card and offered a loan by the cooperative for raising milch cows. He smiled in return, saying he would display the card at the White House. He smiled all the way. Right up to Amber Fort, where 12 elephants had been lined up for him. He was keen on taking a ride but no, said the Secret Service. He had his little dig, though, even if in another context. "How nice to see some friendly elements," he smiled, referring to the Republican symbol.

A few hours later, Clinton and Chelsea flew to Ranthambore sanctuary and were thrilled to spot two tigers. They had gone in open canters with picnic hampers, kicking up a mini sandstorm. The joke doing the rounds was that Union Minister of State for Small-Scale Industries Vasundhara Raje, who went around with the President, would probably be spending the next two days shampooing her hair to get the dust out.

After that, Clinton flew to Hyderabad where he kicked off a health project and visited the Hi-Tec City. Fittingly, he ended his trip to India in Mumbai talking to young entrepreneurs and focusing on the knowledge industry, key areas that would determine the future of Indo-US relations. He then flew to Islamabad for a tough-talking session with Pakistan's Chief Executive General Pervez Musharraf.

At the end of the visit, it was clear that the US recognised India as a major player in ensuring security not just in the region but in Asia itself. More significantly, the US may now increasingly view democratic India as a counter to communist China in the region. Much now depends on the follow through or what former foreign secretary J.N. Dixit calls, " the operational rules" to the vision statement and other agreements signed. There are clearly major differences between the two countries that have to be overcome, especially over the nuclear issue and sanctions. But the trip has gone a long way to build mutual trust and holds the promises of a major shift in relations. Jaswant Singh cautiously calls it a move in the right direction. Now only the destination—and the speed at which it can be reached—has to be decided.

With heavy emphasis on the nuclear issue and terrorism, American newspapers had little room for human interest stories connected with President Clinton's visit. Even then, the few such stories used were taken from Associated Press or Reuters. For instance, the *Chicago Tribune* front-paged on Thursday a story about Clinton's visit to Nayla village. "Clinton Hears About Indian Women's Struggle", the headline declared. On the same page was a picture of Clinton and Chelsea at the Taj Mahal. There were a handful of stories about Holi—with the note that Chelsea wasn't drowned in colours.

The Taj pictures were snapped up by many newspapers. Other pictures that found their way in several publications showed Clinton's reception at Rashtrapati Bhavan, Clinton (looking a bit grim) with a cheerful Vajpayee (which made page 1 of the *The New York Times)* and the scene of the controversial toast by the Indian President.

Politics being on the mind of most newspapers, business stories weren't visible at all. Even *The Wall Street journal* ran political stories. Headline from Wednesday's paper for a story on Page 4: "India Rejects Clinton Plea on Weapons; Gunmen Kill 40 on Pakistani Border". Several stories, while offering a more peaceful scene like Clinton's visit to Mahatma Gandhi's samadhi, immediately reminded readers about the chaos and violence across India. On Thursday, when several big-city newspapers carried the Clinton visit stories on page 1 for the second day, the headlines and the tone were turning optimistic.

The *Washington Times* ran the lead story with the heading, "Clinton Blasts Pakistan, Calls India 'Great'". The bigger and more influential *The Washington Post* declared, "In India, Wooing with Praise". The stories now said that Clinton, after having declared his displeasure at India's nuclear programme in private, was trying to sell his vision by humouring Indian lawmakers. The *Post* also had on page 1 a story about how the Sikhs in Chithisingh Pora were uniting in their grief following the massacre of 40 people. *The Boston Globe,* too, echoed the headlines in the *Post* and other newspapers: "With Careful Speech, Clinton Charms Indians".

The Indian President's remarks during a state banquet found prominent place in several publications, including *The Washington Post* and *The New York Times.* "President Clinton yesterday failed to persuade India to give up nuclear weapons and he drew a remarkable rebuke from his hosts," wrote *The Washington Times.* Television coverage for the most part was fleeting except for Peter Jenning's coverage from India for ABC, and the documentary, *The Dark Horizon: India, Pakistan and the Bomb,* a network "special" which was well-received by the media. ABC has not released the viewership figures. NBC and CBS chose to send correspondents, and not their main anchors, to cover the trip.

Index